Surviving the Bible

Forthcoming in the Surviving the Bible series:

Surviving the Bible:
A Devotional for the Church Year 2019

Surviving the Bible:
A Devotional for the Church Year 2020

Christian Piatt

Surviving
the
Bible

A Devotional
for the
Church Year

2018

SURVIVING THE BIBLE
A Devotional for the Church Year 2018

Cover design: Brad Norr
Design & Typesetting: PerfecType, Nashville, TN

Print ISBN: 978-1-5064-2065-3
eBook ISBN: 978-1-5064-2066-0

The paper used in this publication meets the minimum requirements of American National Standard for Information Sciences — Permanence of Paper for Printed Library Materials, ANSI Z329.48-1984.

Manufactured in the U.S.A.

Contents

Series Introduction

The Bible clearly says . . .

We've all heard this phrase, usually in the middle of some ideological combat about "values." And yet, it seems like we tend to use the Bible to reinforce whatever we already believe. But when we see what we want to see in scripture, it mutates from being a light and path to being a sword and shield.

As Anne Lamott says, "You can safely assume you've created God in your own image when it turns out that God hates all the same people you do."

That, or the Bible feels too big, complicated, beyond our reach. So many people understand it better than we do. At the same time, we have this need to connect, to find wisdom in its pages. We feel a pull back to it, over and again. And in a time of "alternative facts," when we long for something true, something real to offer us some deeper wisdom, we wonder what scripture *really says* about climate change, war, sexuality, gender roles, and money. We would welcome its guidance, if we only knew how to get at it.

I have tried, more than once, to read the Bible from start to finish. Maybe you have too. I can't count how many times I started with Genesis and, by the time I get to the labyrinth of laws in Numbers (if not before), I give up. That's why I'm writing this three-book series called *Surviving the Bible*.

The Bible is the bestselling printed volume in world history. It was the very first thing printed after the printing press was created, and it's sold over 2.5 *billion* copies since. Over 100 million copies are sold or given away every year, or more than 190 every single minute. The entire Bible has been translated into more than 650 languages; the New Testament has been translated into more than 1,400. It's consistently at the top of the list of favorite books in America when people are surveyed.

And yet I'd argue it's also the most misunderstood text in our culture, partly because most of us have never read the whole thing. In fact, only about 9 percent of folks asked claim to have read it all.

My kids love what I call my "dad jokes," or at least I tell myself they love them so I have an excuse to keep telling them. And of course I can't resist sneaking some lessons in there when I can. One of my favorites is "How do you eat an elephant? One bite at a time." Yeah, they roll their eyes but I know they're laughing hysterically inside.

The point is that we don't have to read the Bible all at once. It's not a book written from start to finish, meant to be read like a novel either. It's a collection of laws, stories, history, poems, and predictions written by dozens of different people from multiple cultures and in several languages over thousands of years. It was written for different people with different needs at different times. But the reason we still consider it important today is because so much of the wisdom found, sometimes buried mysteriously like treasure, still rings true.

But who goes looking for treasure without a map? It would be a waste of time. The problem is that so many so-called maps to the wisdom in scripture are more like instruction manuals, telling us what to think and how to believe. Maps, on the other hand, offer a way to find something without telling us what you have to do with it when we get there.

We crave meaning, grounding. We long to separate fact from opinion, to grab hold of something bigger than ourselves. We want to broaden our vision in a time when everyone seems so utterly blinded by the immediate reality, right in front of them. We want answers, but more than that, we want peace. We want to separate fact from opinion and to discern truths that transcend immediate facts, wisdom that has resonated across cultures and generations since we started asking questions as a species about why we're here and what our purpose is.

Fred Craddock was right when he claimed that the Bible can be used to make any point we want. But it's too important a resource to depend on others to tell us what it means. We can think for ourselves; all we need is a guide.

This book is set up like a weekly meditation, breaking down the Bible "elephant" into bite-sized pieces. It follows the church calendar in case you're a part of a church that observes it, but you don't have to be. In fact, you don't have to go to church at all to use this. You don't have to know what you believe either. You don't even have to be a Christian. Use it as a weekly study, or browse the glossary for themes you're curious about. It's an ideal resource to use with a friend or small group, but it's set up to be accessed by anyone who has enough curiosity, openness, and a desire to grow.

Start anywhere. Set it down and come back to it, over and over. There's no "wrong way" to use *Surviving the Bible*. Just open it up, grab a Bible, and take a bite.

Christian Piatt

Look, Shiny!

Lectionary Texts For
December 3, 2017 (First Sunday in Advent)

Texts in Brief
My dog ate my Bible!

First Reading
Isaiah 64:1–9

The prophet, on behalf of the exiled people of Jerusalem, is nostalgic for the time when God has intervened on behalf of the Jews. He also is lamenting the apparent absence of God from the exiles, which, he deems, is because of their sinfulness.

Psalm
Psalm 80:1–7, 17–19

This psalm is structured like most psalms of lament. First there is a celebration of the grandeur and enduring grace of God. Second, the problems of the psalmist's people are laid out. Third, there's the request for God to help. And whether God is angry about the prayers of the people or at the people themselves, divine anger is noted by the author.

SECOND READING

1 Corinthians 1:3–9

Paul writes to the Christians in Corinth, setting an example of thanksgiving to God for enduring grace, and reminding them that their own gifts and abilities are first given by God.

GOSPEL

Mark 13:24–37

Jesus warns his followers to stay alert, to be aware of the distractions of false prophets, and not to fall into such distractions or complacency while waiting for his return after his inevitable crucifixion.

Bible, Decoded

Breaking down scripture in plain language

Grace – In the context of these texts, grace is equated to enduring patience and forgiveness, as exhibited by God toward God's people, who screw up. A Lot.

Lord of Hosts – This refers to a ruler over either earthly or heavenly armies or multitudes. It's meant to affirm God's authority and power and essentially to remind the readers of the text who is in charge (hint: not them).

Clay – The people of Israel are the fundamental elements (in this case, clay) that God uses to make into what they become as people. It's also a reference back to the story of Adam (the first man) who was made out of the same clay. So in a sense, it's an allusion to the fact that, though we're made of earthly elements, we're "inspired" or breathed into life by something not of this world.

Son of Man - This is actually a pretty controversial phrase found in the gospels. Whereas elsewhere, Jesus often is referred to as the "Son of God," this title could be pointing particularly to his humanity, or even his intimate connection with people and the human experience.

Points to Ponder
First Thoughts

There are some interesting themes that jump out among all of these texts. First, the authors are speaking to the people of Israel (the Jewish people) about being without a center, a sense of place. They're neither there anymore, but not yet here. There is a sense of being lost and wandering. In the case of the text in Mark, the loss actually hasn't happened yet, but it will on two levels. For one, they'll lose the temple at the center of Jerusalem that they've been so passionately admiring. But also, they'll lose Jesus, their new leader, all too soon.

So there's this tension of dealing with loss, but also calling for holding out hope for things to improve. It's hard to be hopeful when all you can think about is what you've lost or will soon lose. And yet, the audience in each of the texts is encouraged to be thankful, not necessarily for what is right in front of them, but for what has been provided for them in the past, and to parlay that gratitude into trust that it can happen, yet again.

Digging Deeper

Mining for what really matters . . . and gold

Knowing some context behind this Isaiah scripture can help us understand what's going on. At this point, King Cyrus has beaten the Babylonians, making a way for the Jews to return to the promised land from Babylon. The thing is, the people now living in the territory to be claimed by them as the nation of Israel feel differently. They don't exactly want to uproot and move so these people they don't know can take over their homes. This results in a delay in the establishment of the promised land, leaving the Jews in exile. Isaiah attributes this misfortune to the softening, distracted spiritual lives of his people, which has caused God to turn from them. So he wants them to get right with God in order to get to return to their homeland.

The people who are the audience in this psalm have lost focus too. The author senses God's absence, so God doesn't show up when they need a hand. But as has happened before, the psalmist assures them that God will return to care for them, despite their screw-ups. The author concludes with a request, asking God to return and make things right again.

In Paul's letter to the Corinthian Christians, he suggests that something is causing them to lose their way. Maybe they're falling into the cultural ways and values of the community they're in. Maybe the Christian community they're supposed to build up isn't coming along as quickly as was hoped. Maybe the rejection is discouraging them. Regardless, he senses trouble. So in his greeting to them, he's modeling the sort of thankfulness and faithfulness he expects from them, while also reminding them that all the good in their lives is not of their own doing, but rather is a gift from God.

In the Markan Gospel passage, Jesus knows his followers were ogling the temple in Jerusalem, but he warns them that such love is fleeting, and that it will all eventually crumble. He draws a parallel to his own departure from their midst when he'll be crucified, maybe to remind them not to hold on too tightly to anything physical in their midst. Distractions abound, for both them and those they want to teach. But he urges them to stay alert and to be mindful of the false allure of material, superficial things that draw them off their path.

Heads Up

Connecting the text to our world

These scriptures make me think of Doug, the dog in the movie *Up*. His owner affixed a speaking device to his collar, translating his every "dog thought" into English. And he says a lot of stuff you'd expect a dog to say, like "I don't know you yet, but I love you!" Doug also struggles to follow a thought through once he starts explaining something, inevitably interrupted mid-sentence by yet another squirrel.

We all end up chasing squirrels now and then or, if you're like me, a dozen times an hour when the latest alert pops up on your phone. There's even a term for getting lost down topical rabbit holes online; it's called WWILFing, which stands for "What Was I Looking For?"

There are more existential rabbit holes for us too, like when we get so consumed in the minutiae and stress of daily life that we forget to slow down and be grateful for what we already have in our lives. Sometimes it takes stopping and resting in silence for a few minutes, or offering a silent word of thanks to regain perspective and reclaim our spiritual centers.

This advent—and every Christmas season, really—there are even more distractions than usual. On top of shopping and decorating, there is the seemingly endless stream of social events and end-of-year work items, nagging at our waning minutes. It's so incredibly easy to turn around and feel utterly lost, without a center, without purpose. And a life without a sense of direction and purpose often points to a life that has lost touch with God.

Prayer for the Week

God, it's happening again. There's more shiny stuff and squirrels distracting me from a connection with You than ever. What Was I Looking For? Remind me, then help me find it. Thanks.

Popping Off

Art/music/video and other cool stuff that relate to the text
Up (movie, 2009)

"A New Theory of Distraction," from The New Yorker (article, June 16, 2015) http://www.newyorker .com/culture/cultural-comment/a-new-theory-of -distraction

"Daily Riches: Mindfulness," by Ruth Haley Barton and Richard Rohr (blog, January 25, 2015) https://richerbyfar.com/2015/01/25/daily-riches -mindfulness-ruth-haley-barton-richard-rohr-2/

Are We There Yet?

Lectionary Texts For
December 10, 2017 (Second Sunday in Advent)

Texts in Brief
My dog ate my Bible!

FIRST READING
Isaiah 40:1–11

Isaiah offers comforting words to the people of Israel, assuring them that though their lives have been hard, they won't continue to be forever. Though pain and struggle are temporary, and even life doesn't last, God's word and enduring love do.

PSALM
Psalm 85:1–2, 8–13

The people on whose behalf the psalmist is writing have been struggling, it seems. And in offering a word of praise to God for the restoration of the fortunes of

Jacob and the fulfillment of past promises, they are hoping to strengthen the faith of those who are dealing with hardship.

SECOND READING
2 Peter 3:8–15a

The audience in this text has been waiting for what must feel like a long time. But the author reminds them that what seems like an eternity to them is hardly a blink of an eye to God. They're cautioned to stay faithful and always be ready for God's promised return.

GOSPEL
Mark 1:1–8

The beginning of Mark refers back to our text in Isaiah, in which the prophet notes that God will send a messenger ahead of the Messiah to prepare the way. Then the author notes that this promised way-maker is John the Baptist.

Bible, Decoded
Breaking down scripture in plain language

Repent – Though in our culture we tend to think of repentance as primarily about feeling terrible for things we've done in the past, at its root, the word means to turn away or turn around. So if we're in the process of repentance, it means we're first recognizing we're on a wrong path, and then making it right.

Baptize – Some think of baptism as a kind of "fire insurance," keeping us from going to hell. Others see it as a kind of official stamp of membership in the Christian community. But for others, it's a symbol—a covenant of sorts—between the person being baptized, God, and those watching to help this person live in a new way, in some ways as a new person. The act itself isn't about magical powers; it's a first, small step in a lifelong journey that is no longer made alone, but together.

Zion – Sometimes used to refer to the entirety of the promised land of the nation of Israel, it refers more specifically to a hill on which the city of David was built.

Points to Ponder

First Thoughts

These scriptures get to the heart of what the season of advent is about: waiting and preparing. There seem to be a couple of reasons in the texts why the authors are telling people to wait and get ready.

In some cases, the people are having a hard time, so the authors are assuring them the end of their struggle is coming and to hang in there. In others, there are references back to old promises, and how they are being fulfilled. This means to solidify the people's faith and embolden them with hope.

In both cases, it's worth noting that the actual circumstances for the audience are not changing in that exact moment. Rather, the shift is in their intended perspective and outlook: to get them to look up and out, rather than just down and in.

Digging Deeper

Mining for what really matters . . . and gold

We could think of the prophet Isaiah as a sort of feel-good pastoral caregiver here, soothing the existential "owies" of his people. But actually, the words of comfort are almost given in a sort of reprimanding tone. It's more like "chill out!" or "get over yourselves!" The words of comfort actually are in the form of an order from God, not just an invitation.

The same can be said of the texts in Mark and Peter, and in the psalm too in a way. In each case, the people are being told—it's not a suggestion—to remember that God made a promise, and God does not break such promises. These promises were not one-sided, however. They were part of a greater covenant between God and God's people. When people begin to lose hope or faith, there's the risk they will let their promises slip. So the texts remind them, and us as the present audience, to maintain perspective.

First, there's the perspective of looking back, of remembering, piecing back together the story from which they came and the covenants that bind them to God and each other. Then there's the perspective of looking forward and out, not losing sight of the bigger picture because of present hardship.

Yes, there is comfort and reassurance in the words, but that's not all. It comes weighed with a subtle reprimand to get our heads on right and to persist, to believe we are stronger than even we think, because we are when emboldened by the promise given to us by God.

Some of us try to pin God's promises to particular results or actions. It can be argued that this is trying to put a holy covenant into an earthly framework. But hope persists for its own sake, regardless of outcomes. Its perspective is so far beyond our anticipation of outcomes that it cannot be entirely absorbed. And yet it is sensed, trusted, followed.

Suffering is temporal; death does not have the final word; love is bigger, greater, and far more than the sum total of our brokenness.

Heads Up

Connecting the text to our world

Most of us have been on road trips with kids. I've gone on long ten- to twelve-hour drives in which we haven't even gotten out of town before the inevitable questions come from the back seat . . .

"Are we there yet? How much longer?"

There's really nothing more dispiriting than thinking you're close to the end of a long journey—whether it's a literal or metaphoric one—only to find out you're not even halfway there. And yes, clock-obsession does add to the torture.

Not convinced of the relativity of our perception of time? Spend two hours watching your favorite movie, and then another two trying to hold it when you have to go to the bathroom. Talk about minutes seeming like years!

I used to go hiking with my dad, who made me carry all of my own gear for a multi-day hiking trip. By the end, I was usually wet (I was a klutz and always seemed to fall in the rivers we crossed), tired, and sore. I too fell back into the "are we there yet?" mantra. But instead of letting it get to him, my dad responded with the same thing, every time.

"Just a little bit further."

At the time, I thought he was sort of lying to me. It wasn't just a little bit! I'd go a little bit and he'd say it again. It's lots of little bits. But actually that was the point. If I thought of the rest of the journey in hours and miles, I'd have lost heart. But at any point when it seemed like I couldn't go any more, he'd convince me that certainly I could go just another 100 feet. So I'd do it and we'd celebrate the small victory. Then another, and another. And eventually all of the little bits yielded a completed journey.

It was all a matter of perspective. I could do it; I just didn't know I could. But he knew, which was enough faith for both of us.

Prayer for the Week

God, I do my share of navel-gazing. I get wrapped up in my own pain and problems, until they seem consuming. Help me broaden my perspective, to see the bigger picture, to look up and out, rather than just in and down.

Popping Off

Art/music/video and other cool stuff that relate to the text

"Doubting Thomas," by Nickel Creek (song, 2012)

The Straight Story (movie, 1999)

"Brene Brown on Empathy" (video, 2013) https://www
.thersa.org/discover/videos/rsa-shorts/2013/12
/Brene-Brown-on-Empathy

Stay Thirsty,
My Friends

Lectionary Texts For
December 17, 2017 (Third Sunday in Advent)

Texts in Brief
My dog ate my Bible!

FIRST READING
Isaiah 61:1–4, 8–11
Isaiah is anointed by God to offer hope, justice, and an eternal promise to the people of Israel. They are so closely looked after by God they are like God's bride, he says. So even when things are difficult, they should find hope and endurance in that.

PSALM
Psalm 126
The author recalls how Zion, the capital city of the Jewish people, was restored to prosperity and greatness.

They seek and hope for such restoration for their own people in a time of hardship.

Second Reading
1 Thessalonians 5:16–24

Paul urges the Christians in Thessalonica to remain faithful to their religious practices, and to hang onto a spirit of gratitude. If they need something, they are to ask of it from God. He wants them to continue to tirelessly seek the wisdom and guidance of the prophets that came before them and to be wary of evil in their midst.

Gospel
John 1:6–8, 19–28

The author of the Gospel explains who John the Baptist is as the fulfillment of prophetic writings from the past. Some thought he was the Messiah, but his job, rather, is to make way for the Messiah, to stir up a hunger and to get people ready for his coming.

Bible, Decoded
Breaking down scripture in plain language

Anoint – We can anoint someone with oil, usually on their forehead, often to mark a special, sacred occasion. But someone who is anointed in scripture generally is appointed to a position of special divine authority. In this case, the prophet Elijah and John the Baptist were given specific and important roles in God's work. So they were anointed to go and do it.

Messiah – A messiah is one who is sent to save or liberate others. In the particular context of the Bible, it was generally believed by the Jews that the messiah would come to free them from being captive to their many occupiers. However, Jesus was more intent on liberating and saving them from their own sinfulness, which is part of the reason they were angry at him in the end.

Savior – Obviously, a savior is "one who saves." But we use this word a lot without explaining what people are being saved from. And the answer depends on who you ask: from sin; from themselves; from being lost and without purpose. And though there is the notion within contemporary Christianity of "being saved," as if it's a once-and-for-all thing, in these texts, people seem to need salvation, over and over again, when they lose hope, direction, or when things get really hard.

Points to Ponder

First Thoughts

In some of these texts, like Isaiah and the Gospel passage in John, the hope is found in looking forward to what hasn't come yet. In the psalm, the audience is reminded to look to the fulfillment of promises already made in the past. And in Thessalonians, Paul wants the early Christians to stay grounded in the present business they're about in founding and growing an emerging Christian community.

Sometimes nothing has to change for us to find hope except our perspective. Occasionally, we need nothing more than to get out of our own heads and look at things from a new vantage point. Great leaders and prophets give us this sort of vision, but the capacity to do this is within each of us already. Often, it is more a matter of getting "un-stuck" more than a lack of ability.

Stuck-ness happens usually when things are bad. If history in these passages serves as any example, getting un-stuck requires patience, persistence, and a hell of a lot of practice. But it also requires that we actually *want* to move on. This requires keeping a loose grip on our present situation, and a willingness to sacrifice familiarity for the promise of real hope.

Digging Deeper

Mining for what really matters . . . and gold

If the first forty or so chapters of Isaiah were the "Iron Fist" chapters, this is from the "Velvet Glove" section. Included here are words of reassurance for God's people, and praise to God. It also lays out what some of the people's lifelong priorities should be.

But the positive feelings here, continued into the psalm, are more than just a restoration of brokenness or relief from a long string of bad luck. It's a sort of joy bordering on dreamlike ecstasy. It's transcendent, almost surreal. We don't experience that kind of out-of-body elation just because we have a good day and things go right; it's because something significant has shifted, either in the world or, more often, in us.

But big changes are also disruptive. They interrupt the natural course of things, much like John the Baptist did. And while he didn't always preach feel-good sermons, he certainly made the proverbial ground move under people. He inspired them to change everything and take a different course.

While sometimes those shifts come in the form of fire-breathing prophets or ecstatic revelations, they can also emerge from faithful, steady spiritual practices, like the ones Paul calls his fellow Christians back to in Thessalonians. This is part of the necessary work of way-making that is required for the change we seek.

We could wait around for the next Isaiah, Paul, or John the Baptist to shake us out of our doldrums and set our course straight. We could look to heaven and hope to be struck by the Holy Spirit in a way that ignites a fire in us. Or we can go about the work of preparing, which often seems thankless, unglamorous, even pointless sometimes.

But, the passages here tell us, such faithful persistence yields incredible results, though we may not know how or when. There's a saying that faithfulness is about planting trees under whose shade we won't sit. The true challenge—and the moment when our persistence really becomes an act of faith rather than one of self-interest—is when we decide to try even if we don't get the credit or the good feelings.

It's also been said that both hard work and virtue are, in themselves, their own rewards. Maybe the ecstatic sort of experience described in the texts isn't so much about getting everything we always wanted or having our expectations finally and fully met. Maybe the Jewish people had to wander so long in order to finally let go of every last one of their expectations. An entire generation and then some passed before they came into the promise they had sought to find.

We can't really control or manage ecstasy into happening; it just happens. The best and most important thing we can do, then, is to be ready, to stay aware and make room for it when and if it comes.

Heads Up
Connecting the text to our world

There's a commercial for a beer company whose slogan is "Stay Thirsty, My Friends." It's said in such a cool and congenial way by the uber-suave spokesman that it's easy not to stop and think about what that really means.

Even if I drink his beer, he wants me to stay thirsty? Well, that just sucks. I mean, it's great for him and his business, because if I'm always thirsty, I'll never stop looking for more. Guaranteed win for them.

It's the sort of dream business model every company yearns for; to convince you on the one hand that their product will fix every problem in your life, while creating an unquenchable desire for more of it later. The tech world calls this "planned obsolescence," meaning they want the thing you're buying to meet your needs, but not for too long.

It creates the kind of insatiable desire for more that greases the wheels of capitalism.

The good news is that God's promises aren't empty like those of the marketing messages flooding the media airwaves. They just haven't been fully realized yet. Yes, we do live in the midst of God's love and unlimited grace, here and now, but the assurance we're given in scripture is that this sense of fulfillment we experience on occasion is small compared with the ecstasy of being fully immersed in the fullness of God's presence.

It tends to be the American dream to finally make enough money to free ourselves and our family of the work-for-pay daily grind. But if the needs that cost so much money to take care of weren't there anymore, what a relief it would be to find ourselves liberated from our endless list of wants, and from the desires that seem to keep such a tight grip on us.

That, to me, is something worth striving for.

Prayer for the Week

I'm not so good at releasing myself from my own wants and expectations, and particularly this time of year, it can seem like there are more of them than I can possibly handle. But with help, God, maybe I can replace all of those with a desire to reach for the one true thing that puts to rest all desire and, therefore, all suffering. I can't do it alone. Help me out!

Popping Off

Art/music/video and other cool stuff that relate to the text

2001: A Space Odyssey (movie, 1968)

"Most Interesting Man in the World" (commercial, 2010) https://www.youtube.com/watch?v=L8nt94LCyqY

"Here's the Truth about the 'Planned Obsolescence' of Tech," from the *BBC* (article, June 12, 2016) http://www.bbc.com/future/story/20160612-heres-the-truth-about-the-planned-obsolescence-of-tech

You Just Had to Be There

——————————— ᜏᜟ

Lectionary Texts For

December 24, 2017 (Fourth Sunday in Advent)

Texts in Brief

My dog ate my Bible!

First Reading

2 Samuel 7:1–11, 16

God speaks to Nathan, one of King David's court prophets, telling him that although the Israelites have been a wandering people for so long, they will now have a place, a land, and a community that won't be moved. Evidence of why David should have faith in this is given in God's past promises to David and the Jewish people that have been kept.

Psalm

Psalm 89:1–4, 19–26

This psalm tells of the immovable stability of God's love and faithfulness, and about David being ordained by God to rule over the Jewish people. It's an affirmation of his divine appointment as leader of the Jews.

SECOND READING
Romans 16:25–27

In this letter, Paul claims that Jesus was, in fact, the fulfillment of the promise God made to send a savior of the people. He is tying the early Christians' present work of spreading the gospel to the moment longed for so long ago by their ancestors, and saying that it is to be shared not only with Jews, but with non-Jews as well. Finally, though they find themselves in polytheistic Rome, he reaffirms that there is only one true God.

GOSPEL
Luke 1:46b–55

Known in church-speak as the "Magnificat," sung by Mary, mother of Jesus, this is a song not only of glorification to God; it is a call of rebellion. It's a celebration of the subversive nature of God's justice, finally filling the stomachs of those who hunger, and leaving those who previously have had plenty now empty-handed. This is a perfect example of the often-described "great reversals" that appear throughout the book of Luke.

(or)

Luke 1:26–38

Another landmark Gospel text, this passage known as the "Annunciation" is given to Mary by the angel Gabriel. Gabriel tells her she will give birth to a child she will call Jesus. She's a little confused since she's a virgin, but Gabriel assures her it's really going to happen. He reminds her of other times when women unable to have children were given children by God's direction. So it's both a celebration and a warning for her to get ready.

Bible, Decoded

Breaking down scripture in plain language

Magnificat – Not surprisingly, this translates as "Magnificent" from Latin, which refers to Mary's spontaneous, ecstatic song of praise to God after learning she is to give birth to the messiah of the Jewish people. It has since become the name of a song based on her words used in worship services on the fourth Sunday of Advent, right before the celebration of Jesus's birth on Christmas day.

Annunciation – Another term that is pretty clearly translated. This one, meaning "announcement," is about God's angel speaking to Mary. Think of it as the "big reveal" that we've been building up to through centuries of Jewish history.

Virgin – We assume this always refers to someone who hasn't yet had sex, but it comes from the Hebrew word *alma*, which actually refers to a girl who has entered puberty but who isn't married yet. It can be assumed that this means, then, that she also hasn't had sex, but that's not inherent in the actual meaning of the original word.

Cedar – Cedar wood (particularly Lebanese cedar) is · important throughout the Bible. First, it's believed this strong and durable wood was a gift from God to the inhabitants of those territories. Second, it symbolized the enduring faithfulness of both God and God's people. A house made of cedar would be one built to last that is solid and sturdy; it would also represent a dwelling place inhabited by God.

Points to Ponder

First Thoughts

A theme throughout these passages is faithfulness finally bearing fruit. The Jewish nomads finally get land to claim as their own, David is endowed with the throne as ruler of the Jews, and Mary will give birth to Jesus. These are all examples given of promises kept by God and realized for those who hung in there.

For the Christians in Rome, the theme of the fulfillment of promises is more of a reminder of why they're doing what they're doing. Suffice it to say that evangelizing in the capital of the empire that killed your leader is a little intimidating. I'm guessing Paul realized there was real risk of the entire movement falling apart there for fear of persecution. And while he's trying to encourage them by placing foremost in their minds that this is work of the greatest importance, it also seems like he might be guilting them a little, like "God kept God's promise; will you now turn around and break yours?"

Digging Deeper

Mining for what really matters . . . and gold

From a literary perspective, there's tremendous beauty in these passages (maybe except for Paul's letter, which isn't bad either), all of which revolve around the notion of dwelling places.

First, we have the rich symbolism of houses made of cedar in 2 Samuel, which have two meanings. The first layer of meaning is the "house" of the kingdom of David, whose rule would be critical in the establishment and strengthening of the emerging Jewish territory. This symbolism, then, is continued into the psalms, many of which are by or about King David. Second, David's son Solomon would eventually build God's "house," known to most as Solomon's temple. So the symbolism of the cedars holds these two different meanings together at the same time.

Gabriel's announcement to Mary and her resulting song of praise to God is a sort of consecration of her own body, if you think of it, as the new and incredibly unlikely dwelling place for the "becoming God." If you can imagine her being a physically living and breathing temple, being built and made holy from the inside out, it makes the lyrical quality of the words themselves so much more mind-blowing.

The Christians in Rome may feel like aliens, or even enemies of the state, sharing the stories of their messiah, Jesus. But Paul wants to affirm that their place is right where they are, and that they are home in the assurance that their work is God's work.

The difference between a house and a home is a sense of place and belonging. The dwelling places described in all of these texts are more about creating that sense of place and belonging than they are about the actual "container," so to speak. The difference in all cases here is that God made these people or places special, important, set apart for a purpose. Being grounded in a sense of purpose and belonging gives us life. In some ways, *it is life*.

Heads Up
Connecting the text to our world

Why is so much in these texts presented in a poetic or lyrical form, rather than just spoken or written in regular prose? Art, at its best, helps us elevate and transcend the mundane, giving more breadth, richness, and scope to just the words alone. After all, it's one thing to have someone tell us about an incredible live concert they saw, but it's another altogether to experience the energy and the collective celebration for ourselves.

This is part of what is at the heart of a discipline or medium that's becoming increasingly popular in postmodern philosophy and faith practices called "theopoetics." Whenever God is described in the Bible, it seems like words fall short of capturing the full wonder and awe contained in the experience. This is why we are left with supernatural images of skies being torn open, bushes bursting into flames, voices thundering from the heavens, and other fantastical descriptions of God's presence.

These are all attempts at conveying an experience that is sort of ineffable. It evokes a "you kind of had to be there" sentiment. Through a theopoetic medium like song or poetry, the authors are trying to draw us into that headspace to understand at least a taste of that incredible experience.

In recent history we've tried earnestly to connect with people's minds a lot in worship and teaching contexts. But sometimes a lecture or lesson just can't do what a theopoetic experience can. But it requires an openness to the unexpected, kind of like Nathan's openness to God's message, or Mary when visited by Gabriel. It's not easily choreographed or contained, but we still yearn to live into it and to share it in whatever ways we can.

So what are we to do? Stay awake and aware, open to the possibility that our rational, modern brains may never be able to conceive, or even grasp if experienced. But in those moments when we're struck, broken open by staggering beauty or mind-blowing new perspectives, we can start to understand at least part of the ecstasy that caused Mary to burst out in uncontrollable song.

Prayer for the Week

I'm not always "there" in the moment. Sometimes I wander, work, search, and even bang my head against the wall, trying to make sense of everything. But instead of me trying so hard to find You, help me trust that, wherever I am, if I'm open to it, You can find me.

Popping Off

Art/music/video and other cool stuff that relate to the text

"I Want to Sing" scene from *Monty Python and the Holy Grail* (movie, 1975): https://www.youtube.com/watch?v=g3YiPC91QUk

Magnificat in D Major, by Felix Mendelssohn (song, 1822)

"The 30 Best Retellings of Superman's Origins," by Greggory Basore (blog, Feb. 10, 2012) http://www .therobotsvoice.com/2012/02/the_30_best_ retellings_of_supermans_origins.php

Not Really
What I Had in Mind

———————∿∿∿———

Lectionary Texts For
December 31, 2017, (First Sunday After Christmas Day)

Texts in Brief
My dog ate my Bible!

FIRST READING
Isaiah 61:10–62:3

This passage starts and ends with praise to God. In between is the explanation why: namely, that God will save the Jewish people who have been wronged, and will vindicate them.

PSALM
Psalm 148

The poet here offers a full-throated proclamation of praise to God, not just personally, but calling on all of God's creation to join in the calls of thanks and gratitude. Inasmuch as everthing is God's creation, then all should offer thanks and praise. The author goes further, to say that the people of Jerusalem—God's chosen people, the Jews—should also be praised for their faithfulness and intimate connection to God.

SECOND READING
Galatians 4:4–7
This is from Paul's letter to the early Christians in Galatia. He's reminding them of their special place in the heart of God as adopted children. Though they've been slaves under Roman rule in the past, now their identity is as children under the wing of God.

GOSPEL
Luke 2:22–40
In this text, people are starting to recognize that Jesus is special. Mary and Joseph bring him to the temple in Jerusalem for purification and presentation to God as their firstborn son. When they get there they encounter Simeon, a very old and faithful man who had been told by God he would see the Messiah before his death. Simeon recognizes Jesus as the Messiah right away and bursts out in praise to God. Anna, a prophet and kind of temple ascetic, also knows who Jesus is and tells everyone about it.

Bible, Decoded
Breaking down scripture in plain language
Gentile – Anyone who wasn't Jewish.

Prophet – While some think of prophets almost as magicians, they are actually people of spiritual or religious vision and wisdom who speak to others to help them see things likewise. It's believed that their ability to see and be heard is a gift bestowed on them by God. A simpler way of thinking of a prophet is as a "truth-teller."

Abba – No, Jesus was not a fan of a Swedish pop band from the eighties. In this case, the word "abba" means "father," but in a more intimate, childlike way. It's more like saying "papa" or "daddy."

Points to Ponder

First Thoughts

When we first think about words like "vindication," "redemption," and "salvation" in these scriptures, we have to consider what they mean in context versus what they may mean to us today. Almost sounds like a Chuck Norris movie at first, and some folks writing the texts in the Bible believed that, someday, the bad guys who had done them wrong would get theirs, because God would effectively kick their ass.

But then we have this Jesus figure who comes along and turns all of that on end. He says you don't make violence and wrongdoing right by turning around and doing it to the one who messed with you. Yes, it feels great, and wouldn't it be nice if he gave us the green light to strike people down like we're so often inclined on first impulse? In fact, he upset a lot of people—particularly the ones talked about as God's chosen people here and lots of other places—for breaking it to them that the kind of redemption, salvation, and vindication he was bringing wasn't what they thought. Not at all.

Likewise, we have to ask ourselves what redeeming the world means in terms of our relationships, and the broken economic, political, and environmental systems all around us. If it's not as simple as us winning and someone else losing, what in the world does it look like? And as a result, what does that make of our job description as people seeking the upending worldview Jesus brought to share, and even died to do so?

Digging Deeper
Mining for what really matters . . . and gold

There's a theme of special and particular vision in all of these scripture passages. The authors each see or understand something—whether it's right in front of them, in the past, or yet to happen—that others might easily miss. I've heard people ask why it is that we need the Bible or prophets at all. Why make it so hard to understand the story and intent of God? Why give certain things to some like this, and not to others? Why use imperfect media like written and spoken words to convey these ideas that we seem to need but aren't simply divinely given in the first place?

Part of it may have to do with engineering. We each have the potential and tools for different things. It might also have to do with readiness, like having to stretch before a workout or "learning how to learn" in our early school years. But is it possible that it could have to do with openness and desire too?

In both Matthew and Luke, there are versions of the idea that, if we seek, we'll find what we're looking for. But maybe not if we're looking for the wrong things, or in the wrong places. We're also inclined to impatience.

kind of like when I send my son to his room to find his lost homework, only to have him back in front of me after thirty seconds, insisting he looked everywhere with no luck.

In many of the prophets, there are sayings about looking but not really *seeing*, or hearing but not actually *listening*. That's why so many passages start with words like "Behold!" It's a sort of warning that something heavy is headed your way, and you need to be seeing and listening.

We're on the cusp of a new year and the prospects of a new start. No doubt we already have all sorts of expectations about what will come next. But Paul tells us that we're children of God rather than slaves of human systems, not just because we can make our own choices. It's also a reminder to be open, innocent, wide-eyed, and vulnerable, like a child asking a parent, "What's next?"

Heads Up

Connecting the text to our world

The scriptures, whether from Isaiah or Luke, are written either by or about people who have a tremendous expectancy for God to fulfill some big promises and to witness the coming of one who will enable these things to happen. It's only in Galatians that the audience is a group of people who know what all really went down before and after the crucifixion.

Think any of the "before" people would have been let down by Jesus's way of fulfilling God's promises? Let's consider it in a more current-day, practical way. Think back to a time when you were a kid and you saw the Christmas presents waiting under the tree. Remember how your imagination went wild, thinking of what was in those boxes? It makes me think of the dad in the movie, *A Christmas Story*, who wins a contest from a magazine and his "major award" arrived on the doorstep in a crate.

"It could be anything," he wondered aloud. "It could be a bowling alley!" It's typically human to create expectations in our own minds that inevitably won't be met. And there are a few ways we can deal with such a shock.

One way is like the dad in the movie, who tried to pretend he was just as excited and proud of the leg lamp he found in the crate as he would have been of the hoped-for bowling alley. Another is to kick and scream and vent our feelings of betrayal at God or whoever disappointed us (never mind that it was we ourselves who set up the unrealistic expectations). Or we can try to accept that, sometimes, we are our own worst enemies when it comes to expectations.

In this first Sunday after Christmas, there are plenty of reasons to feel that typical annual let-down. The decorations that were so pretty last week now annoy us with their blinking, tinseled reminders that we have to put them all away. Inevitably some party, gift, or family gathering didn't go the way we'd hoped. Even church has been emptied of all the holiday visitors who come either for a feeling they're seeking or because mom made them.

It's all just . . . blah.

A song by the Rolling Stones comes to mind; to paraphrase, getting what you need sometimes comes easier than getting what you want.

Maybe what we want actually was getting in the way of what we need. Maybe Jesus actually knew what he was doing. And just maybe the next time around we'll remember the old trope about expectations being premeditated resentments and set them down, staying open, trusting that if we try sometimes, we just might find we get what we need.

Prayer for the Week

God, I know what I want, but I don't always know what I need. Help me recognize the difference, and to trust that I'm not always the best judge of my own needs.

Popping Off

Art/music/video and other cool stuff that relate to the text

A Christmas Story (movie, 1983)

"You Can't Always Get What You Want," by The Rolling Stones (song, 1969)

My God, Not Yours

Lectionary Texts For

January 7, 2018 (First Sunday after Epiphany)

Texts in Brief

My dog ate my Bible!

FIRST READING

Genesis 1:1–5

In the first of two creation stories in Genesis, the text proclaims that both the heavens (the skies) and the earth (including land and waters) were created by God. Then it describes the "first day" when God called forth light into existence, creating both day and night once light and dark were separated.

PSALM

Psalm 29

This poem or song speaks to the breadth and power of God's presence. It brings things into creation and down to destruction. It is in all things, and therefore all things should cry out in praise to God. Toward the end, God is more of an elevated figure, lording over all, eternal and in control. Finally, there's a brief and relatively humble request for God to grant strength and peace to God's people.

SECOND READING

Acts 19:1–7

Paul meets a handful of disciples (the text says about twelve of them at the very end) in Ephesus, a coastal city in present-day Turkey where early Christians were sharing the stories about Jesus. Paul asks them what they were baptized in and, reasonably enough, they said "the Jordan River." He explains to them that there's a difference between taking part in the baptism ritual and being consumed by the spirit Jesus was talking about. When he touched their heads, they "caught wind" of the spirit and started speaking in weird languages and about things God had given them a vision to see.

GOSPEL

Mark 1:4–11

This is the story of John the Baptist (Jesus's cousin) shouting sermons with tremendous passion from the banks for the Jordan River and then baptizing those present in a spirit of leaving their sins behind. He was quite a character, with camel-hair clothes and a diet of bugs. Though the telling is brief in this Gospel, it explains that Jesus was baptized by John and that a spirit appeared after the ritual was complete. The spirit claims Jesus as God's son.

Bible, Decoded

Breaking down scripture in plain language

Kadesh – The root of the name of this ancient Israelite city actually means "holy." There are two cities in the Hebrew Bible/Old Testament referred to as "Kadesh," one in southern Israel and another to the east. So this reference could be an assertion of the boundaries and domain the Jewish people, or it could be a statement of God's presence being all across the Jewish territory. The word also is used several times to refer to significant locations in the Hebrew Bible, so it's a testament to the importance of any place that God "touches."

Sirion – The most literal translation of the word is "breastplate" or "body armor." So this reference in Psalms could allude to the notion that God protects and defends God's people against outside threats. Geographically, it refers to Mount Hermon, or more generally the range of mountains at the edge of Phoenician territory. So it's also a possible reference to God's voice or presence making entire mountains shake.

Ephesus – Ephesus was a big deal back in the day. It was a major cultural and commercial hub, kind of like New York. Lots of shipping and roads converged here. Many temples to Greek (therefore pagan or gentile to the Jews) gods stood there too, so it was a ripe spot for trying to get people to sign on with the Christian movement.

Tongues – Speaking in tongues is listed in the Bible as one of several "spiritual gifts" given to faithful people by God. So speaking in tongues would signify being overwhelmed by God's spirit. There is controversy, especially today, about this practice, which some still use in more "charismatic" worship services, because it also says in scripture that it's not a gift from God unless there also is someone present with the spiritual gift of interpreting the "tongues."

Points to Ponder

First Thoughts

It's notable that, in the Genesis text, it speaks of God presiding over the waters. Then in the psalm piece, it says God is enthroned over the flood. This could simply be a reference back to the Genesis piece. But it might also be an assertion that God was in charge of the great flood described in the story of Noah.

There are several references to other scriptures in these writings. One or them is when Paul talks to the disciples in Ephesus about how they were baptized, and they say it took place in the Jordan River. It's not said explicitly, but it could be suggesting that they were baptized by John the Baptist, who is described baptizing Jesus in the Mark passage.

There's also a lot about where God is present in these stories. In Genesis, God is everywhere. In the psalm, God is still everywhere, but more specifically over Israel. In Acts, God appears to and inspires his followers, as beckoned by Paul. Finally, God appears particularly over Jesus at the time of his baptism. Interesting how it goes from universal to very specific.

Finally, it's not insignificant in Acts that the number of disciples described is "about twelve." This matters because the number twelve is used to refer back to the original disciples who followed Jesus himself. So it's symbolically connecting these disciples to those.

Digging Deeper

Mining for what really matters . . . and gold

The practice of referring back to symbols, places, or events that happened before in holy texts is called *midrash* in Hebrew. Basically, when there's a midrashic clue in a passage, it's a sort of alert to pay close attention. The author is trying to say there's something really important to take away from the words.

There's plenty of *midrash* going on this week. Personally, I find *midrash* kind of fun, sort of like finding hidden "Easter eggs" in video games. In these cases, the Easter eggs all point to where we can find God.

It's easy enough to just say offhand that God is everywhere, and leave it at that. But do we really mean it? Is God in my horrible day? The rock I just kicked into the gutter? The mosquito I just squashed on my neck? From these scriptures, we might say yes. Some of us may struggle with this. We want our God to be personal, specific, particular. We don't want God to be equally with "those Muslims" as God is with us. If that's the case, what's the point? What do we get out of all of this?

We can see the narrowing down of God's place in our midst as we move forward through the scriptures. This could suggest either that God becomes more particular about where God deems it worthwhile to be present. It could also point to the desire of those writing the words (and those about which they're being written) to have special favor with God.

Theologian Fred Craddock, among others, I expect, warned against an "either/or faith," opting instead for a "both/and faith." God is in, with, and among all people and all things. Yet at the same time, God is personal, intimate, parental, and close as described last week.

Our problems start when we let our binary way of dividing up the world take over when reading the Bible, as well as when our egos require God to be mine and not yours.

Egos and human frailties aside, God keeps showing up in both terribly powerful and gently personal ways. It's no small relief to consider that God is well beyond our ability to conceive or describe. Not a bad thought to carry us into a new year.

Heads Up

Connecting the text to our world

I hear the phrase "God's country" a lot. Oftentimes we don't mean it with much seriousness, beyond suggesting that the place in question is beautiful, inspiring, or special. The problems come when we start to draw lines and build walls around it.

It's interesting to consider that, in the ancient temples—a practice carried over into modern times by some—there's a special part of a church or temple where "regular people" can't go. This area is supposed to be particularly special, or perhaps a dwelling place for God. Therefore, only those properly equipped can enter. But at the moment when Jesus died, the curtain that divided the special area from the rest where everyone else went was torn in half.

The division between God and humanity created by other people was obliterated. And yet we keep stitching the proverbial curtain back together.

Be it national boundaries, walls of religious exclusion, or labels that make someone "other" or "less than," we're intent on rebuilding the walls that God tears down. So it begs the question whether those who seek to exemplify the ways of Jesus in the world are to participate in the creation, affirming and reinforcing these separating boundaries, or if we're meant for something else. Maybe something quite the opposite.

Prayer for the Week

God, breaker of walls and boundaries, help me let go of my own walls of otherness, whether they're political, economic, racial, sexual, religious, or otherwise. Give me some of the strength and peace they talk about in this psalm to know there's more than enough to go around. Then grant me the resources and conviction to smash some walls I find around me.

Popping Off

Art/music/video and other cool stuff that relate to the text

The Wall (movie, 1982)

Resources on queer theology: https://www.queertheology.com

Who Are You, Really?

Lectionary Texts For
January 14, 2018 (Second Sunday after Epiphany)

Texts in Brief
My dog ate my Bible!

FIRST READING
1 Samuel 3:1–10 (11–20)

Samuel, in the care of Eli the priest, is called out of his bed three times in the night. Samuel thinks Eli is calling him, but Eli finally realizes it's God who is calling him. After the third calling, Samuel tells God he's listening. Then God lays out the bad news about Eli's household and lineage being held to account for blasphemy, for which there's no forgiveness. From there, Samuel becomes known as a great prophet and folks pay close attention to what he says.

PSALM

Psalm 139:1–6, 13–18

The psalmist is singing a song of awe to God for the depth of God's understanding of them, not just who they are, but who they would become. Though a little scared to be so completely known, the feeling also is assuring. And in a final gesture of praise, they give thanks for the assurance that, just as they were with God before birth, they'll also be with God after death.

SECOND READING

1 Corinthians 6:12–20

Paul writes to the Christians in Corinth about reasons to avoid sinful acts that defile themselves. Whereas under Jewish law, it was more a matter of following the law, the rules for behavior as a follower of Jesus have a deeper connotation. Paul's point is that, once we are joined to God through Jesus, we become part of a greater unified body and spirit. Therefore, whatever we do with our bodies from then forward, we also do to God and our fellow followers. So obeying the rules of propriety is not just about self-restraint anymore. It's a part of honoring "God in us."

GOSPEL

John 1:43–51

Philip becomes one of Jesus's early followers. Then when he and Jesus go to Bethsaida, he recruits Nathaniel. Nathaniel is skeptical of Jesus being legitimate because he's a Nazarene, but he comes to realize Jesus is who he says he is. Though Nathaniel is excited to really "see" Jesus—not just with his eyes, but to get it—and to be seen as well at such a profound level, Jesus responds with "you ain't seen nothin' yet."

Bible, Decoded
Breaking down scripture in plain language

Bethsaida – A city east of the Jordan River, along the Sea of Galilee and in the Golan Heights where it's believed the "feeding of the 5,000" took place. One reason it's significant, especially so early in Jesus's ministry, is because it's considered a "gentile" city. So already, Jesus is establishing precedent by reaching out beyond the Jewish people, even for his own inner circle of ministry and leadership.

Rabbi – Simply means "teacher." It's a sort of honorific for someone who possesses particular religious or spiritual wisdom. It's a title of deference.

Fornication – Refers to any sexual or lustful act that is considered a violation of Jewish law, and also can, at least implicitly, refer to acts of sexual hedonism performed in the ritual worship of other gods.

Points to Ponder
First Thoughts

What a crappy deal Samuel got by finally accepting the call to be a messenger of God! His first job is to go tell his guardian, Eli, that he and his entire family are screwed for past acts of screw-ups. So not only does he have to give Eli bad news; it's also bad news for him. Unfortunately speaking difficult truths isn't necessarily the best way to win a popularity contest. But who needs popularity when you're a mouthpiece for God, right? Still, it's hard, often depressing work. I mean, look how it worked out for Jesus, John the Baptist, Paul.... I could go on but you get the idea. It's not a life of glamour, but it is important work. And if it's what we've been made to do, who are we to go against our inner nature for the rest of our lives?

Another striking thing about this Samuel passage is something reiterated much later in the Gospels, and occasionally elsewhere, which is the matter of unforgivable sin. Though we have passages in Paul's letters and in the Psalms that assure us there's nothing we can do to sever the bond we have with God, there is a clear line in scripture beyond which we can't achieve full reconciliation. Blasphemy can mean lots of things, but the way I think of it is that it's an act of willful separation from God. Yes, God never leaves us, but we also have choice. If that choice is to leave God, it's an act of free will. Just because that covenant has been broken doesn't mean the relationship is entirely over, but some things can't be erased. You can't un-ring a bell, as they say.

It's worth emphasizing that this story in John is the first of many times Jesus will go out of his way to reach out to the "others." Much like with Samuel, this doesn't win Jesus any popularity points with his fellow Jews, who feel they should stick to taking care of their own. But some things are more important than living up to others' expectations. For Jesus, reaching across lines is one of those.

Oh, and we can't pass up the chance to get a smile from Nathaniel's jab at people from Nazareth. Being a native Texan from birth (though now an Oregonian by choice), I know what it's like to be judged for where you're from. But it's appropriate that Jesus would be from somewhere that others look down on. Makes for an even bigger expectation-smashing surprise when they realize what he's really about.

Digging Deeper

Mining for what really matters . . . and gold

One of the cultural values we have to consider in reading these passages is that these are tribal people. There's really no such thing as fierce self-reliance. Unlike our valuation of bootstrapping and "self-made" people in contemporary western culture, such self-serving pursuits would have been seen as defeating of the greater whole back then.

Though we value independence, even see it as the brass ring to have financial and professional autonomy, the ethos of the biblical cultures was one of *interdependence*. So whereas it's a long journey for us to go from our contemporary cultural paradigm to one of being an inextricable part of a larger body, this was an extension of an existing reality for the Jews.

We should also not let it slip by us that God calls Samuel three times before he really makes the connection. This is a *midrashic* literary device to symbolize many things, among them the formation of bonds, as well as the breaking of them. Peter denies Jesus three times before he's crucified. Jesus also asks Peter three times if Peter loves him. Even the notion of the Trinity—one God represented in three expressions—suggests this multiplicity coexisting within one greater whole.

This is what we could call a covenant, or a "holy promise." Once Samuel comes to terms with hearing and heeding the call of God, he can't un-hear it. He's forever changed. He's let something in at a deep, personal level that will haunt and transform him the rest of his life.

Is this a good thing or a bad thing? It probably depends on the day you asked him. But it's real, it's thorough, and it's a turning point of significance, to which we're called to pay close attention.

Heads Up
Connecting the text to our world

One of the first questions we usually ask someone when we meet them is, "What do you do?" By this, we usually are referring to what kind of employment they have, as this is something we put a lot of our time, energy, and identity into. It's a safe, somewhat superficial way to try and get to know someone. Even when we talk to kids, we simply adapt the question to ask what they want to be later when they get older.

But we all know that someone's career path doesn't necessarily reveal to us the essence of who someone truly is. In fact, sometimes we hide behind titles and sociocultural roles to keep people from ever really knowing us. Our cultural identities become these masks we wear more and more. We can even get to where we keep them on when we look in the mirror.

It's easy to forget that we aren't our masks. We're not our titles or roles. But letting someone know us more intimately and deeply than that can be uncomfortable, even terrifying. At our little startup church in southern Colorado, I once heard a retired Methodist pastor speak who confessed that he had been hiding behind a pulpit in his ministry for more than thirty-five years. He'd do his weekly sermons, conduct his visitations, attend meetings, but never really let anyone in. He talked about the mixture of comfort, terror, and relief of finally being in a church where people knew him for him.

It makes me think of the Cheshire Cat in *Alice in Wonderland* who, with his creepy all-seeing gaze, keeps asking Alice "Who are you?" Her name and where she's from doesn't satisfy him. Being a little lost girl who fell down a hole doesn't get at what he wants. But the more he asks, the more awkward it gets.

If you've ever really been deeply and thoroughly known by someone else, you can probably relate to the exhilaration and awe of the author of the psalm. There's both a profound comfort and an inescapable sense of presence that comes with being known as well as God is said to know us. Self-deception doesn't escape it. Running doesn't get beyond its reach. Instead, we're invited to resign to it, to fall into it completely and come to terms with the intimacy.

Who are you?

Prayer for the Week

God, you get it. You get me, better than I even get myself. Help me stop fighting it, and in doing so, help me let go of the need to be something else to the rest of the world.

Popping Off

Art/music/video and other cool stuff that relate to the text

Alice in Wonderland (book, 1865; movie, 1951, 2010)

Bruce Almighty (movie, 2003)

Evan Almighty (movie, 2007)

Die, Yuppie Scum

‹mark_waveform›

Lectionary Texts For
January 21, 2018 (Third Sunday after Epiphany)

Texts in Brief
My dog ate my Bible!

First Reading
Jonah 3:1–5, 10

Jonah is ordered by God to go tell the people of Nineveh they'll be destroyed for their evildoing in forty days. They freak out, repent, and God decides not to destroy them since they've changed course.

Psalm
Psalm 62:5–12

King David sings this song of fidelity to God, and God alone. He notes that power comes and goes, as does the money that comes with it and even the people who possess it. Instead, he puts his trust, value, and heart in the hands of God, because he realizes what he puts himself into is what ultimately will come back to him.

SECOND READING
1 Corinthians 7:29–31

Paul's grave warnings to the Christians in Corinth is a reminder to set everything down and release it, including all material possessions and even people they love. He speaks about the end of the world as we know it, which, from this excerpt alone, it's hard to tell if he means the second coming of Jesus and thus the end of all humanity, or if he's keenly aware that those neophyte Christians in foreign territory will soon be martyred.

GOSPEL
Mark 1:14–20

Jesus's cousin, John the Baptist, is arrested for being a religious troublemaker. Jesus continues on, preaching that the fulfillment of things promised by God is nearly complete, which would indicate that things are about to change for everyone. He warns them to get right with God and be ready. He also recruits Simon and Andrew as his new disciples, luring (pun intended) them away from their lives as fishermen to fish instead for people. Finally, he recruits James and John away from their family and their lives in the fishing village to be disciples as well.

Bible, Decoded
Breaking down scripture in plain language

Selah – A holy pause, placed in a text to indicate the reader should stop, reflect, and leave room in silence for God's inspiration to enter.

Galilee – The city of Galilee and the sea for which it was named are central in the Gospel stories in particular. Though it's called a sea, it's actually a freshwater lake, so it's not only a hub of commerce for the region, but also a primary source of drinking water. It was fed by the Jordan River, where John the Baptist ministered to locals, and where he baptized Jesus. So Jesus hasn't gone far from where his ministry started, but he's in the heart of a bustling economic region, telling people to walk away from it all.

Forty Days – Whenever we see this number in scripture, we know there's a connection to other occurrences. For example, the flood story about Noah involved forty days of rain (not that big a deal here in Portland), and the Israelites led by Moses out of Egypt spent forty years in the desert before entering their new homeland. It seems this signifies a time of purging, transition, and even cataclysmic ruptures that yield something entirely new.

Points to Ponder

First Thoughts

By the time he writes this psalm, David has a whole pile of enemies. And suffice it to say that he has come by his enemies honestly. So although by itself, the passage seems to be a song of obedience to God from a man of faith, it's worth noting that, by now, David doesn't have a lot of other places to turn anymore.

We have to keep in mind that Nineveh isn't just any city; it's an Assyrian stronghold. The Assyrians were brutal and prone to war, and were ferocious enemies of the Jews. So Jonah walking into the city and condemning them on behalf of God would be sort of like walking into a North Korean city and telling them God was about to strike them down. It also helps explain why, as we learn later (especially in the book of Nahum) Jonah isn't too happy with God for showing them mercy.

Digging Deeper

Mining for what really matters . . . and gold

The connective tissue among all of these texts this week is pretty evident. We're to get our priorities in proper order before it's too late. In some cases, that comes in the form of God's wrath (even if, to Jonah's disappointment, God erred on the side of compassion instead). In the case of Paul and Jesus, there's reference to the end of everything as we know it, though it's necessary to point out that for both of them and their followers, the end came more or less for speaking of such things. In David's case, his grip on wealth and power, and particularly the means by which he acquired it, left him with no one on his side anymore, save for God.

A more traditional (translated: conservative) interpretation of this might emphasize end-times, striking fear into others and seeking converts to the faith. But it seems there's no real emphasis here at all on making statements of faith or becoming part of some new religious group. Yes, there's talk of repentance, but it's worth digging into the idea of what that means in context.

The type of repentance talked about by and large in this week's passages is an about-face away from business and life as usual. It's about cutting loose the ties that hold us back from connecting more intimately with God and what matters most. And we see glimpses of what lies ahead if we don't. For Nineveh it's being overthrown, be it by God alone, by an enemy army, or maybe both. David gets wise to the fact that he's come into his way of life at much cost to others, for whom he's become a sworn enemy. Jesus and Paul speak more vaguely of things getting bad very soon, and it's not entirely clear if this is in reference to spiritual and existential decline or a demise of the more personal, material sort.

But the particularities aside, the message is resoundingly clear throughout: Being tied to the things of this world leads to nothing but death and decay. In some cases, the call is literally to walk away from it all: even those we love most, which I can't imagine. But even in cases where it's not mandated to leave everything behind, there's a message to not allow our status, possessions, way of life, or even immediate family keep us from the radical, unbinding call of God.

Heads Up

Connecting the text to our world

I was a teenager in the eighties, which was a period of fairly extravagant wealth in the United States. We lived in Dallas, Texas, which probably benefited more than most places from the oil and commercial construction booms that took hold of the economy back then. And as if all of it was going to last forever, people went a little crazy with all their newfound wealth. J. R. Ewing, from the TV show *Dallas*, became a sort of archetype for how far the thirst for more went.

The mentality of acquiring more permeated all levels of the culture. Nearly every day, you'd see a bumper sticker with the phrase, "The Person Who Dies with the Most Toys, Wins." There was even a name for the successors to the hippies of the sixties who now were the driving force in the exploding landscape of American commerce. YUPPIES. It stood for "Young Upwardly Mobile Professionals," but it represented far more than that.

For some, being a yuppie was the proverbial brass ring. It was the sign that you had arrived, that you were finally someone. But there was no small amount of pushback against this mentality that had supplanted the "free love" and anti-establishment movement of the Woodstock era, of protest and calls for revolution.

Soon we began to see more "Die, Yuppie Scum" bumper stickers in response to the "Most Toys" ones. The phrase "Eat the Rich," coined by philosopher Jean-Jacques Rousseau, became the refrain of a popular rock song blasted over the airwaves. For every yuppie, there was an anarchist call to burn it all down.

Not that I think Paul, John the Baptist, Jesus, and Jonah would have advocated cannibalism and arson (well, maybe Jonah would), but we have to wonder which side of this back-and-forth they would have been on. They were the upstart rebels, threatening the status quo that so many had come to value and even worship. Their message was unpopular, yes, but it also resonated with many, especially the poor and dispossessed. We're not all Jonah or John, and we're certainly not Jesus, but we have to consider, if they came upon us today, whether we'd be living examples of the priorities they called people to, or if we'd be on the receiving end of some harsh condemnation ourselves.

Prayer for the Week

God, I like stuff, even though no matter how much I have, it never seems to be enough. Help me find the peace and sense of gratitude to set it aside and release my need for more of its power over me.

Popping Off

Art/music/video and other cool stuff that relate to the text

Wall Street (movie, 1987)

"Eat the Rich," by Krokus (song, 1983)

Chasing Our Fifteen Minutes

Lectionary Texts For
January 28, 2018 (Fourth Sunday after Epiphany)

Texts in Brief
My dog ate my Bible!

First Reading
Deuteronomy 18:15–20

Moses tells his fellow Israelites that there will be another prophet like him from among their ranks and they're warned to do what that prophet says or there'll be trouble. Moses also cautions anyone who might think of seizing on this announcement as an opportunity to claim authority that God hasn't given them because, he says, if God hasn't empowered them to prophecy, the job will kill them.

Psalm

Psalm 111

David is extolling the power, love, and grace of God, also ticking off the promises kept and good things God has done for God's people. Based on this alone, it could be simply a solitary, joyful outburst. But given that it's archived in scripture, we can assume there's a greater corporate meaning to be had. It seems it's a sort of reminder of the goodness of God for those of us (all of us at times, including David), who fall away from a connection with God or whose memory of the good things in our past gets muddled by the present.

Second Reading

1 Corinthians 8:1–13

In this beautiful passage, Paul asserts that just knowing something doesn't do us any good; rather, it's being filled with love, not knowledge, that is the most virtuous and important thing. He does affirm that making sacrifices of food to idols is not what we're called to do, but we shouldn't lord it over those who worship idols on the grounds that we "know better." Rather than feeling better than anyone else (which can set an example that leads people away from God), we're intended to love them, no matter what. In doing so, that's how they find their way to the God we claim has emboldened and filled us with such abundant, unconditional love.

Gospel

Mark 1:21–28

Jesus goes to the temple in the city of Capernaum and amazes the scribes there with his understanding of the Torah. But more than that, they're awestruck when he casts a dark spirit out of a man who comes to the temple. This starts the word-of-mouth churning, and he starts to become a figure of interest. Both his teaching and his miracle of casting out spirits is said to endow him with "authority."

Bible, Decoded
Breaking down scripture in plain language

Horeb – Mount Horeb is where it says in Deuteronomy that God gave Moses the Ten Commandments. In both the book of Kings and Exodus, Mount Horeb is described as the "mountain of God." Generally, when there's a mountain in scripture, it is in reference to something important happening. Mountaintops also are often considered holy places, where humanity and the Divine connect.

Fear – In the context of scripture, the word "fear" as used in the psalm (fear of the Lord) is meant more as respect, rather than being terrified.

Capernaum – This city on the northern edge of the Sea of Galilee was considered Jesus's hometown in the early part of his ministry. So even though this is where his reputation as a man of God really got kick-started, he says later in Mark—and it's echoed in Luke and Matthew too—that a prophet is usually hated and disrespected in his home territory.

Authority – We think of an authority as someone who holds a high office and therefore has significant power and prestige. And though there's power in Jesus's acts and words, there's another way we need to consider the meaning of authority. An author is someone who creates, who summons something from nothing. They make the unseen visible and the unknown clear when they exert real authority. To me, this is the kind of authority that Jesus would be more likely to claim.

Points to Ponder

First Thoughts

It seems worth noting that, in Corinthians, Paul not only holds up love over knowledge; he also values being known over knowledge itself. In particular, it's being known by God that's emphasized, but this begs the question about the importance of connections and relationship over personal edification.

The author of Mark here focuses on the renown Jesus begins to gain for his wisdom, knowledge, and works. But as we go on in the Gospels, we see increasingly that Jesus has no interest in this for himself. His only use for having an audience is to share the stories and messages he feels compelled to give to the world. And when people try to exalt him, he is careful to remind them that his purpose is to point toward God and not himself. He would rather see their adoration and devotion directed to God, and his example of self-lessness and being a path toward something greater than ourselves is our aim.

We can imagine that some people heard Moses's warnings about false prophets claiming authority and responded with serious eye-rolls. *Who does he think he is, anyway? That guy can't even talk without stumbling on his own words. So being the leader is good enough for*

him, but not for us? He's just worried we'd be better at it
than he is. In fact, I'm pretty sure I could. . . .

But his warnings really are in our best interests, if
we're able to see beyond our own egos and desires. He
realizes that it takes far more than what tools we have
on our own to carry out such a heavy mission. And yet
our response to such warnings is about the same that
parents get when they tell kids they're doing something "for your own good." At least, I know how I used
to respond to that phrase, and it definitely wasn't with
deference.

Digging Deeper
Mining for what really matters . . . and gold

We think of prophets today as pretty unique. It's not
every day we meet someone who has PROPHET on
their business card. But back in biblical times, it was
common for leaders to have scores, or even hundreds,
of prophets to call on for guidance. We have to believe
that, among these were more than a small number of
false prophets, those who saw claiming such authority
as a way to get in good with their leaders, and so gain
special privilege or status. But for the prophets in our
stories here, that's not so much the case.

Each of them—Moses, David, Paul, and Jesus—had
those "Who, me?" or "Why me?" moments. Moses tried
to say no to God's call because he didn't think he could
handle it. David was a kid out in the sheep pastures.
Paul was struck blind by God's presence. And even
Jesus asked at least once for the call God had presented
him with to be taken away.

And yet each of them had a special gift, a set of tools they may not even have been aware of themselves entirely. People around them doubted as well. Jesus faced this a lot, with people constantly questioning his authority. And why not? False prophets abounded at the time and, for many, it was hard to know who was legitimate.

In our psalm, David recalled the promises made and fulfilled in Exodus, and of which Moses spoke. Paul had David's, Moses's, and Jesus's legacy and stories to lean on.

The difference between our garden-variety prophets and the truly great, culture-shifting ones has to do with seeing ahead to what will come as they follow their path through to completion and doing it anyway. It's about remaining faithful to their call when the fame, admiration, and wealth fall away. It's about taking to heart the notion asserted throughout the Gospels by Jesus to get over ourselves, and that the work we're called to isn't just about us. It's about having the vision to see our greater purpose and to find a sense of humble duty in it, leaving all else as secondary to what matters most.

It's a rare person who can fulfill such a role. But when you're called and the tools have been afforded you, the only right response is to go.

Heads Up

Connecting the text to our world

In a recent study, a number of pre-adolescent children were asked what they wanted to be when they grow up. The number one answer was "famous." We've become a culture in which fame celebrates itself, as is evident during the movie, TV, and music awards seasons in particular. But with the opening up of media channels, combined with the explosive popularity of "reality" television, it seems that fame, in and of itself, is reason enough to be famous.

The viral nature of online media causes things to gain momentum like an avalanche, with more people watching simply because others are watching. The result is the vaulting of people like the Kardashians to media powerhouse status, simply for being . . . them.

But to what end? The attention may give us a degree of power or wealth, but the veneer is thin, and people's attention often is superficial and fleeting. We can examine the public record, too, for the effects of such immense fame on the human psyche, and of its inevitable absence later on.

Jason Russell, better known as the maker of the 2012 Kony video, suffered a public emotional break-down under the pressure of such sudden, fierce global attention. More former child actors than not litter the shoulders of Hollywood's star-studded streets. The list of lives lost due to emotional decline, drug abuse, and other related responses to fame seems endless. And yet we crave it.

I have a friend who owned a record label in the Pacific Northwest back in the 80s and 90s when grunge music was emerging as the newest force in rock. He played in bands with some of the most famous musi-cians in the world. Today, he lives with his wife and son on a few acres in a pastoral exurb of Portland, happy to have left the entertainment world far behind him. He speaks to me of his own spiraling struggle with abuse back then, as well as all the friends and loved ones he's lost to the ever-hungry fame machine.

The lure of admiration, status, power, and renown is fiercely strong in our culture. And yet it leads to death and decay. We know this, and still we long for it. Had Moses been able to pass his mantle along to another, I expect he would have done so with gratitude. David is king, but everyone hates him. Paul is a figure of great influence among early Christians, but he'll pay for it with his life. And Jesus . . . well, we know how that ended.

Prayer for the Week

God, I see rich and famous people, and I find myself envying them. Sometimes, I may even go out of my way to get a taste of what they seem to have. Help me keep my head straight. Help me remember where those roads lead.

Popping Off

Art/music/video and other cool stuff that relate to the text

Heavier Than Heaven: A Biography of Kurt Cobain (book, 2002)

A Band Called Death (movie, 2012)

Almost Famous (movie, 2000)

"The price of fame: pop stars are more likely to die young" from *The Independent* (article, Sept. 3, 2007) http://www.independent.co.uk/arts-entertainment /music/news/the-price-of-fame-pop-stars-are -more-likely-to-die-young-463836.html

Fighting True North

Lectionary Texts For
February 4, 2018 (Fifth Sunday after Epiphany)

Texts in Brief
My dog ate my Bible!

FIRST READING
Isaiah 40:21–31

This passage is in three sections; the first and third start the same, with the author of Isaiah seeming a little baffled that his audience hasn't absorbed the scope and endurance of God's power and presence yet. In section one, he reasserts God as creator and destroyer of all things, for all time. Then God speaks directly to the audience, wondering why they feel they're not heard by or in reach of God. Finally, Isaiah's voice returns, assuring listeners that God will strengthen them and give them endurance if they place their trust in God.

PSALM

Psalm 147:1–11, 20c

A song of God's power and wisdom, the beginning speaks of justice coming to the good and wicked alike. Many attributes of God are listed, including grace, mercy, and strength. In the second part, the psalmist notes that God's not impressed by skill and performance, but rather by devotion, respect, and obedience.

SECOND READING

1 Corinthians 9:16–23

Paul offers two brief lessons in this short passage. First is a reminder not to take personal pride in our own accomplishments. Rather, we're always to defer to the priorities God gives us and keep the perspective that all we can do, we do as a gift from God. Second, he offers a quick lesson in cultural competency, telling his fellow Christians to really understand—and integrate with—the culture in which they find themselves. This is done, not in order to be affirmed and to fit in, but to gain credibility when we share what is at the center of who we are, as informed by the gospel.

GOSPEL

Mark 1:29–39

Jesus heals Simon's mother-in-law of a bad fever, which leads others to begin bringing sick and infirm people to him for healing. After a while, he heads out into the wilderness on his own to pray. When his disciples find him and tell him there are lots of people looking for him, he says that it's time instead to move on and to share what they have to share in other parts of Galilee.

Bible, Decoded

Breaking down scripture in plain language

Jacob – In the Isaiah passage, there's a reference to people crying out, "O Jacob, O Israel. ..." Jacob was the grandson of Abraham, the man with whom God made a lasting covenant for him and all his descendants (the Jewish people). Jacob (with the help of his mother, Rebecca) stole his brother Esau's birthright as the first-born son. God gave Jacob the new name of "Israel," which means "he who struggles with God."

Jerusalem – This city is mentioned more than 800 times in scripture. In the Gospels, Jesus is brought to, and goes to, Jerusalem quite often. For Jews, it's considered the holiest city in their faith, much like Mecca for Muslims. In ancient times, it was believed that God-on-earth dwelled in Jerusalem.

Galilee – Jesus's home turf, Galilee is effectively the entire northern section of Israel. It's an area with a high concentration of people, commerce, and culture. It would have been the region where Jesus really began his ministry in earnest.

Points to Ponder

First Thoughts

The concept of place is very important in the Bible for multiple reasons. First, understanding both geographically and culturally more about these cities and regions helps us understand why they're worth mentioning at all. Second, there is rich spiritual and historical significance to keep in mind, particularly when we talk about places like Israel, which also refers to an entire people descended from Abraham, and sometimes even Jacob himself.

When Paul talks about how God is not wowed by our individual abilities and accomplishments, I can't help but think back to my kids when they were toddlers, whose mantra at the time seemed to be, "Look what I can do!" Imagine us working our butts off all our lives, achieving the highest ranks of prestige among our peers (or even, say, writing books to establish a legacy), and God pats us on the head, offering a "that's nice" in response.

Though there's a biblical basis for "sabbath" (rest) outright, I like to think that this is lived out many times by Jesus. For example, in this Gospel text, he goes out into the wilderness for some alone time. This is also encouraging for introverts like me. Makes me feel less antisocial and more like Jesus! Or something like that.

Digging Deeper

Mining for what really matters . . . and gold

All of these passages are studies in contrasts. In each of them, there's a distinct difference between humanity's priorities, power, and stature compared with that of God. All things in this world are temporal, but God is eternal. Nature is volatile; God is a constant. Our priorities pale in comparison to what really matters in the larger picture. And where we think we ought to go next may actually stand in the way of what's best for us and others.

This is a common device used throughout scripture, including by Jesus when he challenges the degree to which people give weight to written religious law. When he uses phrases like "Scripture says _____, but I say _____," we can count on whatever he's going to say to be surprising and maybe even a little bit subversive.

Oftentimes, we're working hard at trying to unlock the secret formula hidden away in the Bible, hoping to reveal unearthed wisdom that will change us forever. We want to work our way into peace, accomplish our way into a sense that all is right with us and the world. If we just do a little bit more, work a little harder, we'll get there.

If the patterns in these texts are any guide, though, we should recognize what our impulses are and consider doing something really different. Of course, we want to know what that thing is we need to do instead, but sometimes it's just to stop, be quiet, and pay attention.

It's frustrating how often our natural impulses lead us astray, even when we may have the best intentions. It seems, though, that a lifelong pursuit of God consists of an ongoing series of missteps and course corrections.

No degree of will or effort in the world can make a compass naturally incline itself anywhere but magnetic north. We can yell at it, spin it around in circles and turn off the lights. Still north. We can try to convince ourselves and others that north is actually south, but it's not the case. We can know it's pointing one direction and still choose to go another. But true north is, was, and will be enduring, constant, unchanged.

Heads Up
Connecting the text to our world

If there's one four-letter word in the English language that isn't generally considered to be profane but should be, it's "WAIT." I hate that word, or at least what it connotes. Waiting usually means you're at the mercy of someone else, unable to have any control over your situation. I'd much rather be in control than to wait on anything or anyone else.

I'm more in line with what Dr Seuss says about waiting in *Oh, the Places You'll Go!*, where he describes the "waiting place" as a most useless place. Everyone is waiting for a train to come, a plane to go, waiting for a yes or no, or waiting for the snow to snow.

EVERYONE IS JUST WAITING.

If you like waiting, you're probably either a sloth or koala. Otherwise, it sucks.

And yet, it's what we're guided to do in three of the four passages. It's more obvious in the Isaiah passage, but also implied in the psalm and Mark. Part of faithfulness and obedience is patiently, silently waiting for what's next. It means being open, willingly giving up control over the future and our own lives. Like Jesus says in the garden at Gethsemane . . .

Not my will, but Thine be done.

So even Jesus waited. Even when there's a whole crowd of people wanting his help, he retreated into the solitude and silence to sit, wait, and listen. When he did, the mandate for what came next was very different than what the rest of his followers expected. In this time between Advent and Lent, we're in one of those in-between spaces. And even when Lent begins, what do we get? More waiting.

But waiting patiently, preparing, and listening don't go well with constant, hectic busy-ness. Yes, there's always more to do, and much or all of it seems terribly important in the context of our daily lives. But God's vision is broader, and to get even a glimpse, we have to look up, sit with silence, and wait.

Prayer for the Week

God, give me patience, and give it to me right now (just kidding, kind of). You know I hate waiting, but I'll do it if for no other reason than as a gesture of trust. If it was good enough for Jesus, it's probably good enough for me.

Popping Off

Art/music/video and other cool stuff that relate to the text

Everything Belongs: The Gift of Contemplative Prayer, by Richard Rohr (book, 2003)

Noise, by Rob Bell/Nooma (video) http://nooma.com /films/005-noise

Superman's Fortress of Solitude (Wiki) http://super man.wikia.com/wiki/Fortress_of_Solitude

Eat the Goat

Lectionary Texts For
February 11, 2018 (Transfiguration Sunday)

Texts in Brief
My dog ate my Bible!

FIRST READING
2 Kings 2:1–12

The prophet Elijah and his follower, Elisha, went to the Jordan River. Elijah struck the water with his garment and the river parted. As they went across, Elisha asked for a double portion of the blessing Elijah had received from God, and Elijah said he had to witness his ascent to heaven in order for this to be granted. Then an angel in a chariot came down and swept Elijah up. After he was gone, Elisha tore at his clothes in mourning.

Psalm

Psalm 50:1–6

In this poem, David paints a picture of a fantastical and pretty fearsome God, tied to imagery of fire and raging storms, but also unspeakable beauty. God also is portrayed as a beckoning voice, calling all members of heaven and earth together, to be held as one body within a covenant—a holy promise—which was sealed by a sacrificial offering to show commitment and devotion.

Second Reading

2 Corinthians 4:3–6

Paul explains that, though some people will be blind to the illumination that comes from really "getting it" when it comes to God's message as framed in the life and teaching of Jesus, it's not something to be proud of or lord over the blind when we do see it. Rather, we're meant to humbly be light bearers, and to act as instruments of that kind of illumination in our world so that others who don't yet see it might have a chance to experience what we find to be so special.

Gospel

Mark 9:2–9

Peter, James, and John climb up a mountain to be alone with Jesus. At the top, Jesus lights up in a brilliant white glow. The prophets Moses and Elijah appear alongside him. Just then, God's voice proclaims to them that Jesus is, in fact, God's son. The disciples freak out (understandably), and suddenly it's just Jesus standing with them again like normal. On their way back down the mountain, he makes them promise not to talk about what they saw until after he is killed.

(Same text is offered on the second Sunday of Lent in this volume.)

Bible, Decoded
Breaking down scripture in plain language

Mantle – The type of garment Elijah struck the water with. It's a kind of cloak that indicated being part of the priesthood, sort of like a clerical collar or stole indicate today.

Bethel – From the Hebrew *beth el*, which means "House of God." About ten miles north of Jerusalem, this was a "border city" for the Jews in biblical times. It was named by Jacob after he had a vision there of angels and a ladder ascending all the way to heaven (AKA, "Jacob's Ladder").

Son of Man – This is an interesting phrase that has its roots in Greek. In general it was a vernacular way of someone referring to themselves. Translated more literally, it means something like "human being" or "the human one." It's used more than eighty times in the Gospels and only by Jesus referring to himself, or to something he said about himself. Some biblical scholars understand this to be an affirmation of Jesus's humanity, to be considered in balance with the expressions of him as also divine in other places.

Points to Ponder

First Thoughts

When I was in Jordan I actually went to the site called Elijah's Hill, next to the Jordan River, where the story was believed to have taken place. The hill is no more than fifteen to twenty feet high. When I heard this story as a kid, I imagined it as a tall, dramatic mountain. It's funny how we take our myths and change them into something so much bigger in our minds.

The significance of Elijah dividing the water isn't that they didn't get wet. It's a *midrashic* nod to the story of Moses when he parted the Red Sea. At least today, the Jordan where they would have crossed is nearly narrow enough to jump across. But it suggests that Elijah is part of the priestly and prophetic lineage of Moses, and therefore, particularly favored and chosen by God. It's worth noting, too, that just after this passage in Kings, Elisha goes back across the Jordan River, but not before parting the waters himself. By this act, he was given the priestly mantle carried before him by Moses and Elijah.

Oh, and just in case we haven't picked up on the Elijah/Elisha/Moses connection on our own yet, by the time we get to this passage in the Gospels, Jesus lights up like a glow stick and appears with Elijah and Moses at his side. Talk about a sign! So they're all connected. Moses was called and empowered by God; Elijah picks up that same priestly mantle. Elisha carries it following Elijah's passing; and finally, Jesus completes the circle, carrying the story to its completion and bringing it all back to God.

Digging Deeper
Mining for what really matters . . . and gold

There are several different images of the holy and of God in these stories. Generally, they involve fire or light in some way, and are just almost unbearable, even for those who claim the God of Israel.

The imagery of fire is especially interesting in these passages. The story of Elijah is tied directly to the exodus of the Israelites, led by Moses, out of Egypt. In that story, a pillar of fire guided them to safety during the night. But fire also is tied symbolically to the offerings given to God by God's faithful at times, in the form of "burnt offerings." So fire or light is a symbol for God as guide, but also as consuming force, devouring all that is not steeled against its destructive, overwhelming nature.

So whether God is comforter and guide or destroyer depends on who you ask. But clearly, the choice is theirs.

It's worth considering the comparison of God's spirit with fire a bit more, because often, it gets seen as a terrifying thing that's associated with torture and suffering. But in his letters (not this particular one, but others), Paul talks about God's fire being one of purification. It's a force that strips away all the things that don't matter, getting down to the purest, bare essentials. In a sacrificial context, fire does consume, but as a holy act, not a punitive one. It's a sort of contract between us and God, that God accepts what we have to offer.

Fire also represents salvation or hope, as a beacon or guide. It points a direction and, if we consider its role in nature and our lives, fire is essential to survival, really.

When we think of God in the form of brilliant fire in these ways, it's not so necessarily terrifying. In fact, the multitude of ways to understand it are actually pretty beautiful.

Heads Up

Connecting the text to our world

When we were still just engaged back in the nineties, my now-wife, Amy, went on a mission trip to Venezuela for a couple of weeks. She, like a lot of folks, went on the trip hoping to make a difference. She knew she was going into areas of profound poverty and environmental exploitation. She wanted to do her part to make things right, as she had a heart for reaching out and caring for "the least of these."

When she got there, a few experiences struck her so deeply that they still linger with her today, nearly two decades later. There was the time she went to a small village in the rural outskirts of the capital where they slaughtered a goat to make soup for their guests. She saw the source of their dinner, lying on a table only feet away—less than appetizing—and what appeared to be something eyeball-shaped floating in her bowl. Then a woman stuck her hand in front of Amy's mouth and invited her to take a bite of something they believed was very special.

It was raw goat intestine.

Everything in her wanted to politely decline, but a small boy next to her explained that he was so glad she had come to visit. He told her that, because they were all so poor, they usually kept goats to use for their milk.

The only time they actually got meat to eat was when someone was gravely ill or they had visitors. She grimaced and took the bite.

Another was when she attended a worship service at a neighborhood church. During the service, they invited a small, frail boy up from the crowd, explaining that he had lost the rest of his family and was wandering from village to village, simply trying to survive. Within seconds, the church surrounded him with love and hugs, promising to adopt him as a community and to raise him as their own.

These people who had so terribly little were more extravagant in sharing what they had than anyone she knew. It was almost like they'd read the stories and admonitions in the Bible and taken them seriously!

During her time, Amy helped dig some ditches and install some shelves, but more profound than the impact she had on them was the change that took place within her. In this week during which we consider transfiguration, it's easy to get caught up in the fantastical imagery of the stories, and to marvel at the brilliance of Jesus and of God's chosen prophets. But maybe the real transfiguration we're meant to come away from this week with is something more personal, intimate, internal.

How we are transformed by the stories we encounter and embrace in scripture, as well as those we encounter every day in the world can't be known until it has already happened. We're invited to stay open to transfiguration, even by those we hardly know, regardless of what we will become and for what purposes we will be used.

We wait, wonder, remain open, and hope to find out.

Prayer for the Week

God, I keep waiting for the world around me to change, for you to do the heavy lifting. But maybe it's me I'm actually waiting on. Help me find the strength, vulnerability, and clarity to be that change the world needs, and to allow it to change me.

Popping Off

Art/music/video and other cool stuff that relate to the text

"Waiting on the World to Change," by John Mayer (song, 2006)

American History X (movie, 1998)

Gran Torino (movie, 2008)

Love Is a Setup

Lectionary Texts For
February 14, 2018 (Ash Wednesday)

Texts in Brief
My dog ate my Bible!

First Reading
Joel 2:1–2, 12–17

The author of Joel paints a grim, solemn picture of what the coming of God's kingdom looks like. However, this is not the point of the passage. Rather, it's saying that it is never too late to turn to God, to make right our wrongs, and to humble ourselves in a spirit of repentance.

and

Isaiah 58:1–12

God is speaking through the author, and then the author speaks, somewhat interchangeably. There is a

sense of exasperation at people whose religious rituals are empty, or even self-serving. There is frustration
when people ask God for judgment against their enemies, and yet don't live out the values at the heart of the
Law. Rather, we're meant to give away what we have in
a spirit of selfless generosity, with the assurance that
what we really need will be provided.

PSALM

Psalm 51:1–17

This is a song of desperate beseeching David offers to
God, asking for the very transformation and strength to
turn from old ways called for in the two passages above.
Once redeemed, David promises to be a model and a
crier of the abundance of grace offered by God to others, and to encourage them to do likewise.

SECOND READING

2 Corinthians 5:20b–6:10

Paul echoes the sentiments offered in the Joel text,
exhorting his audience to have a sense of urgency
about their job as children of God. They're urged to
mend brokenness, to heal wounds, and to make things
right with God and, by extension, within themselves
and with others.

GOSPEL

Matthew 6:1–6, 16–21

Jesus warns against superficial, false, empty acts of religious piety. If we go through the motions of religious
ritual to be noticed and admired by others, they're

worthless. If we conduct ourselves in religious ways, and yet don't do the "soul work" of changing from the inside out, what's the point?

Bible, Decoded
Breaking down scripture in plain language

Sackcloth and ashes – Sackcloth was a garment (kind of like burlap today) used in a ritual of mourning or repentance. Ashes were more particular to repentance for transgressions of an individual, but also during times of national crisis. Often when disasters occurred, it was believed this was a result of God's wrath for the sins of the community.

Hyssop – Hyssop is mentioned in scripture all the way back to Exodus. It's used in lots of different contexts, including during Jesus's crucifixion. The branch that held the sponge with sour wine he was given just before death was a hyssop branch. In the psalm, it is referred to as a sort of purifying agent. Its pungent, minty odor was believed to be useful for lepers to cleanse themselves of infection, and it was also used with dead bodies to cover up the smells of death.

Points to Ponder
First Thoughts

Interesting to note that in 2018 and 2024, Ash Wednesday and Valentine's Day fall on the same day. In some ways, the darkness and lamenting spirit surrounding Ash Wednesday is so starkly in contrast with the superficialities of the pink and red hearts, chocolates and flowers we associate with Valentine's. Given the choice, I expect most people would pick hearts and flowers over sackcloth and ashes. But there's a reason we lament and repent before we celebrate, just like we can't exactly appreciate the full scope of resurrection without first visiting the crucifixion.

Similarly, the fullness of life and love—beyond the trappings and distractions of fleeting romance—can be lost without first unburdening ourselves of the lingering specter that we're here for little more than a handful of moments, many of which we screw up. We're not perfect, and as such we're vulnerable, dependent.

But to be loved, even in our imperfection, is a more authentic, pure sort of love. Can we accept it? Do we feel worthy? Love only works when we're prepared to accept what is offered. Sure, we'll take the card and candies, but what about unconditional acceptance? Sometimes, going through the repentance of Ash Wednesday, unburdening ourselves of the yokes we place on ourselves unnecessarily, help ready us to take in the love that's offered without exception and, in turn, give it away again.

Digging Deeper

Mining for what really matters . . . and gold

There is more than one way to interpret the notion that "God's kingdom is at hand." Many of us heard some form of this, framed as a grave warning, to get right with God before it's too late. A downpour of fire and fearsome beasts would descend on us, chaos and violence would tear the unrighteous limb from limb, and the wails of the unclean would echo from canyon to mountaintop. Our only hope for not finding ourselves among the Great Unwashed was to fall down on hands and knees, wailing and mourning and seeking forgiveness at the eleventh hour of the coming judgment.

But there's also the possibility that we've got it backwards. Maybe instead of us waiting for God to make things right, God is waiting on us. Instead of sulfur and bloodshed, the fulfillment of God's kingdom-come is love made complete, and humanity made whole. Consider the possibility that the one thing keeping the world from love being fully realized, here and now, is our own blindness to our capacity to offer and embrace without exception.

I'm not entirely sure that God "needs" our rituals of humility and forgiveness-seeking. Seeing God as so small and petty that resentments are held, grudges are kept record of, and we have to crawl in supplication in order to appease the Divine says more about us than about God's true nature.

This, after all, would make love and forgiveness conditional, and therefore, absent of grace. Grace is only grace when no strings are attached. This, after all, is why resurrection is made possible; Jesus went through the worst of what humanity had to offer and came out on the other side of it, absent of any burden of resentment, hatred, or judgment against those who crucified and betrayed him.

As author and speaker Brene Brown points out, we tend to see such vulnerability—like forgiving one's enemies, even as our final breaths escape us—as weakness. We spit at it, taunt it, and ridicule it. But in fact, summoning the will to be vulnerable, especially when there's the most at risk, is a tremendous sign of strength.

It's open-ended, though, without complete resolution. We give up control, and we don't like it.

And yet, it's given to us, over and over. And God waits.

Heads Up

Connecting the text to our world

One of the hardest things I've ever witnessed was when my wife imposed the ashes on the forehead of our then-six-year-old daughter during an Ash Wednesday service. We give both of our kids the option of participating in our worship rituals, including communion and this. Of course, if it was hard for me to watch, I can only imagine how difficult it was for my wife. The ashes represent two things. First, they're a sign of repentance, turning away from the ways that lead us further from God and from the spirit of openness to accept radical, extravagant love.

They also represent the ashes and dust we came from, and to which we're certain to return. It's just not fair, bringing such a beautiful spirit into the world, only to snuff it out again. Sure, it may be years or decades from now, but it will come.

Love is a setup for a broken heart. It never ends well, ultimately: a romance veiled in tragedy. Life and death, joy and sorrow, are commingled in ways that can't entirely be separated. The paper hearts and grocery store cards are so much easier. They don't cut too deep, and therefore, don't risk as much.

But more is offered, and more is expected of us. We're expected to bring it all to God, offer it up in the spirit of love and vulnerability. We ask for strength to repent and trust because it's hard—even terrifying—on our own. We trust for the sake of trust, love for the sake of love. We're broken, and yet re-membered, brought back to wholeness and completion, if we allow ourselves to be.

Love is not an insurance policy. We'll break these promises to reconcile, to make right what has been broken. It all will end. But the question isn't whether love and forgiveness can come without suffering. The real question is: *Is love worth it?*

Prayer for the Week

God, I screw up. I'm not perfect. I don't even really understand this idea of unconditional love and forgiveness. I know I don't even have to ask for it; it's just there. Give me the strength and humility to accept it.

Popping Off

Art/music/video and other cool stuff that relate to the text

Phenomenon (movie, 1996)

"The Power of Vulnerability," by Brene Brown (TED talk, 2010) https://www.ted.com/talks/brene_brown_on _vulnerability

Choosing Weakness

Lectionary Texts For
February 18, 2018 (First Sunday in Lent)

Texts in Brief
My dog ate my Bible!

FIRST READING
Genesis 9:8–17

After the floodwaters recede and Noah, his family and the animals emerge from the ark, God establishes a promise with humanity and the rest of creation; there will never again be a flood that will destroy humanity and its other inhabitants. The sign offered to symbolize this covenant is a rainbow.

PSALM
Psalm 25:1–10

David asks God for three things: protection, wisdom, and mercy. He concludes with several lines of praise for God's greatness and forgiving, abundant nature.

SECOND READING
1 Peter 3:18–22

In a reference back to the covenant established between God and Noah on behalf of all living creation, God has offered a new covenant, symbolized in the death and resurrection of Jesus. As Jesus was buried bodily and transcended death, we express our intent to die to our old selves and ways through the ritual of baptism, rising from the waters into a new life, unburdened by sins and missteps now left in the "grave" of the past.

GOSPEL
Mark 1:9–15

With typical Markan brevity, the author of Mark covers a lot in a few sentences. Jesus is baptized in the Jordan River by John the Baptist, God's spirit descends on him in the image of a dove, and then drives Jesus into solitude in the desert. John is arrested and Jesus enters Galilee to begin his ministry in earnest.

Bible, Decoded
Breaking down scripture in plain language

Resurrection – We all know what resurrection means in the literal, bodily sense, and we are likely familiar with the Christian tradition of faith that Jesus was physically resurrected from the dead after being crucified. However, some believe that this is a device meant to be understood more as a spiritual resurrection, with his spirit escaping and confounding the bonds of death. Still others consider it more of an existential resurrection, in that Jesus never succumbed to the death-dealing ways inflicted upon him by humanity. Literally, the word from the Greek, *anastasis*, means "stand up again."

Christ – Though we might think from popular culture's example that "Christ" is Jesus's last name, it's actually a title that comes from the Greek word *christos*, which means "anointed." It is meant to suggest that God chose Jesus –or anointed/blessed him—with his particular ministry to all of humanity.

Points to Ponder

First Thoughts

In this era of such environmental upheaval and crisis, it's worth considering that, in the Genesis story, God makes the covenant with all living creatures, and not just humanity. While some Christians make a case from scripture that the world is both our playground and trashcan, there's also a compelling argument that God feels all of life is worthy of protection and preservation. Curious that we would consider ourselves to be exempt from such values.

We Christians today have it really easy. Maybe that's part of why it's harder to convince people this "Good News" thing is really that important. After all, my son, who is a musical prodigy, doesn't really get the same reward from mastering an instrument or piece of music that someone who has to work and sweat for it. Instead, he flits around from one to another, firm in his knowledge that the next thing will come just as easily as the last. And yet there's so much need in the world, so much brokenness and suffering, even if our own roads are relatively smooth by comparison.

Compassion is about more than sympathy or pity. It means when one hurts, we all hurt. It seems Christianity in the contemporary West suffers from a compassion crisis. We don't need to live under the threat of death or imprisonment to take seriously this kind of compassion to which we're called.

Digging Deeper
Mining for what really matters . . . and gold

In this Genesis passage, God makes a covenant with Noah and the entirety of life on earth. It's important to clarify what a covenant *is not* in order to better understand what it really is. A covenant is not a two-way agreement or a contract. There's no negotiation or dealmaking. It's intentionally and firmly unilateral. God doesn't say that, if humanity behaves, there will not be another flood. There just won't be one, period.

In a way, this would be like telling a kid that they'll not be grounded ever again, no matter what they do. This certainly leaves the covenant open to exploitation, or even to be patently ignored, taken for granted.

It leaves God vulnerable to us.

As we enter into the Lent season, which takes us through Jesus's ministry and to its conclusion at the cross, we're well served to take time to consider this vulnerability God demonstrates, and to which he calls Jesus, John the Baptist, Paul, and others. These guys don't do what they do as Jesus-followers for the paycheck, the benefits, or the glory. In fact, it ends the same for each one of them: death.

In his book *The Weakness of God*, John Caputo suggests that our images of Jesus as conqueror, God as fearsome tyrant, or even Christians as members of a spiritual army don't reconcile with the staggering, voluntary weakness Jesus/God demonstrates at the crucifixion.

If this is true, if we truly believe it, then the way of Jesus is a path of peace—at all costs. We're not just to choose peace when it suits us, when there's little or nothing at risk. It's when the stakes are at their highest that the decision to choose peace as vulnerable examples has the greatest chance of shifting perspectives and turning hearts. It means giving up on the notion of winning in the conventional sense, setting our vision instead on a longer, broader horizon.

What lies beyond that barely visible horizon is God's kingdom-on-earth, waiting for an invitation to dwell among us.

Heads Up

Connecting the text to our world

We've all been punished, or even simply had natural consequences come our way, for things we've done. We don't necessarily like it, but sometimes we get what's coming to us. As I recall from the many times I heard it growing up, this is called "learning the hard way." And some of life's greatest wisdom can be learned first by doing it wrong. Ever stuck a Lite Brite peg into a light socket? I did, but only once. How about checking to see if your plate actually is hot, even though someone told you already?

For being the smartest species on the planet, we sure do some stupid stuff.

But then there are the unearned consequences: the bad fortune and suffering we encounter, even when trying to be good and do right. Hardly seems fair, but it happens. John the Baptist was living out his call as a prophet to the fullest, and for it he got jail and beheading. Jesus fully embodied a message of peace, forgiveness, and righteousness; in return, he was tortured to death. The early Christians who are the audience in the passage from 1 Peter were being treated similarly, all for claiming allegiance to God first, rather than Caesar.

In the story of Noah, God vows not to destroy the earth with a flood, but this isn't a guarantee that we'll be immune to suffering. Unfortunately, perhaps, the thing God doesn't save us from is ourselves. The things human beings do to each other—sometimes even in God's name—are chilling.

In Buddhism, it's believed that at the heart of all suffering is desire. This aligns pretty well with Christianity really, but neither says that others' desire won't lead to our suffering. The toughest part of being part of a larger human family is that, just as we can raise each other up, so can we tear one another down.

So what good is God's promise then, if not to serve as a perfect deflector shield to keep out all the bad stuff? Maybe, like Jesus, if we put God first we'll find at the heart of our lives something that actually helps make all the gross stuff worthwhile.

Growing up, I was a really picky eater. But if I knew there was dessert coming, it made some of the yucky parts more bearable. For some, the dessert may be the promise of eternal life in the "sweet by and by." Personally, I like to think the payoff is more immediate, in the form of a life of substance, real perspective, and a vision that there's so much more at stake than our suffering.

On Ash Wednesday, we asked if love was worth it. Today, we have a chance to offer a response. It's easy to say "yes" to God when nothing comes at a cost; it's a lot harder to stick with that "yes" when the stakes are raised, even if our lives depend on it.

Prayer for the Week

God, remind me that Love isn't easy or safe, but it's always worth it.

Popping Off

Art/music/video and other cool stuff that relate to the text

"Manifesto of the Brave and Brokenhearted," by Brene Brown (video) www.brenebrown.com

The Weakness of God, by John Caputo (book, 2006)

Wax On, Wax Off

Lectionary Texts For
February 25, 2018 (Second Sunday in Lent)

Texts in Brief
My dog ate my Bible!

First Reading
Genesis 17:1–7, 15–16

When Abram is ninety-nine years old, God speaks to him, telling him he will be the forefather of many nations. He will make his family tree extensive, and he and his wife Sarai will have a son. God gives Abram the new name of Abraham, and renames Sarai as Sarah.

Psalm
Psalm 22:23–31

Once again, David offers a song in three parts. First, he honors the descendants of Jacob, who was the grandson of Abraham and Sarah. He acknowledges the honor given to them by God, and therefore, his respect is given to all who come from him as members of the people of Israel. Second, David proclaims that the poor will be fed and that any who long for God will be compelled to irrepressible praise. Finally, he offers a poetic exaggeration for effect, claiming that even the dead will sing God's praise, and those yet to be born will hear the stories of God's greatness.

SECOND READING
Romans 4:13–25

Paul notes that Abraham's inheritance as father of the nation of Israel wasn't decreed in written law, but rather was a fruit borne from his faithfulness. He encourages his audience, the early Christians in Rome, to do likewise, not living by rule of law, but by a discipline of lifelong faithfulness modeled after their ancestor. God did for Abraham what seemed impossible, and in following his example, we too are reminded to employ such faithfulness in trusting in the promise of God's mercy, expressed through Jesus.

GOSPEL (1)
Mark 8:31–38

Jesus speaks publicly about what the future holds for him, and in doing so, implicates Jewish temple officials and Roman leaders in unjustly jailing and killing him. Peter gets nervous and tells him to stop, but Jesus accuses him of speaking evil because he's worried about human problems rather than getting the bigger picture. Later, Jesus teaches Peter and his disciples that "dying to self" actually gives them a clear path to rich spiritual life. Jesus isn't advocating suicide or glorifying physical death; he's simply saying that they have to overcome the power of human desires, including the instinct of self-preservation.

Gospel (2)
Mark 9:2–9

Peter, James, and John climb up a mountain to be alone with Jesus. At the top, Jesus lights up in a brilliant white glow. The prophets Moses and Elijah appear alongside him. Just then, God's voice proclaims to them that Jesus is, in fact, God's son. The disciples freak out (understandably), and suddenly it's just Jesus standing with them again like normal. On their way back down the mountain, he makes them promise not to talk about what they saw until after he is killed.

(Same text is offered on Transfiguration Sunday in this volume.)

Bible, Decoded
Breaking down scripture in plain language

Abraham – Abraham's family is considered the starting point of the establishment of the nation of Israel. His name means "father of multitudes." His original name, Abram, means "high father" or "exalted father."

Sarah – Sarah's original name means "quarrelsome," but her God-given name of Sarah means "princess."

Satan – Though we think of the words "Satan," "devil," and "Lucifer," as interchangeable, the word "Satan" in Hebrew actually means "adversary," "enemy," or "one who resists." So though Peter thinks he's caring for Jesus by trying to silence him, he's actually resisting the call to share the story of Jesus with all, no matter the cost.

Points to Ponder

First Thoughts

Much like the names Adam (earth) and Eve (to breathe or live), names like the ones in today's Genesis story are essential to the symbolism of the story itself, and so they're worth understanding better. In the story of Abraham and Sarah, knowing their names' meanings, we see that Sarai started out as argumentative (which we'll see when Abraham tells her she's going to have a child in her old age) to being royalty of sorts to their descendants. Abraham was a man of high regard and honor as Abram, but God endowed him with a blessing of many in his family line. So we can see the transformation they go through just in their names.

It's also helpful to know that three faiths—Judaism, Islam, and Christianity—consider Abraham and Sarah to be their ancestral beginning point. This is why we refer to all three as the "Abrahamic religions."

Digging Deeper

Mining for what really matters . . . and gold

One recurring theme both in these passages and in other texts in which something new is revealed and everything changes, is this complex but important relationship of past-present-future. There are two parts to be considered.

First is how the present affects both past and future. We think most immediately of how it affects things going forward. Obviously if I get a new job today, that changes what I'll be doing tomorrow. But it also changes the past, at least inasmuch as it alters or reframes how we look at the past. Expanding on the job example, the job I just got might help me look back at my past experience and see how something I saw as not that important at the time prepared me for what I'll now be doing. In the context of a faith journey, sometimes a present revelation can help make sense of things that seemed senselessly bad or pointless back when they took place.

I want to clarify that I'm not slipping into the lazy thinking of "everything happens for a reason," as I think that divests us of responsibility for our own choices, and it also places God in a position of playing chess with our lives. However, I do believe that, given enough time, vision, wisdom, and perspective, almost everything can be made sense of.

The second consideration here is the notion of both fitness and readiness to serve, and to say "yes" when it is required. The fitness comes from past practices and disciplines, be they spiritual practices, self-care, or mental engagement (or likely some combination of all of these). Abram, Jesus, David, and Paul all studied the stories, ideas, and traditions of those who preceded them. They developed their own spiritual life to the point that it became internalized and not just another to-do on their daily list of chores. And they all went about taking what they learned from all of this and applied it in real life.

Readiness, however, is not the same as fitness. When we've done all of the work on our own fitness, it seems we've invested enough that we deserve to have some say and control over what happens next. For example, if I practice guitar every day for ten years, it's because I want to be a guitar player. But it's possible that all of that practice has unexpectedly prepared me for something else I just haven't imagined yet.

If I am so hell-bent on realizing my own anticipated outcome, I might miss the amazing thing that could have been.

Readiness requires a vulnerable openness to a future outcome over which we willingly surrender control. That in itself is an act of faithful trust. In fact it may only be then that the truly remarkable things begin to happen around us.

Heads Up

Connecting the text to our world

This whole thing about fitness, readiness, and trusting that there's more to the world and even our own lives than we can sometimes see reminds me of *Karate Kid*. Daniel wants to learn Karate so he can kick the ass of some bullies in his school, so he asks Mr. Miyagi to train him. Instead, Miyagi makes him prune a tiny tree. Then he asks again to learn Karate, but Miyagi makes him paint the fence. Again, he asks for training, but Miyagi makes him wash an entire lot of cars.

What Daniel doesn't realize the whole time is that all the seemingly mundane tasks he's being forced to do instead of taking part in his karate training *actually is his training*. Not only are the focus and repetitive motions he's been employing for these chores useful in combat; they've also taught him focus, self-discipline, how to take orders, and how to trust. Miyagi also taught him, without Daniel realizing it at the time, that to be great, he first had to practice the art of smallness and humility.

The reason Daniel kept on believing in Miyagi, even though he nearly quit many times, was because he knew Miyagi believed in him. So finally, Daniel relented and laid himself bare, letting his master do with him what he saw fit. And that is when he, too, became what he sought to be. Not only that, but he ended up being so much more than just another kid who could stand up to bullies. He became something more than he could have imagined on his own.

I know this is a lot to read into an otherwise cheesy eighties movie, but this is what makes it such a great film. The spine of the story reaches back millennia, back to Jesus, to King David, all the way to Abram and Sarai, figuring their lives of faithful service were soon coming to quiet ends.

When we let it, real life is an ongoing series of beginnings and ends, little births and deaths. The tiny deaths are scary and unknown by nature, but if we forestall them with all our might, we never make room for the new life to emerge. In this Lenten season, when we're surrounded by so many thoughts of death and endings, let's not lose sight of the hope, whatever it may look like, that will carry us to the other side.

Prayer for the Week

God, when all I see is death, loss, or ending, you imagine life beyond my ability to conceive. Help me imagine it in moments and ways I can, and to trust when I can't.

Popping Off

Art/music/video and other cool stuff that relate to the text

"Closing Time," by Semisonic (song, 1998)

Karate Kid (movie, 1984)

Words Matter

Lectionary Texts For
March 4, 2018 (Third Sunday in Lent)

Texts in Brief
My dog ate my Bible!

First Reading
Exodus 20:1–17

God speaks to Moses on Mount Sinai, giving him what we know as the Ten Commandments. These are the Israelites' essential rules for daily life going forward.

Psalm
Psalm 19

Pulling again this week from the Psalms of David, we find that in the first section the psalmist tells of how the very scope, grandeur, and elegance of creation stands as a wordless testament to God's own beautiful hand. He goes on to assert the sovereignty of God's law, as it is complete, enduring, and perfect. Finally, David asks to be made free of flaw and frailty like God's law is.

SECOND READING
1 Corinthians 1:18–25

Paul downplays the efforts of any who try to apply intellect when understanding the role of the crucifixion of Jesus. In fact, he suggests that over-intellectualizing matters best approached through a lens of faith will lead people further away from the understanding they claim to want.

GOSPEL
John 2:13–22

Jesus drives the traders and moneychangers out of the temple. Then he proclaims to those watching that the temple will come crumbling down, but that he will raise it up in three days. They're confused because they don't understand that he's referring to his crucifixion and resurrection rather than the physical building they're in.

Bible, Decoded
Breaking down scripture in plain language

Moneychangers – In Jesus's time, each region had its own royal bank and currency. Therefore when someone came into a new region (for example, during higher holidays like Passover) moneychangers would set up shop in high-traffic areas to convert their currency. So in a sense they were symbolic of the state, or the ruling forces. The animal dealers were selling animals of different sizes and cost for temple sacrifice.

Sabbath – Stemming from the Jewish tradition, it is expected that every seventh day (from sundown Friday to sundown Saturday) is a day of rest from all work. This is meant to be a day given to God, used for religious observance. It is modeled on the creation story in Genesis in which God creates the universe in six "days" and rests on the seventh.

LORD – You've likely noticed that this word is written differently in different places. It actually appears in all caps 6,000 times just in the Old Testament. When Moses asked God for God's name, the response was "I am," as in God is the foundation and center of all being or existence. The word *yahweh* or *yhwh*, directly transcribed from Hebrew, means "I am." However, as time went on, Jewish people felt God's name was too holy to say, therefore they tended to say *adonai* instead, which means "Lord." But because there are different root words translated in English as "Lord" throughout the Bible, this is how we can tell which original word the name came from.

Points to Ponder

First Thoughts

I'm the kind of person who prefers to be given the specific steps to do something right, so I can just do it and not leave all these loose ends lying around. But faith is inherently messy, incomplete, never ending. And though we like to create statements of faith and religious rites of passage that make us feel like our faith life is a goal we can reach and then know we've arrived, a lifelong pursuit of Jesus's ways and example is never that easily compartmentalized. The good news is that it means it also can't be owned and controlled by dogma or any religious leader or institution. Ultimately it comes down to God and us.

In a time when it seems words are increasingly trivialized and anyone can say what they think or feel on impulse, it's important for us to remember that words matter. How we read, discuss, and live out scripture matters. How we internalize and adopt the teachings of Jesus matters. What we think the crucifixion means matters. But too often Christians—let alone others—fall back on trite phrases or well-rehearsed "isms" rather than digging deeper into what the meanings are behind the words. Words can be pretty and impressive, but the impact they end up having depends on the spirit in which they're offered.

Digging Deeper

Mining for what really matters . . . and gold

Sometimes, timing is everything. This week in the in-depth section, I want to focus just on the John passage, rather than necessarily tying them all together. So in John here, Jesus cleanses the temple as one of the very first acts of his ministry. But in the Gospels written earlier in which this story was told (Mark, Matthew, and Luke) it happens toward the end, just before he's handed over to the Roman authorities for trial and crucifixion.

What John's Gospel does here is something we see repeatedly throughout the letters of Paul, which is that Jesus is calling for an end to sacrifice as a religious ritual to satisfy God. Jesus is repudiating more than people profiting in the temple: he's rejecting the entire notion that death-dealing is the way of God's people.

Rather, he makes known his intent to enter into death, and yet emerge on the other side of it. Maybe even more important to this particular moment is that Jesus calling himself "the temple" is a big deal here. We have to keep in mind that this is *the* temple, not just any temple. It was basically the holiest site the Jews had, and it was believed to be the place where God dwelled. But Jesus co-opts this, saying, in effect, that this temple they care so much about isn't God's house, but his body is the temple where God really dwells.

This would have shocked and angered a lot of people. He's discrediting their entire tradition of sacrificial atonement, and doing so in their holiest space during their holiest holiday. And as if that wasn't enough of a shakeup, he also claims to have God residing inside him, and not where they thought.

So he's throwing down the gauntlet, challenging the Old Ways, and the guards and stewards of it, right away. Talk about a mic-drop moment.

Given that we're entering into our holiest time of year as Christians, it seems fitting that we'd heed his warning and not invest ourselves in the value of the rituals themselves. Instead, we are to use them as an orientation toward the real thing, to help us focus on the holy revealed in Jesus, and subsequently in each of us.

We are the church. We are the reflection of God in the world. We are the flicker of life and hope in a world dealing in death. If only we muster the faith first to believe it's real.

Heads Up

Connecting the text to our world

I'm not what you might call a typical theologian, but in reading these texts, I couldn't stop thinking about the scene in the movie, *The Princess Bride*, when Vizzini, who fancies himself the intellectual superior of everyone he comes across, is forced to adjust his view of things. He loves to use big words, even when a small one will do, and his favorite word is "inconceivable." After the third or fourth time using it around Inigo Montoya, Inigo calls him on it.

"You keep using that word," Inigo says. "I do not think it means what you think it means."

It happens all of the time in scripture, which by its very nature is open to broad and widely varying interpretation, hard as some may try to argue that it has one single and absolute message for all people, over all time. It happens to Jesus all the time. He speaks in poetic hyperbole or parable, and people scramble for the exact, literal meaning. It's like the student at the front of the class, writing down every word the professor says, asking "Will this be on the test?"

Given that most people didn't read back in the days when Jewish law originated, the Ten Commandments whittled this huge mass of 613 original laws down to a few that anyone could understand and follow, without having to rely on the intellectual elite to tell them if they were doing it right. In this way it was an act of subversion of authority, handing power directly to the people.

Paul also warns against our inclination to hide behind, or even elevate, the importance of our intellect or education, when the simplicity of uncomplicated faith sometimes will do the job. Likewise, we can hide in the mundane repetition of religious ritual until it just becomes something we have to mark off our list once a week. After all, we can't be smart enough, clever enough, or rich enough that God will sit back and think, "Wow, how'd they do that?"

Trying hard to impress and win the approval of others gets us no closer to a full, meaningful life based on vulnerable, humble faith. So this Lent, let's set the fancy words and elaborate rituals aside. God isn't impressed by our worship services or how well we can spout Bible verses on demand. A daily practice of faith may be simpler, but it's not necessarily easy.

Prayer for the Week

God, I struggle to see you at all sometimes, let alone within myself. And sometimes I'm fast and loose with my words and religion. Help me to strip down all that doesn't matter, so that I can better see the simple call to let go of everything else and follow.

Popping Off

Art/music/video and other cool stuff that relate to the text
The Princess Bride (movie, 1987)

"Oh Lord, You Are So Big!" scene from *Monty Python's Meaning of Life*, (movie, 1983) https://www.youtube.com/watch?v=fINh4SsOyBw

Cake or Death?

Lectionary Texts For
March 11, 2018 (Fourth Sunday in Lent)

Texts in Brief
My dog ate my Bible!

First Reading
Numbers 21:4–9

Moses is leading the Hebrews in the wilderness, but they get restless and start to complain. God sends serpents into their midst that bite—and kill—them in their sleep. They ask Moses to pray to God to make it stop, which God says will happen if Moses affixes a figure of a snake to his staff. The serpents didn't disappear after that, but their bite was no longer lethal.

Psalm
Psalm 107:1–3, 17–22

A song of thanks to God, calling on the story told in the Numbers text.

Second Reading
Ephesians 2:1–10

Paul refers to the same theme, recalling how human failings have led them into a future of mortality and trial. Yet God offers grace as a gift without condition to all of humanity for those who will have it. This grace makes good for the collective sinfulness of our being, and we can understand the breadth of this grace and unconditional nature of God's grace as it's expressed through what Jesus endured at the hands of humanity, responding with love and mercy.

Gospel
John 3:14–21

Jesus draws a parallel between himself (referring to himself as he often does in third-person) and explains that he is the new embodiment of God's covenant with humanity to offer life, despite their choices that have led them into suffering and death.

Bible, Decoded
Breaking down scripture in plain language

Serpent – Throughout scripture, serpents represent human temptation and frailty. Though some like the idea of it being "the devil," there's no particular basis for this. Also, doing this divests us of the personal accountability that our choices are entirely our own, and that it's not some supernatural external force making us do it. So in a sense, we're each part-serpent.

Trespass – Technically, this just means "to cross a boundary." This could be seen as the boundary between right and wrong, or life and death, good and evil, etc. Wouldn't it be great if sin was as clearly marked as this, with a big, red line that said "STOP HERE!"? But by its very nature, sin and falling short of our ideal selves comes in incremental choices, justifications, and denials. Yes, sometimes, it's a clear line, like rape. But most sin is trickier than that, and God doesn't stand over us with a ruler, slapping our knuckles with it when we screw up. We're expected to learn, to know better and, therefore, to do better.

Points to Ponder

First Thoughts

Taken at face value, this Numbers text (and lots of Numbers texts, really) is weird and, frankly, makes God out to be a jerk. You complain, you die. And then there's the bit about Moses making a bronze figure that helps immunize people from snake venom. First, that's weird. Second, isn't that idolatry? But if we approach it metaphorically, it recalls the Genesis story in which the serpent (sin) leads humanity into a future resulting in death. However, God offers mercy, not in the form of eradicating sin, but by offering a way out of it, if people will accept it.

The risk in these passages is that we take them as a get-out-of-jail-free card. We still have to deal with the complexity of our relationship with death, suffering, and all that it means to be fully human. That isn't taken from us, covenant or not. And I don't really want it to be. Life makes sense in the context of death, and peace is understood through the dark veil of conflict.

We still have to wrestle with the serpent; its bite still stings. But our own cycle of destruction and despair is not the end of the story. So in the midst of the richly nuanced, sometimes tragic human narrative, there's a light of hope shining through.

Digging Deeper

Mining for what really matters . . . and gold

So far we've focused on the promise of salvation in its many forms and the home that comes with it. But those people in Numbers who died before Moses crafted the bronze serpent just . . . died. Here, God's just mean if you ask me. This is the old, vengeful, jealous, almost petty God many of us learned to fear in our fundamentalist Bible study days. The God of my childhood, while having a forgiving side, was largely a fearsome sadist. And even though there was "good news" in the story of Jesus, the idea that God required the spilling of Jesus's blood to make up for our evil doesn't sit any better.

The big theological term we're wrestling with here is "substitutionary atonement," or the idea that Jesus had to die in order for our sins to be forgiven. Those of us who struggle to reconcile this theology with our understanding of God as infinitely loving and merciful tend to want to cover our eyes this time of year as Good Friday approaches.

Side note: Let's all agree that calling the day Jesus is tortured to death "good" is, in itself, eerily morbid.

But we have to contend with the crucifixion, as it's central to the Christian story. We need to witness the suffering and the bloodletting and not allow ourselves the luxury of looking away. Not because we need to understand that God was willing to kill God's own son for us (sorry, but we didn't ask for that). It's because nothing expresses the breaking open of our sinful nature and our violent, fearful, scorning response to grace and love more than the crucifixion.

We killed Jesus. Not you or me, specifically, but it's in our collective nature to look at something that divests us of all control—which is the really scary prospect of unearned Love—and extinguish it. And yet even despite our best efforts, that Love is renewed, reignited. The covenant between God and humanity is offered again, and again, whether we're able to internalize it or not.

And as author Frank Schaeffer once told me, he needs the cross in his story of faith, not because God's bloodlust was satisfied, but because it demonstrates, beyond what words could ever do, how profoundly Jesus/God meant what he said about loving and forgiving infinitely and freely.

Heads Up
Connecting the text to our world

I can't help but think of the comedy routine by Eddie Izzard in which he jokes about Marie-Antoinette's "let them eat cake" quip. Eddie is a brilliant British comedian who performs in drag, transcending all assumptions about the superficiality of stand-up comedy. The quote from Marie-Antoinette was from her response when her associates told her the French people in the late eighteenth century were dying of starvation because of a bread shortage. Her response: "Let them eat cake."

Izzard goes on a long routine about her emissaries going out into the community making the offer to people of "cake or death?" Not surprising, most people say "cake, please," though one smartass jokes he'd prefer death, only to pivot quickly back to cake.

"Sorry, you already said 'death,'" they responded. "So I'm afraid it's death for you."

Then Izzard supposes what might happen if they ran out of cake too.

"So," her emissaries explain to the people, "we're all out of cake, I'm afraid. So your choices are . . . or death."

Not much of a choice.

God's grace, or God's ability to "forget" our misgivings and transgressions as it says in the Bible, thankfully isn't so finite. The choice is never ". . . or death?" There's always more cake.

The thing is, it's not your cake to claim and keep to yourself. You don't get to store all the cake in your church or denomination and tell people they have to say or do the right thing to get some cake. It was never your cake to begin with. So share the cake as if there will always be enough.

Prayer for the Week

God, if the idea of thinking about sin scares me, the cross freaks me out even more. Help me be able to accept what you offer, even if I don't feel equipped to take it. Transform me in ways I can't on my own.

Popping Off

Art/music/video and other cool stuff that relate to the text

"Cake or Death?" by Eddie Izzard (monologue from "Dress to Kill" sketch) https://www.youtube.com/watch?v=rMMHUzm22oE

Dress to Kill, by Eddie Izzard (book, 1998)

Saved! But from What?

———————/\/\/———————

Lectionary Texts For
March 18, 2018 (Fifth Sunday of Lent)

Texts in Brief
My dog ate my Bible!

FIRST READING
Jeremiah 31:31–34

Jeremiah speaks on behalf of God, foretelling of a time soon when the Jewish people will have God's "law" impressed within them, rather than having to follow written law. It will be considered a new pact, or covenant, between them and God. They won't have to be taught how to understand and love God; it will be inborn.

PSALM
Psalm 51:1–12

King David begs God for forgiveness for his transgressions. He feels dirty and burdened with sin, and asks

God to wash him clean, likely of the weight of his own guilt. He claims to have been born into sin, and asks God to remake him as a sinless being, from the inside, out. Finally, he begs God not to give up on him.

and

Psalm 119:9–16

David is making his commitments of demonstrations of faithfulness to God. These psalms are primarily dedicated to teaching his son, Solomon, the ways of following God as a faithful Jew.

SECOND READING
Hebrews 5:5–10

The author of this letter is asserting that Jesus is, indeed, the Messiah because he is of the "Order of Melchizedek (explained below)." He is not, however, appointed to his role as priest or king by humans; he was born into his titles directly from God. However, he also notes that Jesus grew into his role by taking on his role as a suffering servant, and since he did so completely and selflessly, he was the salvation the Jews had been seeking.

GOSPEL
John 12:20–33

Some people came from Greece to meet Jesus, but he told his disciples and others gathered with him that he was done ministering to people in the way he had been doing. Instead, he was preparing to be handed over to the Roman government for trial and death. Though it would be very hard, he handed trust over to God. God spoke to Jesus before the crowd, and Jesus explains the voice is meant to help them understand that the things coming were sanctioned by God. Jesus told them that after his death, people of all nations would be drawn to him.

Bible, Decoded

Breaking down scripture in plain language

Order of Melchizedek – A designation within the "Abrahamic religions" (Islam, Judaism, and Christianity, all of which began from descendants of Abraham) for those who hold both a kingly and priestly role. King David was such a ruler, and given that Jewish prophecy told that the Messiah would come from the lineage of David, he is indicating here that Jesus is part of this same order that reaches all the way back to Aaron, the older brother of Moses. This is the line from which all legitimate Israelite priests were to come.

Salvation – This is one of the most loaded and misunderstood words in the bible. While we tend to think of it as personal, individual salvation, ancient Jewish culture was more collective in their thinking, particularly about salvation. As for "salvation from what?," contemporary thinking generally assumes we mean the more fundamentalist understanding of being saved from hell, or saved from an eternity of death. Back in Jesus's time, they were most concerned with their messiah saving them from the brutal rule of an occupying force, especially since they had been under outside rule for so long.

Points to Ponder

First Thoughts

This psalm takes place after King David sees Bathsheba bathing on the roof of her house and is smitten. So he can have her, he sends her husband off to war, then takes her and uses her.

How we think about, and talk about salvation, is of more than passing importance. In a lot of ways, it tells us a lot about how we see God and our relationship with God. If we talk strictly about life-after-death salvation, we risk focusing on the future and not addressing needs of the present. If we focus only on salvation in the forms of reconciliation and social justice, we risk robbing our service of the necessary spiritual component that undergirds it. If we focus on personal salvation, we neglect our accountability to greater society. If we only talk of collective salvation, we can rest in broad "we" statements and not take personal responsibility. And finally, salvation is not simply another item on our wish list to God. Salvation is a collaborative mandate with mutually binding responsibilities, like the covenant we've previously discussed.

Digging Deeper

Mining for what really matters . . . and gold

The idea in biblical cultures of the primacy of firstborn sons can be problematic in our contemporary, more egalitarian culture. It ignores daughters and negates children who are just victims of birth order. It's easy to look at their seemingly more primitive, patriarchal settings and reject them out-of-hand as inferior to our more enlightened present views and values. I know I struggle at times with the wisdom of Paul, particularly because it is often couched in what seems to be misogynist language. Never mind that there are serious debates about whether some of the more controversial texts apply to our own historical context.

But we need to consider the importance of these things in the tribal cultures of the time for Jewish people. Historically they were constantly displaced, overthrown, fighting for survival and a place in the world. They were shepherds and tradespeople, artisans and farmers. Sometimes maintaining some basic sense of community order was essential to life itself.

We don't have to accept all of the norms and values of Jesus's culture to be changed by the essential truths of the stories they lived and told. We don't have to throw out every one of Paul's letters because we don't like how he talks about salvation or how women are to behave in church. They presented themselves in ways, and spoke in ways, that could be heard and internalized by their audiences at the time. And just like we can see humanity's relationship with God, and the shift from life-under-law to life-within-covenant over the course of scripture, we can evolve and grow in our view of God, Jesus, Paul, David, and our understanding of what it means to be saved.

Finally, we should be mindful not to fall into the sort of binary thinking that sets an "either/or" trap for ourselves. Truth doesn't have to be bound to a static take on the Bible and Christianity in order to be central to our lives. As the old gives birth to the new, we should acknowledge with gratitude the stuff of death that may have only given us that life in dying and finally giving way. And yet we needed it; our very lives depended on it.

Thank God for life, death, and rebirth. And the cycle continues.

Heads Up

Connecting the text to our world

One of my favorite movies of all time—well, at least in the top fifty or so—is called *Saved!* To me, it is the most spot-on sendup of the evangelical Christian youth experience. Mandy Moore as the self-appointed chief soul-winner hides behind her pious Christian-soldier veneer as a deeply scared, insecure, and, frankly, bitterly angry young woman. One of the best moments of the film is when someone accuses her of being less than Christlike in her crusade to make everyone more like her, to which she flings her Bible at them in fury, screaming, "I am FILLED with Christ's love!"

I'm sure part of the appeal of this for me is that my youth minister threw a Bible at me just before inviting me not to return to church when I was a kid. But there's more to it than that. Mandy Moore's character was desperately seeking something to make her feel like she was somebody, like her life mattered. When she found it in being an emissary for Jesus, she jumped in all the way, presuming all the while that everyone needed what she now had, in the way she had it, and nothing would stop her from spreading it, far and wide.

But mostly she was just an arrogant, obnoxious joke to the people around her who saw through it. And if we really consider the example Jesus set out for us, her model of evangelism wasn't Christlike at all. Sure, Jesus preached and taught, but he was more invested in what we might now call a ministry of attraction, rather than promotion. He lived out what he believed and valued more than he just talked about it. He let people come to him rather than forcing his ideas on them. And more than talking to them about salvation, he demonstrated it by addressing their most immediate present needs.

He treated those who often were relegated to the garbage heap of "other," and treated them as equals. Suddenly his words carried weight. This guy really believes what he's talking about! Sorry Mandy Moore, but I'm going with the Jesus method on this one.

Prayer for the Week

God, it would be so much easier to talk about you and salvation rather than go about the hard daily work of salvation in the real world, a little bit at a time. Help me keep things in priority and find the endurance to stick with it.

Popping Off

Art/music/video and other cool stuff that relate to the text
Saved! (movie, 2004)

"I am filled with Christ's love," scene from *Saved!* (movie, 2004) https://www.youtube.com/watch?v=umLUKBlpyoY

I Didn't Deserve This

———⟋⋁⋀⋁⟍———

Lectionary Texts For

March 25, 2018 (Annunciation of the Lord)

Texts in Brief

My dog ate my Bible!

FIRST READING

Isaiah 7:10–14

God grants Ahaz freedom to ask anything he wants of God as a sign that he is the one, true God. But afraid he would be putting God to the test, he declines. God then gets impatient and deems there should be a sign anyway. This is when Isaiah prophesies about the birth of Jesus.

PSALM

Psalm 45

In the part of the Psalms that is called the "Book of Psalms," this was a "song of the day" to be recited to music on the sabbath. It's a song of praise to the king, but verges on being a love song.

Second Reading
Hebrews 10:4–10

This letter—more of a sermon, really—nullifies the use of any physical offerings or sacrifices to cleanse people of their sin. This, the author claims, is only achieved through Jesus, particularly because he was willing to fulfill his role in the story of salvation of humanity through his death and resurrection.

Gospel
Luke 1:26–38

One version of the annunciation story, in which the archangel Gabriel tells Mary, who is a young girl engaged to be married, that God will give her a child to bear who will be savior of the world. She's understandably baffled by this news, but Gabriel continues to explain that her cousin Elizabeth will also have a son even though she's beyond childbearing years. After this, Mary accepts her role in this, offering gratitude for being chosen for such an important task.

Bible, Decoded
Breaking down scripture in plain language

Ahaz – King of Judah (a territory south of the kingdom of Israel) at age twenty, he reigned for about sixteen years around 750–530 BCE. The capital city of Judah was Jerusalem, which later became a central hub of commerce in the region. Ahaz was the son of

Jotham, who also ruled for sixteen years starting at age twenty.

Points to Ponder

First Thoughts

It's worth noting that, in the Luke passage, Joseph is described as "Joseph, of the house of David." Though it seems strange to drop the family line of a man into this story who doesn't yet have a role to play could seem strange. But we have to keep in mind that the prophecy of the coming of the Jewish messiah foretold that he would come from the house, or lineage, of David. Curious, of course, since Jesus isn't supposed to be genetically related to Joseph according to the way the story goes. But because Jewish culture didn't allow women's names to be entered into genealogical records, we have Joseph's bloodline instead. This doesn't keep people from trying to tie Mary back to David too. Some say she is the same "Mary, the daughter of Eli" mentioned earlier in scripture, while others suggest her father was Joachim.

Interesting in both Luke and Isaiah that God (in Luke, by way of Gabriel) offers a gift that at first is refused. And yet God continues to offer. It's generous to offer a gift anytime; it's extravagant generosity to offer it even if the person receiving turns it down. To keep offering something with no possibility of an equally matched gift in return is truly selfless. To give because it is in one's very nature to give without expectation except to express a deep love is the kind of divinely inspired state of being we're called toward.

Digging Deeper

Mining for what really matters . . . and gold

Why in the world would we have these stories about the announcements of Jesus's birth—arguably a theme that belongs in Advent instead of Lent?

This passage in Isaiah, especially pulled out in such a small, isolated excerpt, can seem so convoluted that we pass over it, save for the fact that it includes the prophecy about Jesus's coming birth. But it's worth understanding a little bit more about the backstory here. Ahaz had been attacked by Israel previously, and in order to protect himself against the threat of invasion, he had formed an alliance with the king of Assyria. He had even taken treasure from the temple and given it to the Assyrian king as a gift.

So not only was he an enemy of Israel; he had also effectively stolen from God. And so it's likely his refusal to ask anything of God had less to do with pious observance of the law, and more to do with his own guilt and a sense that the last thing he deserved is to be asking anything of God. So although the "annunciation" prophecy is important, it's also necessary to understand the context in which this announcement of such an extravagant offering from God comes.

Ahaz doesn't deserve anything from God, and yet God gives it. And here's where we get to why this is an important part of Lent. We're getting ever closer to the culmination of the story of Jesus, which we all know ends in agony and bloody tragedy at the hands of people, and yet he is given. Not only this, but he enters into this covenant willingly, with eyes wide open.

The story of Ahaz is here this week, not so we can look down on a king who has turned against God. But the extent of God's forgiving and extravagant grace is made clear only when it's done despite our inability to come close to deserving it.

Forgiveness is remarkable when it's unearned; love is truly selflessly given when it's not reciprocated. It's a messy, lopsided relationship in which one party has to carry an unreasonably heavy share of the burden. But it's in this burden-bearing that our own burdens are made lighter.

Heads Up
Connecting the text to our world

We tell our kids that "giving is better than receiving." Tell that to a nine-year-old just before an Easter egg hunt, birthday party, or Christmas morning. Though it's a nice thing to say, we all really like getting things. It's only in time, as we begin to have a deeper sense of our place in the world and the joy that comes from giving happiness to others that it becomes closer to true.

Still, when we give something, even if we don't receive in return, there's usually a little ledger in the back of our head that keeps track. And if that ledger gets too far out of balance, particularly to the benefit of someone else, we're likely to develop a lingering resentment.

Resentments, though, come from unfulfilled expectations. And expectations are no one's making but our own. It's a rare person who really can give without any expectation tied to it, over and over again, especially to people they find—how should we say it—particularly hard to love. Sure, I can keep giving to my loved ones, even if they don't even the proverbial score. But give extravagantly to the person who lets me down, over and over again, or worse, who has betrayed me?

Thanks, but pass.

Good thing I'm not God.

Prayer for the Week

God, giving without strings attached is really hard. Help me be more like you in how I give, extravagantly and without expectation.

Popping Off

Art/music/video and other cool stuff that relate to the text

"Jack's Death Scene" from *Titanic* (movie, 1994) https://www.youtube.com/watch?v=OGhK4014JNE

"Captain America" comic by Steve Rogers (#25, 2007)

Resurrection for Dummies

Lectionary Texts For
April 1, 2018 (Easter Sunday)

Texts in Brief
My dog ate my Bible!

Gospel
Luke 24:1–12

Jesus's tomb is empty. The women who discover he's gone, and then Peter, are baffled.

First Reading
Acts 10:34–43

Peter speaks to Cornelius and a group of Gentiles about the resurrection and about God showing no favor to a particular group of people.

Psalm

Psalm 118:1–2, 14–24

The stone rejected by builders is now the foundation stone. The psalmist also rejoices in God's victory over death.

Second Reading

1 Corinthians 15:19–26

Since death came through a human being, the resurrection of the dead came through one too. Death is the last enemy.

Bible, Decoded

Breaking down scripture in plain language

Galilee – Territory in what is today northern Israel where Jesus lived most of his life. It was known in his time for being a region replete with political unrest, independent attitudes, and even the occasional politically motivated act of violence.

Cornelius – A "God-fearing man" known to be a pretty good guy among the Jews, even though he himself was a Roman soldier and a gentile (outsider). Although in this text in acts, he and Peter are only talking, this leads eventually to Cornelius being baptized as one of the first gentiles to become a Christian. This is considered a big deal in the birth of the early Christian church.

Points to Ponder

First Thoughts

Peter's name, given to him by Jesus, meant "rock." He was one of the disciples used as an object lesson in denying Jesus three times before his death. And yet he's also the first disciple to visit Jesus's empty tomb, and he is responsible in large part for Cornelius being baptized. The psalm talks about the stone that is cast away by the builders becoming the foundation stone. Given Peter's name and importance in starting the church, it makes sense to think of this reference in the psalm as a prophecy of Peter's role.

If you wrestle with the idea of resurrection, you're not alone. Jesus tells Peter that he'll build the church on his ministry, and yet he comes away from the tomb bewildered by its emptiness. The women, who seem to be the most faithful to Jesus before and after his death, seem to have developed amnesia about the resurrection prophecy. Good to know I'm not alone in scratching my head when it comes to resurrection.

I love the idea that Paul puts forward in the Corinthians text that Jesus/God has triumphed over death, our final enemy. It's beautiful, hopeful, and so liberating. However, his language in the few verses just before this scripture (1 Corinthians 15:12–19) sound a whole lot like the "if-then" ultimatums that ran me out of the fundamentalist church. Basically he says if you don't believe Jesus was raised from the dead, everything is pointless. Let's put a pin in that and come back to it.

Digging Deeper
Mining for what really matters . . . and gold

Lots of ministers love preaching about the risen Christ on Easter Sunday without talking about what he went through to get there. It's a bad habit we Protestants have, but plenty of us skip right over Maundy Thursday and Good Friday to Easter. Part of this is because we don't like to have to deal with the darkness of Jesus's crucifixion, suffering, death, and burial, but it's also because we don't really understand the resurrection.

But in Corinthians, Paul is basically putting us all on notice, saying that if we don't believe in the resurrection, the whole of Jesus's life and our lives as followers of him are meaningless. Hey Paul, let's back up the ultimatum truck, okay?

Growing up, I heard this sort of "if you don't believe _____, then _____ terrible thing is going to happen." It used to scare the crap out of me because I wanted to believe, but it seemed like there was no room for questioning, doubt, or nuance in our understanding. Either you believed or you didn't, period.

But I wasn't sure I did. Not in the way my church wanted me to, anyway.

The thing is, we doubters seem to be in decent company. It's not as if all of the folks right around Jesus got it right away either. In Luke, the women show up and are surprised that Jesus isn't there. It takes a little reminder from the two guys in white (some say they're angels, but the Luke text just calls them men) that Jesus told them this would happen, back in Galilee. Kind of a big thing to forget. They came with oils and spices, fully expecting him still to be in that tomb, and yet these are the women who stood by at the foot of the cross, and Mary Magdalene was the one who washed Jesus's feet in precious oil not long before.

Then along comes Peter. Sure, he gets points for being the first disciple on the scene, but what is his reaction? The women have already told him that Jesus's body was gone, and I'm guessing they reminded him of the whole resurrection thing. Then he goes and sees for himself that, sure enough, the body isn't there. And yet he's bewildered.

It seems like someone as faithful as Peter, the one on whom the church will be built, should get it. But Resurrection is a mind-blower. It makes no sense. There's a part of us that, no matter how earnestly we want to believe, whispers in the back of our minds that resurrection is impossible.

For me, resurrection is a process, rather than a one-time event. It's more like how Martin Luther King spoke of history's arc, bending toward justice. God's arc for the whole of humanity is long, chaotic, and sometimes even violent. But it bends toward hope. It bends toward life and love. That love, though not yet fully realized, is a restoring love that is greater than the sum total of the destructive forces humanity can muster.

Resurrection literally means to make something right again. Though we are bent, bruised, and bloodied by life's darkness, God's love makes us upright once again. Maybe not today. Maybe not tomorrow. But faith in resurrection means that our entire existence bends toward God's fullness.

Heads Up

Connecting the text to our world

I'm an Olympics junkie. Not only that, but I'm also ardently pro-American when watching them. My wife, Amy, and I were watching synchronized platform during the last summer Olympics (honestly, when else would we do that??) and she said she was kind of pulling for the team from Mexico to medal, even though it might mean pushing the Americans out of the running.

"What the hell are you talking about?" I said, more than a little incredulous.

"We win so much already," she said. "This is a rare chance for Mexico."

"If you root for another country," I grumbled, "the terrorists win."

I'm usually a fan of the underdog, and I'm not exactly a sports fanatic, but something about the national zeal, combined with the athletic excellence, brings it out in me.

Of course, there's a part of all of us that loves a winner. There's a reason why so many people wear the jerseys of their favorite teams or players (way more when that person or team is on top than not, by the way), why we revert to a sort of tribal level of passion, painting our faces, screaming rabidly, and why we practically make a religion out of our sports. At one level, it's inspiring to see someone achieve what appears to be unattainable. The idea of doing what most Olympians do—or all professional athletes, for that matter—is hard to comprehend. But when we get to witness it, it serves to embolden our faith in humanity a little bit.

Yes, we screw up a lot, we fight each other, and we're warming up the planet at an alarming rate. But once in a while, it's transcendent to watch someone do something amazing, beautiful, a little bit closer to perfect.

Then there's a baser drive at play too. After all, if it was just about athletic ability, inspiration, and beauty, we'd have no need for medals and the whole "competition" thing. We love winners particularly because there are losers. In fact, the more losers there are, the sweeter the winners appear. I expect this taps into some very basic evolutionary stuff for us. Though we don't toss people into gladiator forums to fight to the death any more (though we get pretty close), we love to pit two individuals or teams against each other to fight it out in an all-or-nothing decision.

We shower the victor with adoration, attention, and treasure, while the loser, no matter how slim the margin, fades into obscurity.

We crave a means of determining who is the best, so that we can identify ourselves with them. Once we know Michael Phelps, the New England Patriots, or whoever are the best, we can buy their uniform, eat their cereal and drink their sports drink, all the while, feeling like we possess a little piece of them.

But without all that work, practice, and emotional tribulation stuff.

It's not unlike making an alliance with the pack leader, really. Once we know who the alpha is, we know who to cozy up to so we ensure our own safety and survival. It's funny that, on one level, sports can be so inspiring and transcendent of the basic human condition, while also appealing to our most primitive selves at the same time. No wonder they're popular.

Then there's Jesus, hanging out with the losers, the sick, the criminals; the kind of folks you would not likely see climbing to the top of the medal stand. And although I'd love to identify as often as possible with the big winners, more often than not my heart lands in the losers' camp too.

That's reason enough for me to love Peter. He tries really hard. He wants so desperately to believe and do the right thing. But he screws up . . . a lot. Jesus gives Peter his name (which means "rock") because he's a man of solid faith. Not perfect faith, but solid. He even names that Peter will be the cornerstone of the new church that will come next.

Despite that, it wasn't so long ago that Peter denied Jesus, and he was among the disciples who fell asleep while Jesus was praying in the garden of Gethsemane. These are only a few examples. Remember the whole "sinking in the lake" thing? That was him. Suffice it to say that, in spite of his faithfulness, he's kind of a loser.

The good news is that God loves losers. In fact, the entirety of the Christian faith was built with them. The psalmist predicts this in our Psalm text, noting that the stone cast aside by the builders will become the cornerstone of the church. That's Peter.

We've all been Peter at one time or another. We've messed up, lost, fallen short, felt unworthy, doubted . . . you name it. And it would be easy enough in those moments to justify our own uselessness. *God can't use a loser like me. I'm supposed to have it all together, to have all the answers, to have scripture memorized and to believe every word it says. I'm just not ready for all of that. I can't do it.*

If we waited until we all were fit to serve God, there would never have been a church to begin with. Yes, we'll screw it up. Yes, people will get hurt. But that's not a reason to sit on the sidelines, telling ourselves all the reasons why we're of no use.

Prayer for the Week

God, I know I'm not perfect. Sometimes I don't even know what I believe. There are times when I feel like Peter, the outcast, tossed to the side, discarded. But I'm still willing to try to do right, to understand, to discover all that I was made to be. I'm still not entirely sure what this whole resurrection thing means, but I do believe that your creation is imbued with love and with goodness. Yes, there's evil in the world—and sometimes I'm a part of it—but I don't want that to keep me from taking part in the beautiful, amazing moments. Help give me the courage to do, to try, to wonder, even when I don't feel like I can.

Popping Off

Art/music/video and other cool stuff that relate to the text

E.T. (movie, 1982)

Rocky (movie, 1976)

"Hallelujah," by Jeff Buckley (song, 1994)

"Easter Again," by Leo Kottke (song, 1986)

"Roll Away the Stone," by Kelly Joe Phelps (song, 1997)

Show, Don't Tell

Lectionary Texts For
April 8, 2018 (Second Sunday of Easter)

Texts In Brief
My dog ate my Bible!

First Reading
Acts 4:32–35

All of the people who were a part of the post-resurrection Jesus community lived communally. Everyone gave all of their possessions to the disciples, who gave them back out to anyone who needed something.

Psalm
Psalm 133

The brief text offers poetic comparisons that suggest the holiness of people unifying and living together in community. Not only is it good; it is sacred, blessed by God, as humanity was intended to live.

SECOND READING

1 John 1:1–2:2

There are several themes in this text. First is another emphasis on the value and necessity of strong community, especially centered around holding each other up in our faith practices. The remainder focuses on warnings not to make claims about living a life of faithfulness, while not actually living it out. Finally, though we're supposed to try and live without sin, we will inevitably fall short of that. We're reminded to ask for God's forgiveness when we do.

GOSPEL

John 20:19–31

The disciples, who were in hiding after Jesus's death, were visited by him. He inspired (literally says he breathed on them) and endowed them with the power to forgive sin. They later explained this to Thomas, the disciple who wasn't there. He doesn't believe it, and says he only will when he can attest to it personally. Jesus appears and criticizes Thomas's skepticism, saying that belief without proof is greater in God's eyes.

Bible, Decoded

Breaking down scripture in plain language

Hermon – A mountain on the border of what are now Lebanon and Syria, it is considered to be the highest point in Syria. So something from such a high place would be, at least poetically speaking, akin to be pouring down from God.

Thomas – Though most of us know Thomas as the doubting apostle, fewer know that he was a fervent missionary for the Christian faith after this experience. He traveled east, beyond the Roman Empire into what is now known as India to tell the story of the gospel (a really long way by ancient standards). This is why there are so many celebrations of him in the orthodox Christian and Catholic traditions.

Apostle – We use this word when we mean disciple sometimes, but while a disciple is a student or follower, an apostle is a messenger or someone who is sent on a mission. So although the disciples also became apostles, this is why Paul, who wasn't a disciple, can still be an apostle.

Points to Ponder

First Thoughts

Most sermons I hear about this gospel text focus on Thomas being a skeptic and how it's a cautionary tale for us not to await proof from God before believing. But I think more interesting is that Jesus appeared to the assembled group and not the individual. Maybe another, sometimes-missed meaning here is that God's inspiration and presence emerge when we come together with a common purpose. Otherwise we have no foundation on which to build anything we may believe.

In a privacy-obsessed and capitalist-driven culture, it's easy to gloss over the really difficult challenges placed in front of us in these passages about living communally. Some might even argue that texts like the ones in Acts make a compelling Christian case for socialism, though there's no explicit mention of government beyond the disciples managing resources.

We talk a lot these days about "intentional community," or community built around a common purpose or set of values. What that could or does look like in today's world depends in part on how we begin to think more communally, and to what end, beyond our own lives.

Digging Deeper
Mining for what really matters . . . and gold

The word *kibbutzim* in Hebrew is literally translated as "clustering" or "gathering." It was a type of collective living arrangement in the Jewish tradition in which everything is shared and no one owns anything just for themselves. The concept was built around the idea of sharing crops, but far more is shared when people give to each other without keeping score, and when they share meals together and, really, their very lives.

It may seem scary to many of us now. We could be taken advantage of. We might turn everything over, only to have someone steal it, or others might get lazy and not do their share. Times will come when there's only one of something and two people need it. Or what if we just won't like them? Once they already have all our stuff, we're stuck!

Part of this was done out of basic survival in a culture where there could be plenty one moment and little-to-nothing the next. But it was modeled also on a tradition valued in the culture: *they really meant this stuff.*

But there's something wonderfully subversive about *kibbutzim*. It's not a meritocracy. It doesn't matter who your parents were or how much you inherited.

Titles are irrelevant and, perhaps more than that, so is money! There's no need for it. And though we value it most of all (part of why Jesus spoke about it more than anything else), it's a tool that gives away our power to government. They print or coin the money, by and large they determine its worth, and we work like hell to get it.

Remove the money, remove the power. Bloodless, nonviolent, quiet. All it takes is changing the entire way we live and our whole value system. Now, I write this in my own private house, on a computer than I personally own, so I'm not above calling out my own hypocrisy. But I think we have to begin to wrestle with the spiritual, strategic, and social importance of *kibbutzim* and what it might look like, at least incrementally, in today's world.

Good or bad, we're in it together.

Heads Up

Connecting the text to our world

The morning of September 11, 2001, is one I'll always remember. I was home sick and Amy came back to our apartment in a panic. She turned on the TV, which showed us one flaming skyscraper, followed by another. The images are still burned into my memory. The entire city of Fort Worth, where we lived at the time, was deathly silent. Everyone was bracing for what was going to happen next. More attacks around the country? Retaliation, leading us into war?

Most people hid away, quietly waiting, wondering, praying.

As people began to emerge, though, something was different. It didn't last forever, but it was real and palpable. We were different with each other, even those of us who disagreed or never associated with each other. We were kinder, more thoughtful, more grounded. If anything good came of the tragic events that day, it was that we were one people, however briefly.

Soon enough, the events were politicized and we identified the person and group who we would pursue in response. But like the disciples, huddled away, many of us also experienced some deep spiritual presence. Jesus breathed on us, in a manner of speaking. And while some of us may have focused on retaliation, others felt driven out to heal old wounds and build new bridges among various faiths and cultures.

There doesn't have to be crisis in order to sense God's inspiration. But it does take intention. The whole "Wherever two or more are gathered, there I am also" text sounds good, but that puts the responsibility on us. Just like Thomas we need community, faith, and a call or mission. The community is there, and it's important, even sacred. But if that becomes "the thing" and we end up being religion junkies, coming back once a week for our regular God-fix, we won't get what we need, even if we think we're getting what we want.

Prayer for the Week

God, it's so easy to think of "we" after I feel like "I" am taken care of in all the ways I want. Help me step more boldly into the "we," trusting that, where "we" are, there You are.

Popping Off
Art/music/video and other cool stuff that relate to the text

"One," by U2 (song, 1991)

"Doubting Thomas," by Nickel Creek (song, 2005)

"Art Kibbutz" Artist Community http://www.artkibbutz
.org

I Don't "Know" Know Him

Lectionary Texts For
April 15, 2018 (Third Sunday of Easter)

Texts in Brief
My dog ate my Bible!

FIRST READING
Acts 3:12–19

Peter criticizes the Jewish audience for not yet understanding Jesus's resurrection, and condemns them, too, for turning on him at his time of trial. He then claims the ancient Jewish prophecies for a suffering and resurrected messiah have been fulfilled, and urges them to change their ways and ask for forgiveness.

PSALM
Psalm 4

David opens the psalm with a lament over the lack of righteousness of his people. He then urges them not to try to escape their own shame for sinful acts by falling into more sin as a distraction, but rather to reflect and learn from their mistakes. Finally, he criticizes their apparent blindness to all God has already provided them, offering gratitude as an example of what they should do, and asks for nothing but peace and protection from God.

SECOND READING

1 John 3:1–7

God's children are misunderstood as they are a reflection of God in the world, who also is misunderstood. So the author speaks to readers/hearers like children, not because they are sinless, but almost as an assumption that they haven't learned and don't yet know any better. The theme of this week resonates, calling for turning away from sinful behavior and seeking purification from God. It's also noted that it is sin itself that pushes us further from God.

GOSPEL

Luke 24:36b–48

Jesus appears among the disciples who are fearful and in hiding after his crucifixion. He offers a blessing of peace and asks for something to eat. He recognizes their bafflement, so he opens their minds to understand that he is, indeed, the fulfillment of the prophesied messiah from their tradition.

Bible, Decoded

Breaking down scripture in plain language

Fish – Fish are ever present in biblical stories, in part because they were central to the culture itself. They're explicitly mentioned in one of the Genesis creation stories, and Jesus mentions—or deals with—fish in many gospel stories. The *ichthus* (Jesus fish symbol) becomes the secret symbol to signify belief in Jesus after his ascension, so there may be some significance in Jesus asking particularly for fish in this text in Luke. But it could also simply be evidence that he is, indeed, still human with physical needs.

Author of life – Here, the use of this term is meant to suggest that not only was Jesus put to death; God was crucified as well. But there's also a wonderful implication about the meaning of the word "authority." We hear the fundamentalist claim that the Bible is authoritative, which often tends to suggest legalism and absolutism. However, authors create something from nothing (yes, I'm biased, but it's true). And inasmuch as God said "let there be . . ." and creation came from the void, this paints God as the Great Author. In this way, we can resonate with the authority of scripture, given that it evokes life and meaning where it was previously absent.

Points to Ponder

First Thoughts

This text in Acts and how it's used today is a good example of how we co-opt scripture and turn it into something ugly. Peter's condemnation of his audience can be, and has been, used to fuel anti-Semitic sentiment. However, we run the risk of warnings offered elsewhere in scripture of feeling superior, twisting our prayers of thanksgiving into something more akin to "Thank God

I'm not like those guys." In all honesty, how many of us would have let fear and second-guessing take over when faced either with keeping silent at Jesus's trial—or even joining in the chorus—or face the same torturous demise he did?

David's warning not to fall back on sinful habits to distract from the shame of previous sin sounds much like the seeds from which life-taking habits come, or even addiction. We drink too much, so we feel guilty, and can't deal with the guilt, so we drink. . . . So though it feels like harsh judgment in a way, the censure also offers a path out of a lifeless cycle of futile escapism.

Digging Deeper

Mining for what really matters . . . and gold

In Acts, Peter is drawing what seem to be some pretty clear lines between those who are *in* (followers) and *out* (the rest of the Jewish audience). Though there is a call in this toward transformation and repentance, there's a real risk in this sort of message being co-opted and used as a tool within the church to claim that what we have is what they all need. Therefore, our sole mission is to make them more like us.

No.

There are many distinctions here, actually. There's the difference between Christ, the person, and the rest of us, as he is the only one who went willingly all the way to the cross. There's the separation that our errant ways have placed between us and our divinely desired union with God. But there's also the priority we tend to place on self over other. Too often we allow the latter to be compromised for the sake of the former, justifying our actions with willful ignorance and broad, hasty judgments.

Authors or speakers in each of these texts decry such separations, be it interpersonal or in our relationship with God. The separations themselves are the sin we're to overcome. Therefore simply by affirming some Christian/non-Christian boundary and fighting to pull people across to the right side, we're called to reflect on, sit with, and then go about the hard work of destroying all such boundaries: of class, race, orientation, or whatever they may be that divide us and sever our connection with the holy.

We are called as healers to mend brokenness, within ourselves and in our midst. It may feel more gratifying to work as recruiters rather than healers, but it's what is at the core of our call as Jesus-followers. It's hard, thankless, never-ending work, and first, we have to apply it to ourselves. Shakespeare once wrote, "Physician, heal thyself," because a doctor who is in need of care won't be much good to anyone else. During this time of reflection following Easter, maybe our mantra should be "Christian, heal thyself."

Heads Up

Connecting the text to our world

Today's social media culture offers a social fabric that is miles wide and inches deep. We stay "connected" to people by clicking a thumbs-up on a recent picture or clever statement, or offer a heart emoticon of sympathy when they are struggling. But it's all safe, expedient, superficial. It doesn't demand more from us than we're ever willing to give. Moreover, we can customize the flow of information coming to us by who or what we pay attention to and what we choose to ignore. We build insular, self-affirming echo chambers that indulge static ways of thought and affirm that acquaintances, rather than deep relationships, are the new normal.

It could be argued that I know more people now than ever before. I know at least something on a cursory level about them, yes, but as the saying goes, I don't "know" know them. I'm willing to click "like" on something, but I'm not really investing in them, or they in me. If things really got difficult, it's safe to say that my circle of friends would shrink dramatically.

Jesus and Peter, both, express dismay at the lack of ability people seem to have to get it when it comes to what he's really about. If they did, after all, they would have been transformed in a way that their response would have been different. Our convictions and interpersonal bonds run only so deep; everyone has that point at which what we stand for falls victim to a more visceral sense of self-preservation.

Of course, when coming to terms with the harsh reality that we all—every single one of us—fall short of the ideal we'd like to imagine for ourselves, it would be easier to distract ourselves from the sense of shame or frailty by jumping on our Facebook feed or scrolling through texts. But as the psalmist exhorts, it's best to sit with the sense of fragility, to wrestle with it and let it begin to change us. We're not to be martyrs, victimized by our own sense of worthlessness. We can change, thank God.

As singer and libertine Dean Martin once said, good judgment comes from experience and experience, well, that comes from poor judgment.

Prayer for the Week

I screw up, God. I know you, but sometimes I have to admit I don't "know" know you. It's easy just to feel bad and then run from my guilt. Help me sit with the discomfort instead, learning and growing for the better from it.

Popping Off

Art/music/video and other cool stuff that relate to the text

"You Don't Know Me," by Son Lux (song, 2012)

Groundhog Day (movie, 1993)

The Matrix (movie, 1999)

Inconvenient
Christianity

Lectionary Texts For

April 22, 2018 (Fourth Sunday after Easter)

Texts in Brief

My dog ate my Bible!

FIRST READING

Acts 4:5–12

Though it has already happened before this text starts, the disciples have healed a crippled man who had been begging at the entryway of the city for a long, long time. This gets the attention of government and religious officials, who challenge their authority to perform such miracles. Peter claims the authority of Jesus, referring to him as the stone the officials had rejected, and upon which the church would be built.

PSALM

Psalm 23

This is one of the most famous psalms in the bible, namely because it is read at most funerals. The tone is one of comfort that God remains with us, despite the trials, darkness, and hardship we face.

SECOND READING

1 John 3:16–24

This serves as a reminder of where our priorities lie, or should lie, as Christians. It claims that, if we learned anything from Jesus, it's that there are things more important than life itself: compassion, service of others, being an example of what is necessary to bring real, lasting healing into our midst. And if it takes our lives to follow through on it, that's why Jesus set the example first. The conviction that we are standing in righteousness in doing so gives us the strength necessary to face all the difficulties that come with such a path.

GOSPEL

John 10:11–18

The Gospel uses the metaphor of sheep and shepherd to illustrate why it's so important for figures of authority/responsibility to stand their ground when times are hard. If not, there is nothing to stand on in behalf of the innocent and vulnerable. This is our mission. Those who succumb to the fears inherent in such risk, it claims, aren't trusting thoroughly in the promise God makes to all who hold fast.

Bible, Decoded

Breaking down scripture in plain language

Shepherd – We talk about Jesus as shepherd a lot. But when he was gone, the job wasn't finished. It was passed along to his apostles. The "sheep" they were protecting were those who were so easily ground up by the political machine they were in. But wolves always go after the sheep; it's in their nature. And it's in the shepherd's nature to be the firewall against such a threat. The good news is that Jesus was that shepherd, showing us the path through the valley of the shadow of death. The challenge, though, is that now, we are the shepherds.

Abide – This is an interesting word that pops up a lot in the Christian faith. In some contexts it means to follow, more as a child does a parent or a student follows the teacher. However, it can also mean to resonate with on a deep level, or to be in harmony with something or someone. Abiding in Jesus, then, doesn't stop simply at following him. It means stepping into those proverbial shoes to help finish what he started.

Stone – It's poetic that Peter refers to Jesus as the rejected stone on which the church would be established, especially since his name, Peter, given to him by Jesus, means "rock." Jesus also said, upon this rock, I'll build my church. So we can see how seriously Peter is taking Jesus about being that rock, rejected or not.

Points to Ponder

First Thoughts

Peter has gone through an incredible turnaround in what seems to be a pretty short amount of time. He went from being this fumbling, faltering disciple who tried to hold Jesus back from persecution to stepping into a similar role himself. I guess he finally got it.

Digging Deeper

Mining for what really matters . . . and gold

We've talked about the symbolic importance of mountains in scripture, but now let's talk about valleys. If mountaintops are, in fact, the experiences of the holy we seek, then the valley would reasonably be the chasm that stands between them. And though we may want to hide in the safety of the mountaintop, a point at which we feel at peace, safe and close to God, we're called, over and over, back down into the dark valley. Jesus required it of Peter, and we shouldn't expect any different.

But beyond that, it's helpful to consider what valleys represented to these people in particular. There's one valley they would all be familiar with nearby called *hinnom*. It was where they dumped all of their garbage. It was gross. But also, it was where pagans often would go to conduct ceremonial animal—even human—sacrifices in secret.

At the base of the valley of *hinnom* was a lake, and suffice it to say no one wanted to drink the water there. In fact, because of all the oils and fats from the remains left from the trash and sacrifices, there was believed to be a thick, toxic oil slick on top of the water, which would have killed anything trying to live below the surface. So not only was the valley a symbol of death all around it; even under the water's surface, everything was dead.

Even more fascinating is that there are stories about the lake catching fire when a flame or lightning strike would get close. This, as we hear Jesus talk about, is quite literally a "lake of fire" they would all know—and care to avoid. The references to this valley as *Gehenna* have been rendered in many scriptural translations as one of the many synonyms for "hell." It gives new meaning to "hell on earth," especially for the audiences of the stories told here.

Heads Up

Connecting the text to our world

Easter is the one good part of Lent, really. The only sort of fun part anyway. We trudge through weeks on end of solemnity and self-denial, only to get to the message that we're all going to die.

Well, yay.

And we just endure Good Friday the whole death-and-torture thing, but honestly, we'd rather find a loophole if we could to get around it. Who doesn't like cute new spring dresses, a joyful Easter celebration, and the hope that comes with new life, raised from the still-smoldering ashes of death?

But without death, there can be no resurrection.

Without a desolate winter, spring loses its context. Without sorrow, joy lacks its poignancy. Without pain, we cannot embrace healing.

The only way out of the darkness is to walk through it, one step at a time.

And yet, we just got through Easter—haven't even eaten all the chocolate bunnies and picked up the Sunday clothes from the dry cleaner, and we're already face-to-face with adversity and threats again. Remind me why we signed up for this Christianity thing? It just seems so . . . dark, depressing.

When we're down, deep in the valley of oppression, addiction, doubt, darkness, rejection, or even death and loss, it's hard to see anything else. The world just got done witnessing the resurrection of the man they still doubted was who he claimed to be, and now the few who stayed closest to him are facing likely similar persecution for carrying on his work.

Well, that's just not fair. All they did was heal a guy who was without hope for an independent future. And it's not like they *had to say* why they did it. They could have just scattered, or distracted them with a flourish and a "TA-DA." Why the hell, when you're facing yet more darkness, would you seem to welcome it? Just ask God to make it all go away, fix it, destroy the darkness, once and for all.

But if God destroyed all darkness, humanity as we know it would go with it. We are creatures of light and dark, intertwined. It's around us, among us, within us. Peter and the other apostles know the mission ahead of them and the risks inherent in it. And they do it anyway, emboldened by the sense that doing what is right is more important than doing what is safe.

In the 23rd Psalm, it would be nice if it said that, when down in the valley of the shadow of Death, God will just turn the light on and make it all better, or maybe airlift us out and drop us safely on the other side of the valley. But the comfort Peter finds to steel himself against the powers that be (AKA, the Darkness) is not that they'll be struck down and no longer will pose a threat. They'll tread once more through the deep dark of the valley.

But they rest in the comfort that they won't be doing it alone.

Prayer for the Week

Eternal light, I don't ask you to get rid of the darkness, but rather to guide me through it as my companion, my hope, and my strength.

Popping Off

Art/music/video and other cool stuff that relate to the text

"Holy Grail," by Jay-Z (song, 2013)

Der Herr ist mein getreuer Hirt, BWV 112, by Johann Sebastian Bach (song, 1731)

God Chooses
Weakness

Lectionary Texts For
April 29, 2018 (Fifth Sunday after Easter)

Texts in Brief
My dog ate my Bible!

First Reading
Acts 8:26–40

God tells Philip to go from Jerusalem to Gaza. Along the way he meets the treasurer of the Ethiopian Queen, reading Isaiah. Phillip joins him and starts explaining it, going on to tell him about how Jesus was the fulfillment of these prophecies. The man asks Philip to baptize him and he does, then disappears, "relocated" by God to a region called Azotus to spread the gospel there.

Psalm
Psalm 22:25–31

A prediction by the psalmist that all people of the world will come to know God and worship God.

SECOND READING

1 John 4:7–21

Love, life, Jesus, and God are all intertwined. Knowing—and deeply living into—a life informed by love leads one to God and to a life of meaning. Jesus was sent by God, who is called Love interchangeably, to reveal that path to such a life. There is a deep, intimate coexistence described of God in us and us in God. Love was perfected among us in the form of Jesus's example, and such perfect love leaves no room for fear. Finally, we're warned not just to say we love, while not actually living it out.

GOSPEL

John 15–18

The Gospel text continues this notion that we must be part of a greater whole in order to be what we're made to be: the embodiment of love in the world. Like a vine clings to its source, we are part of the larger plant. We're also to allow ourselves to be "pruned," allowing all that doesn't lead us to this more perfected expression of love to fall away.

Bible, Decoded

Breaking down scripture in plain language

Eunuch – This is a word that gets interpreted in many different ways. In some cases, it's referring to men who were castrated involuntarily. For others, they apparently chose to do so on their own. Finally, there are those born without testicles—or at least without descended or fully developed testicles—from birth. Another interpretation is that this simply refers to a chosen life of celibacy. Finally, even others believe when Jesus refers to eunuchs as those who are "born this way," he is referring to any man who does not feel sexually attracted to women. Castration or celibacy in non-Jewish cultures sometimes was done as a sign of faithfulness to a religious order or service to a ruler. More specifically, they would often serve in the bedchambers of their leaders.

Vine – This symbol is used throughout the Bible namely because they were known to everyone in the cultures. They refer to Jesus and humanity, the church and its congregants, or God and creation. The idea is that they are more than connected; they are interdependent. The vine can't bear fruit without being attached to the larger vine, and the branch yields nothing without the fruit the branches yield.

Perfect – This word is distorted all too often in our current culture because we think of it as meaning "without any error," or "never making any mistakes." Actually, the word comes from the Greek, *téleios*, which means "fully developed," "full-grown," or "complete in all its parts." In this way, perfection is more accurately understood as the idea that the whole is greater than the sum of all its parts.

Points to Ponder

First Thoughts

I think we can find these texts both comforting and disquieting at the same time, depending on how we look at them. The idea of how deeply and profoundly we are interconnected with God and one another is a source of assurance, especially when we inevitably feel isolated, unknown, and misunderstood. This happens increasingly in our highly mobile, too often insular world.

But the idea that God depends on us, or more specifically on me, for *anything* is more than a little nerve-wracking. This puts a big responsibility on us. What if I screw it up? Actually there's no "what if" about it; I will screw it up, guaranteed. I often wonder why God would choose to trust a fallible person like me with such important work.

The flipside of this is that God willingly chooses to be vulnerable, even given the reality that it won't always go well. This chosen vulnerability of God, though, is precisely what is expressed in the death of Jesus. We choose sometimes to focus on Jesus as king or victor, conquering death and confounding those who sought to destroy him. But in this period after Easter when we're still seeking to process what went down, it's worth spending some time with this idea that *God chooses weakness* in order to make room for relationship with us.

Digging Deeper
Mining for what really matters . . . and gold

Though I've mentioned in earlier studies that Acts is primarily focused on the growth and spread of Christianity, there are sections of sorts within it to be aware of. The first seven chapters particularly focus on the growth and emboldening of the gospel's influence among Jews. In this chapter, we see Peter beginning to baptize and minister to Gentiles, or non-Jews. In the next chapter, we encounter the conversion of Paul, a Jewish Roman citizen who ends up being critical to the church's future and the credited author for much of the New Testament. Then in chapters 10–11, we read what is called the "Gentile Pentecost," where Christianity really begins to catch on outside of the Jewish community in a real way.

But it all starts with Peter following God's call south, and then being willing to connect with a man along the way very different than he is.

Though we can get caught up in the idea that our mission is to spread Christianity far and wide, I think it's important to start by looking at *how* this all takes place first, as there's an important order to things. Imagine it almost like circles expanding outward, if you will.

First Peter encounters Jesus. In him he sees a spark of the divine revealed he's not encountered before. It's so profound that he drops everything and changes the direction of his whole life. Then he becomes part of this tightly knit cohort of Jesus followers known as the disciples. From there, they reach out and minister to those nearest to them, serving them and teaching. It then expands throughout the Jewish communities, and from there, beyond that to the so-called Gentiles.

But it all traces back first and foremost to Peter's profound, transforming connection to God through his commitment to Jesus. Without that, there is no anchor, no vine, from which to grow these other branches that yield fruit sprouting into new life, and so on. Without this, there is no Paul, and likely no churches established and cultivated by him and his colleagues.

The next depends on the one before.

Heads Up

Connecting the text to our world

I was invited to a screening of Martin Scorsese's movie, *Silence*. Though it was rich in beautiful imagery and deep theological and social themes, honestly it felt more like homework than your typical Hollywood entertainment piece. At nearly three hours long, with minimal soundtrack and sparse dialogue, it took some effort to get through. But the themes throughout it resonated with many we see this week: chosen celibacy, willing weakness, and even the clash of cultures that happens when our religious fervor takes us into unknown territory.

The story takes place in seventeenth-century Buddhist Japan, a period when several western nations were sending Christian missionaries there to convert them to the Christian faith. The Japanese, wary of the risk of colonization, outlaw Christianity and turn violent against converts and those who spread it. Two Jesuit priests go in search of their mentor, a fellow priest, who supposedly renounced his faith and disappeared into the Japanese social fabric.

Most fascinating to me was this relationship between Ichichiro, a Japanese peasant and Christian convert, and Rodrigues, a young Portuguese Jesuit priest. Rodrigues needs Ichichiro in many instances throughout the film, though Ichichiro repeatedly lets him down and betrays him, only to come back, over and again, to ask him to indulge him in confession. Though Rodrigues grows weary of his weakness, he obliges, knowing full well Ichichiro will turn on him again.

Someone should tell him he's being taken advantage of! He's taking unnecessary risk by allowing this man who has shown he can't be trusted into his inner circle. It's crazy to keep doing it. He ought to turn Ichichiro away, tell him he's had enough chances, and to go elsewhere, far away from the priest!

But he doesn't because it's part of his calling, and it's in his nature to do this. Yes, he'll be exploited and betrayed, and yet he offers himself. He does it because it's what he sees in the example of Jesus, and to what he is called as part of that greater Body of Christ in the world.

Prayer for the Week

God, help me love in spite of the risk, and in doing so, become a more fully developed, perfect part of this larger communion for humanity with you that you seek.

Popping Off

Art/music/video and other cool stuff that relate to the text
Silence (movie, 2016)

No-Limits Love

Lectionary Texts For
May 6, 2018 (Sixth Sunday after Easter)

Texts in Brief
My dog ate my Bible!

FIRST READING
Acts 10:44–48

Peter, who was speaking in a foreign territory, had many gentiles who were moved to be baptized. Others (presumably Jews) seemed to take issue with this, but he reprimanded them, suggesting it wasn't for them to decide who was worthy and who wasn't. So the gentiles were baptized and he stayed among them for days.

PSALM
Psalm 98

A poem of jubilation, calling people to sing a new song of praise to God, in order to bring all of creation into a chorus honoring God.

Second Reading
1 John 5:1–6

The author calls for both faithfulness and obedience, and says that truly living out a life that demonstrates love of God will, by extension, show a love for God's children, or all of humanity. They suggest that the world is won through such obedience and faithfulness, as this is what Jesus revealed by doing it himself.

Gospel
John 15:9–17

Jesus levels the playing field by referring to those following him as friends, rather than being servants or in more of a parent/child relationship with him. He asserts the importance of adherence to God's commands, but clarifies that putting another's life before our own in an act of selfless love is the greatest expression of obedience to God we can offer.

Bible, Decoded
Breaking down scripture in plain language

Lyre – A handheld harp-like instrument with seven strings. It can be strummed like a guitar or plucked like a harp. It's believed this was the instrument, or one of the instruments, David played.

Baptism – Though we know baptism as a symbolic act to signify formal entry into a life committed to following and resembling Jesus, it has historic ties to a Jewish ritual known as a *mikveh, mikva,* or *mikvah.* This is a Jewish ritual bath used for purification. Though beliefs varied/vary about how it is performed, some Jews believe that full immersion is necessary to achieve ritual purification. In Christianity, it can be seen as a similar cleansing act of past sin, but also is seen as a way of symbolizing death to our old selves and rebirth into a new life: a miniature death and resurrection, of sorts.

Points to Ponder

First Thoughts

It's worth asking who or what baptism is for. It's such a central act in Christianity, and yet done and understood so differently. Some believe it has to be done by a priest, while others feel like it's entirely between the person being baptized and God. Some do full immersion; others "sprinkle." Many Christian traditions practice infant baptism (I was baptized as an infant in the Episcopal Church), while many believe there's no reason to baptize before the person reaches the so-called "age of accountability" when they can choose for themselves and know what they're doing.

We have to consider why do we do it, for whom, or whether we believe God requires it in order to find us acceptable. We may get baptized to unburden ourselves of sin, to feel we've left it behind, or as a sort of "fire insurance," to keep from going to hell. We might do it just to make others happy, or to have them help hold us accountable to our promise. Maybe it's a sort of contract, a holy promise we're making with God. Like any symbolic act, it can be taken many ways. And though the meanings are often powerful and their implications profound, we have to be mindful not to assume that our meaning is shared by everyone else.

Digging Deeper

Mining for what really matters . . . and gold

In Acts, we see the tension of what Peter is telling his followers, which is that God shows no favor to one group over another, and their long-held tradition that they are God's chosen. Whereas it's easy to draw parallels to nationalist fervor or our political resistance to immigration, we need to understand that, for generations on generations, it's been at the core of Jewish teaching to believe that God, indeed, does choose sides.

And now not only are they being forced to reconcile that with what Peter—and really, Jesus—is claiming; they are called out to actively minister to the "other" and to welcome and nurture them into this emerging new community of Jesus-followers.

This, in a sense, is the "New Song," referred to in Psalm 98. Obviously these aren't happening at the same time, as they were written centuries apart. But the fact that it's reiterated like this demonstrates the cyclical nature of human behavior, falling in and out of sync with God's intent for overcoming division, hierarchy, and distinctions of class, race, nationality, or even religious identity.

In the 1 John text, we see a common theme in the book of Jesus as conqueror—one that's difficult in many ways to reconcile with the reality of Jesus in the gospels—the first word in the text is *"everyone."* The other key word, it seems, comes soon after, which is *"chooses."* The important power balance here is that the choice is in the hands of the "other," not us. We're not the ones who have authority to deem anyone's worthiness of God's grace and love. Our job is more as preparers of space, stewards of a path, and radically hospitable family members.

Finally, Jesus models this by breaking down the hierarchy even within his own group of disciples in the Gospel text. *We're no longer master-servant*, he says, *but now friends*. That makes them equals.

Equals. With God incarnate. Consider the implications of this. Talk about not feeling worthy! But it also illustrates the depth and breadth of the extent to which God goes to widen the so-called circles, or even destroy them altogether. Our response, then, must be to do so in our midst, every day.

Heads Up

Connecting the text to our world

I was christened in the Episcopal Church when I was a baby, as I mentioned above. Neither of my parents were Episcopalian; it was for my grandmother's sake (who was *really* Episcopalian) that they went through all the classes and got it done. She came and watched when it happened, but for my mom—a Baptist—it wasn't really what mattered. For her, I needed to be baptized when I was older, full immersion preferably, when I chose it for myself.

I know some people that are practically baptism junkies, going in for a spiritual cleanse, almost like they're going to the nutritionist for fiber pills. But it's not an oil change, and honestly, between you and me, I'm not sure the water where or how you do it even matters. Heck, I got baptized in a swimming pool, and I turned out alright. I mean, sort of alright at least.

I'm also not one for the whole "get out of hell free" card idea. To me, that lets us off way too easy. In fact, getting baptized, and even going through classes beforehand if they're required, isn't hard, really. It's everything we're supposed to be and do afterward that's tough.

I think about Jesus's call to what is known as the "Greatest Commandment," which this passage in the Gospel according to John seems to be referring to. Loving other people with our whole selves, and following through on living that love out regardless of the consequences, is way harder than trying to stick with a handful of rules. I mean, I can tell you I have at least half of the Ten Commandments nailed, really without even trying!

We talked in last week's study about the biblical idea of perfection, and how it doesn't mean completely without any mistakes all the time. It has more to do with something completely coming into itself in every way. It's about growing up. And once we grow up, we're responsible for knowing what's right and wrong. We choose to get baptized or not. We choose whether it's a one-off ritual, or if it's the beginning of a new way of trying to be.

Jesus didn't come to trash the old rules and laws. Scripture says he came to perfect or fulfill them. So in a way he is helping them become fully mature, complete, realized as what they were meant to be.

Prayer for the Week

God, I like being special, favored, singled out. But help me come to terms with the fact that being part of a greater, co-equal whole is far more precious in the end.

Popping Off
Art/music/video and other cool stuff that relate to the text

"One," by U2 (song, 2006)

Contact (movie, 1997)

Contact, by Carl Sagan (book, 1985)

Grow Up, Already

Lectionary Texts For
May 10, 2018 (Ascension of Jesus)

Texts in Brief
My dog ate my Bible!

FIRST READING
Acts 1:1–11

The author of Luke writes of the physical presence of Jesus among his disciples after crucifixion. Jesus tells them to stay in Jerusalem until they are encountered by God's Holy Spirit. While they're focused on knowing when God will restore Israel (and therefore them, the Jews) as the capital of the Jewish territory, he warns them against trying to know things that aren't for them to worry about. Instead, they'll be dispersed among surrounding regions to teach and minister after God's spirit empowers them, which is a nod toward the moment called Pentecost. Jesus then ascends and leaves them.

Psalm

Psalm 47

Another song or poem of praise, this one's focus is on "God beyond" or "God above." Though others are more intent on either "God within" or "God among," this one is different. In this way, it goes with the ascension theme of the week.

Second Reading

Ephesians 1:15–23

Paul offers gratitude for the faithfulness of his fellow Christians in Ephesus. He also prays for vision and wisdom to be afforded to them in their ministerial work. He claims that such power is demonstrated in the life, death, and resurrection of Jesus, declaring it as a transcendent power, above and over all people or any human laws or power. Finally, he refers to Jesus as the head of a larger body, with the church as the greater body.

Gospel

Luke 24:44–53

This series of events in Luke are the ones referred to above in the Acts text.

Bible, Decoded

Breaking down scripture in plain language

Theophilus – From the Greek, this literally means "God-love." But in this case, many historians believe it's an honorific for the person to whom this book (and Luke) were written. There's a fairly solid consensus among religious scholars, too, that both Luke and Acts were written by the same person, and to the same audience. It's even suggested that originally they were written as one single work, which is one reason we'll often hear them referred to as "Luke-Acts."

Ephesus – This ancient Greek city has a lot of historic, and no small amount of biblical, significance. It was a wonder of architecture, with facilities that could accommodate tens of thousands at a time. It also is the site of the Temple of Artemis, known as one of the Seven Wonders of the World. It's also one of the Asian churches referred to in Revelation.

Points to Ponder

First Thoughts

Personally, I struggle with the "God above" or "God beyond" concepts. It feels lofty, abstract, unreachable. And it also feels so different than the intimacy of the Jesus portrayed just last week in these studies, where he was saying he wasn't a master, but a friend. I'm grateful, for this reason, for the comparison Paul makes to Jesus being above all in the way that a head is above the body: elevated but not entirely removed. In this way it also resonated with the caution that the disciples should not to stand in awe, eyes turned to the sky. Rather, they're meant to take their charge as living, vital parts of this Christ-body and get to work fulfilling their mission.

Above, but not removed. Elevated, but still belonging. Like many things with regard to Jesus, there is no simple either/or understanding of him. God is within, among, and beyond, all at the same time.

Digging Deeper

Mining for what really matters . . . and gold

We tend to reflect more on the miraculous implications of Jesus's ascension. But what about those left behind? Bear in mind that this is the second time in a short period of time they've lost Jesus. First, to the Roman cross, and now, to God. This man to whom they've pledged their lives has now departed, charging them with the most difficult work they've ever embarked on. On top of that, they likely know the ultimate consequence of their evangelism throughout Roman-occupied territory.

So just when they need Jesus the most, and just when the threat against their lives is the greatest, he disappears. It seems their task is made even more daunting, given that now they will be speaking of this resurrected messiah that everyone can no longer see and touch for themselves.

It seems there are two spiritual and personal disciplines the disciples are called to exercise here. The first is patience, as Jesus did not give them a specific agenda before leaving them. Rather, he tells them to wait, holding fast to his promise that they will know what to do when the time comes. Anyone who has waited without a concrete end-date knows how maddening that can be, but patient trust is required, nonetheless.

Second, though they have been looking to Jesus for wisdom, strength, and guidance, now they have to look more intentionally inward. The entire time Jesus healed and taught among them and the others he met, he repeated his mantra that the power of God was within them. But now they have to put that idea into practice. They're growing up as people of faith, in a way. Maturing, becoming more perfect, as we've talked about in recent studies.

Growing up isn't always fun, but it's necessary. If Jesus stayed with them, it's likely they would cling to him, rather than evolving in their own spiritual lives. Now, to borrow a phrase, it's time to practice what they've been preaching.

Heads Up

Connecting the text to our world

As the father of two kids, I think I can safely say that the hardest part about parenting is letting go. Though I know my kids likely feel alone and vulnerable, even a little scared, when I leave them on their own to figure out something difficult, I feel at least as scared and vulnerable.

What if they mess up? What if they get hurt? What if something irreparable happens that can't be undone? What if people think I'm a bad parent, even though I'm trying to do what I think is best for them? So many unanswered questions hang over me when I pull back from them and, more often than not, I don't feel like a good dad.

I feel like a jerk.

There's a story about a man born with no arms who now lives on his own. When asked how he survives, let alone performs many daily functions most otherwise abled people have to do, he credits his mother. For his whole life, he had depended on his mom to pick his clothes out and dress him, until one day when she didn't. He protested, yelled and cried, and yet she didn't open the door of his bedroom to come in and help him. It sounds like a heartless thing to do, but to her, it was the only way he would ever learn to dress himself. But it was also the first step toward him believing he could ever be independent.

It took him half the day, screaming in frustration and struggling with his clothes to get dressed, but he did it. Looking back, he said, that was the moment at which he knew he was his own person and that he was not helpless. He talked about the experience years later with his mother, who confessed that, the entire time he was in his room, she was leaning against the other side of his door, weeping.

Distance isn't always easy, but sometimes it's necessary. Maybe in those moments when we feel God's distance, we're meant to be finding that potential within ourselves to be God-among-us, rather than standing, staring at the sky waiting for help.

Prayer for the Week

God, I tend to pray and expect results. It's not often that I like to hear the thing I'm waiting for is myself. Help me see my own full potential and to use in ways I am intended to.

Popping Off

Art/music/video and other cool stuff that relate to the text

My Left Foot (movie, 1989)

Big (movie, 1988)

There Is No Spoon

Lectionary Texts For

May 13, 2018 (Seventh Sunday of Easter)

Texts in Brief

My dog ate my Bible!

First Reading

Acts 1:15–17, 21–26

Peter announces to a crowd that the place among the apostles previously held by Judas needs to be filled. Joseph (Justus) and Matthias are the top candidates. So Peter prays for guidance; they cast lots and select Matthias.

Psalm

Psalm 1

The good and evil are compared to trees: the good are planted by a stream, and the wicked dry up and wither. Those who are righteous bear fruits—or spiritual gifts—as they are meant to, whereas those who don't follow a faithful path have lives that lead to death or meaninglessness.

Second Reading
1 John 5:9–13

The author compares the values of human claims over claims and promises offered by God. God's word, as reflected in Jesus's words and life, are life-giving. Humanity's claims and promises, however, are not eternal.

Gospel
John 17:6–19

Jesus offers a prayer to God as he is to be separated from those to whom he has ministered. He asks God to fill them with the kind of joy he has, to protect them from evil, and to sanctify them in their ministry of spreading his gospel message.

Bible, Decoded
Breaking down scripture in plain language

Casting Lots – A way of helping discern the will of God from ancient times, much like the use of rune stones later on in Europe and elsewhere. The sticks or rocks had symbols inscribed on them and were thrown like dice. The result, combined with prayer, was meant to help determine God's desire. The fact that the roman guards at Jesus's crucifixion cast lots for his clothes can be seen both as a way to mock the Jewish tradition, or might also be read as a metaphor for determining if Jesus's death was divinely ordained.

Sanctify – To make something sacred or holy. Generally reserved in the past for places of worship and external symbols, here Jesus asks for a similar sacred status to be bestowed on people directly.

Points to Ponder

First Thoughts

Fun Fact: Our son was named after the disciple Matthias (minus the "h") who we affectionately call the disciples' benchwarmer or sixth man.

It's so easy to be seduced by human promises, regardless of whether they are founded in reality, or if they're good for us or others. Though God's promises speak to the heart of what we really need, they don't always fulfill our most immediate desires for satisfaction, escape from suffering, or even just hard work.

If we need yet another example of how Jesus is set apart, consider that he's praying for others and thinking about their well-being at the moment when he is in greatest personal danger.

Digging Deeper

Mining for what really matters . . . and gold

These scriptures come just days after the recognition of Jesus's final ascension in the lectionary calendar. It seems, then, that it's timed this way because of the concern that people would lapse into depending on human wisdom instead of divine guidance. Chronologically, obviously Jesus is said to have offered this prayer prior to his ascension. But it was a theme of his ministry, as it clearly was something the authors of scripture were mindful of for centuries.

It also taps into this sort of dualistic idea, echoed throughout theology and philosophical texts by many over many centuries, that there are dual, separate existences: the physical and the spiritual. It seems potentially to run up against the ideas we've discussed recently about God abiding in us and us, in God. The danger of the physical/metaphysical dualism is that we come to hold the entire physical world, or even other people, in contempt. This can lead to dehumanizing attitudes such as those seen in the Crusades, or the environmental neglect we see today.

There is great wisdom, though, in warning against the potential deception of following the latest charismatic speaker or self-help guru. Sometimes, it's easy to incline ourselves to follow someone whose words feel good or tell us what we want to hear. Sometimes it's a relief to surrender to someone who claims the foresight and authority to provide for us, as long as we give them our power.

Following the laws placed within us is harder, and we don't get the luxury of blaming someone else when things go wrong. We have to stay alert, accountable, even vigilant against false teaching. We have to know the difference between a wise person and the breadth and depth of divine wisdom. The difference, though seemingly subtle at times, is the difference between a path leading to a life of fullness and meaning, versus one that leads us nowhere but in circles, with nothing to show for our efforts in the end.

Heads Up
Connecting the text to our world

In the movie, *The Matrix*, Neo is a man who is part of the rebellious resistance who is slowly coming to terms with the fact that he is more than just a guy. For his people, he is "The Chosen One" whose destiny is to lead the remainder of humanity in a successful overthrow of the machines that have taken over the earth. In order to do this, he has a lot to learn.

In one instance, he's given a Wonderland-like choice: take a red pill and wake up back where he started, or take the blue one and see where his path leads him. Such a small difference between one pill or the other, but the consequences could not be more dramatically different.

Another of his challenges is overcoming the illusions that bind him to false assumptions about the world in which he lives. While waiting in a lobby to meet The Oracle, he meets a young monk. In his hand, he holds a spoon, which melts and wilts when the boy concentrates on it. He offers it to Neo to try, but focus as hard as he may, nothing happens.

The boy then explains that, in order to master control over the physical properties of the spoon is first to understand that "there is no spoon." The thing that is holding him back from his potential is a false construct, an illusion. And therefore the limitations he experiences don't come from the world around him; they come from his own mind.

In order to become the Chosen One, he has to embrace that the material world is illusive. He has to let go of all he is told and all he has been taught in order to search within himself for what is really true. Only then does he begin to live into who he is meant to be.

Like a lot of popular culture stories, they borrow on biblical themes, even portraying a Christ figure in various interpretations. But at the same time, especially inasmuch as we're called to continue to be the expression of God in the world that Jesus fully realized, this is a reflection of us as well. At least it's a reflection of what we aspire to. We have to be discriminating in teasing apart the substance from the superficial, and false wisdom from divine vision.

We're empowered with both the privilege and responsibility of choice. Yes, it would be nice if everything was more cut and dried, but it takes the wisdom of a serpent, as scripture says. Certainly there are those who will claim they possess the Truth, and there's appeal in letting them tell us what to do. But the spoon is set before us. Only we can decide if it's real or a deception.

Prayer for the Week

God, I know I can't just divest myself of the responsibility of making good choices. But please help me summon the wisdom to be able to tell the difference between human wisdom and yours.

Popping Off

Art/music/video and other cool stuff that relate to the text

The Matrix (movie, 1999)

Alice in Wonderland, by Lewis Carroll (book, 1865)

Drunk on Spirit

Lectionary Texts For

May 20, 2018 (Day of Pentecost)

Texts in Brief

My dog ate my Bible!

First Reading

Ezekiel 37:1–14

Ezekiel has a vision in which God places him in a valley of bones. God tells him to preach to them and they will come back to life. The bones gather and flesh appears on them, but they're not yet alive. Ezekiel does as he is told and God summons the winds to restore life in them, vowing to restore them to their homeland, Israel.

Psalm

Psalm 104:24–34, 35b

A song of praise to God as the creator of all life and the master of both life and death.

SECOND READING
Acts 2:1–21

The disciples and a crowd of others are gathered on Pentecost when a wind fills the space and what appears to be fire rests above them. They begin speaking in different languages they don't usually speak in, and skeptics suggest they're drunk. Peter explains, rather, that they're overcome by God's Holy Spirit. He says this is a foreshadowing of the prophecy from the book of Joel, in which God's spirit is poured out over all people and all who seek God will find salvation.

GOSPEL
John 15:26–27; 16:4b–15

Jesus speaks to his followers about his imminent departure and says that the Holy Spirit will come to reveal all that needs to be known to them. Only then will the world come to understand the faults of their lack of faith in Jesus and the real implications of his wrongful death. Their eyes will be opened to the truth people rejected from Jesus.

Bible, Decoded
Breaking down scripture in plain language

Advocate – From the Greek *parakletos*, the word has many translations, including "Advocate," "Paraclete," or "Comforter." Jesus prophesies that the Holy Spirit will stay with the disciples to guide and give them wisdom in their work. It also can mean "one who speaks on our behalf," almost like in the context of a trial or judgment. This stands in notable contrast to "Satan" or "the Adversary" mentioned in Job, who is more like a prosecuting attorney.

Pentecost – In the Christian tradition, we recognize Pentecost as the day the Holy Spirit touched the disciples and emboldened them with the courage and vision they required to go out into other regions to preach and minister. In the Jewish tradition, it's the recognition of the holiday known as *Shavuot*. This holiday recognizes when God gave Moses the Ten Commandments on Mount Sinai. It also takes place in the Christian calendar ten days after the ascension of Jesus is observed. Literally translated, Pentecost means "fiftieth day," because it comes fifty days after Easter Sunday (counting Easter).

Points to Ponder

First Thoughts

The events described in the Pentecost scene are fantastical, even bizarre. It would be hard not to be freaked out if we were present. Hell, I get nervous in charismatic worship services!

We wonder if all of this really happened or if it was something akin to magic. Seems awfully flashy for Jesus who will, at other times, keep parts of his ministry secret. More significant than the actual events at the time is how people responded to what clearly struck many there as a "God event." Some wrote them off as deluded drunkards. Maybe they figured they were still drowning their sorrows after their so-called Messiah was taken from them.

Others, though, bore witness and saw God in it. Not only that: it moved them, changing the course of their lives and those of countless others. While it's all too easy these days to approach the inexplicable and wondrous moments in our lives with skepticism or try to rationalize them away, it takes real, vulnerable openness to possibility to see something else. It takes even more to allow such an experience to transform us.

That choice is at the heart of faith.

Digging Deeper

Mining for what really matters . . . and gold

On the day of Pentecost, some were perplexed, some amazed, some sneered. It's okay to be perplexed or to question what we're experiencing. The trick is not to get stuck there. Pentecost is chaos, and chaos is inherently disorienting, decentering. It's radical, in the very essence of the word, which means "changed down to the root."

This is all new. There's no precedent for it. Though the day and the Jewish holiday it represented has history, the descent of the Holy Spirit and the effect it has is without roots in the known, explicable, rational world. *It is unreasonable.*

It's a crowded place, and in come violent winds and tongues of fire. It's a time for the outpouring of spirit, truth-telling, visions, and dreaming dreams. "God declares, that I will pour out my Spirit upon all flesh. . . ."

And yet we all see what we choose to see.

The disciples' drunkenness is not a drunkenness of denial but a euphoria of hope. Though humans crucify, God resurrects. Though humans divide and dominate, God communicates. God has the last word, and the word is wild. It changes everything. It rebuilds broken community. It breaks boundaries and enlarges the house. It makes possible understanding where before there was blind ignorance.

The Spirit comes when the light is almost gone, turning the sun dark and the moon like blood. Pentecost, however, is not an event to be wished for lightly. The Spirit is somewhat cranky and given to its own thing. As it says in John 3:8-9, "The wind blows where it wills, and you hear the sound of it, but you do not know whence it comes or whither it goes; so it is with everyone who is born of the Spirit."

The body of Christ receives and shares the same gift that the disciples received. This gift of the Spirit is as fresh today as it was at Pentecost. That is a promise, and it still holds for those who will wake up.

Poet Ellen Cuomo writes, "Faith is risking what is for what is yet to be. It is taking small steps knowing they lead to bigger ones. Faith is holding on when you want to let go. It is letting go when you want to hold on. Faith is saying yes when everything else says no. Faith is looking beyond what is and trusting for what will be."

Such faith takes vision, which the Spirit affords them. It takes openness, which their spiritual disciplines have equipped them with. And it requires a willingness to go when called, which Jesus trained them for in their years together in ministry.

Heads Up

Connecting the text to our world

My wife Amy and I went to Cane Ridge, Kentucky, once for a conference. It was the place where our denomination, now called the Christian Church (Disciples of Christ) came from. What began there in the early nineteenth century as a revival ended up lasting for several days. People preached from tree stumps and sang, while others were so consumed by spiritual ecstasy that they were said to have fallen to the ground, barking like dogs.

I'd like to say that, if I had been there, I'd have stayed open to the experience. But I'm keenly aware of my own tendency to question and remained reserved, rather than getting swept up in something that, God forbid, might make me uncomfortable. I don't know if that stuff actually happened or not, but something profound enough to give life to a new frontier church movement took place, and it was profound enough that people there were forever transformed.

Nothing like that exactly happened to us while we were there, but we did experience something that has stuck with me for years. No, I didn't start speaking Swahili or have my head light up with fire (though that could help explain the baldness). And as far as I could hear, there was not a single bark. And yet, I am as sure as I've been at any time in my life that I encountered a sense of overwhelming presence of God's spirit.

We met in the small church on the property for a worship service to finish out the conference, and a handful of us sat up in the balcony to watch from above. But before we started, our black colleagues—all of whom were running the service that night—asked us to come down.

"Ain't nobody sitting in that balcony tonight," they said. So grudgingly, we agreed. It was only during the message that we understood their request. This church where we worshiped had been a whites-only congregation on the lower level; they made all slaves crawl up outside ladders to sit in the balcony. For that reason, the worship leaders decided that all should worship, unified, in a gesture of solidarity.

Suddenly, the moment's significance changed. We had been sitting in the slave seats, and our African American friends declared the power to relegate others to second-class citizenship as unwelcome, at least in that moment and in that place. Their music dripped with sorrow, praise, and beauty, and the speaker's words evoked a passion that brought me, of all people, to my feet. I realized toward the end that I had been moved to tears.

No fire. No foreign languages. No wine. But God was there with us. At least that's what I choose to believe.

Prayer for the Week

God, I question, grow skeptical, and even doubt. Help break me open, over and over, to be available to wonder, transformation, and to be okay with not always understanding what moves me.

Popping Off

Art/music/video and other cool stuff that relate to the text

"Faith Is," by Ellen M. Cuomo (poem)

"Pentecost: The Iconography" from *Christian Iconography* (article, 2015) http://www.christianic onography.info/pentecost.html

"Changes," by David Bowie (song, 1971)

You and Me, Kid

Lectionary Texts For
May 27, 2018 (Trinity Sunday)

Texts in Brief
My dog ate my Bible!

First Reading
Isaiah 6:1–8

Isaiah has a brilliant, fantastical vision of God, surrounded by angels, and he feels unworthy. He decries the use of his improper words and associating with people who are sinful. He feels like he shouldn't be allowed to see God and be in God's presence. An angel places a burning coal to his lips and purifies him, making him now worthy of being in the presence of God. And when God asks for someone to speak on God's behalf, Isaiah eagerly volunteers.

Psalm

Psalm 29

A song of praise depicting God as creator and destroyer, and overseer of all of creation. There's a particular reference to God breaking the "cedars of Lebanon," which refers to a symbol in this culture of strength, nobility, and even royalty, going all the way back to King Solomon.

Second Reading

Romans 8:12–17

Paul explains in no uncertain terms that ways of flesh lead to death, but ways of the spiritual don't. We're adopted spiritual children of God, so intimately close to God that we even call out almost like we would call to "daddy" as a young child.

Gospel

John 3:1–17

Jesus is preaching about the need to be reborn, and Nicodemus gets confused. He imagines a somewhat graphic scene in which he tries to crawl back up inside his mother's womb. But Jesus explains that what he means is they must set aside the norms, values, and ways of the physical world and choose instead the ways set forth for them as followers of Jesus's new way.

Bible, Decoded

Breaking down scripture in plain language

Seraph – Seraphs are angels of a special sort. Namely, they are a kind of guard. In the case of the Isaiah text, they are the guards on the top of the Ark of the Covenant, said to contain the Ten Commandments. So in a way, seraphs are glorified security guards.

Holy – This is a word we use a lot, often without knowing really what it means. Basically it means entirely different, "other." So if you have animal, vegetable, and mineral on a multiple choice, God is D: none of the above. There's God, and there's everything else. This is why God is described as holy.

Nicodemus – A Pharisee who was part of the Jewish Sanhedrin, doesn't seem to be down with destroying Jesus like some of his peers. In fact, he talks with Jesus several times, and even shows up after Jesus is dead. Nicodemus only appears in John's Gospel and not the others, so it's possible he's a literary device to represent something more. He is also likely rich, given that the burial spices he brought for Jesus's body weren't cheap. And though compelled by Jesus, he wasn't easily swayed either.

Points to Ponder

First Thoughts

Isaiah talks about some pretty freaky stuff in this text, what with flying angels, burning coals on lips, and such. But I think the key to the whole thing is that, in a sense, Isaiah is us. He's a man of his people. He is sinful and he feels unworthy of being in God's presence. And yes, there he is, right there with God. And when God asks for volunteers, Isaiah doesn't grumble or self-doubt like Noah, Moses, and others in scripture. Right away, he's like the kid in the front row with his hand shooting up, yelling, "ooh, ooh, pick me!" Kinda like Horshack from *Welcome Back, Kotter.*

Psalm 29, like lots of psalms, is a song or poem. Some commentaries on the psalms note that the intentional repetition of choice words and phrases throughout are meant to make it catchier and easier to remember. Kinda like the "ear worms" from pop songs you can't get out of your head no matter what you do.

It's actually important to remember in this Romans text that Paul wrote this specifically to citizens under Roman law, for whom their inheritance (they were some rich folks, mind you) was a big deal. So families who wanted to keep it in the family would make sure to have babies. Those who didn't have kids would adopt babies to keep the family line going. But Paul says, "Yeah, you have to do this to get and keep what's coming to you here on earth, but you're already set." This is in the spiritual sense, in contrast with the rule of physical law, because God takes care of God's own if they're led by the example of Jesus, and that's that. Done deal.

In the Gospel text in John, Nicodemus is either a wise guy or a hapless doofus. When Jesus talks about being born again, he gets hung up on the fairly unsettling image of crawling back into your mother's womb (calling Dr. Freud!). After a forehead smack, Jesus explains it's a spiritual rebirth, not a physical one. So now, we understand where Paul got his whole "born into a spirit of adoption" gig later in Romans! Guess who was paying attention? Hint: It wasn't Nicodemus.

Digging Deeper

Mining for what really matters . . . and gold

Some "higher" theological interpretations of this week's texts will focus on the so-called triune Godhead, or the three-in-one expression of the divine in Father, Son, and Holy Spirit. After all, it is Holy Trinity Sunday, so it's expected. I can't help but notice, though, that the texts seem to lean more Pentecostal than Trinitarian in my reading. If you'll recall, Pentecost was marked by the event in scripture when the Holy Spirit descended on the disciples, who were hiding out after Jesus's death and talking about what to do next. They go from fear and freak-out mode to divinely inspired inspiration, charged with the mandate to go out and give birth to this thing that would become the Christian church.

It's a born-again story of sorts, resurrecting the body of Christ in the church, overcoming the fears of earthly consequences after being inspired by something more compelling than that fear. Isaiah's account isn't dissimilar, and the other texts—particularly in Romans and John—are loaded with spiritual resurrection stories.

All this aside, though, I can't help but think that the most overlooked theme here is the repeated message that God and humanity are directly connected, with no need for an intermediary. Isaiah is offered forgiveness by God in this sort of face-to-face encounter, and both Paul and the author in John encourage their audiences to shed the skin of earthly legalism and protocols, opting instead for the more liberating immersion in a love offered without exception or condition, save for accepting it.

In a way, it's God's way of saying, "It's just you and me, kid. Stick with me and we'll go places."

Heads Up

Connecting the text to our world

There's a serious temptation for leaders in organized religion, and for their followers too, to fall into the trap of believing that the religious leaders are necessary for us to experience God and the messages the gospel offers. Leaders enjoy having the power, and those they lead benefit by not having to take as much personal responsibility for their own faith development.

It's a transaction of sorts, but it's not what God seems to require. In fact, Jesus pushes back against the merits of a religious go-between on many occasions.

We do this with politics too. Reduce our patriotic duty to voting and paying taxes, so when something goes wrong, we have someone else to blame. But following Jesus's path is not done passively; you can't call Uber or wait for someone to take you there. We're expected to walk it ourselves, to do the hard work and to take responsibility for our own spirituality. It's liberating, yes, but it's also hard.

Fortunately, we don't have to do it alone. Yes, we have to engage God, our faith, and everything it calls us to head-on, but we have guides, support, and friends and loved ones to hold us up. Like the U2 song "One" says: we get to carry each other. It's both a privilege and a responsibility, but one inspired and empowered by something way bigger than any of us alone.

Prayer for the Week

God, when there's work to be done and you call for volunteers, help me have the strength and courage to step forward instead of back.

Popping Off

Art/music/video and other cool stuff that relate to the text

The Blind Side, by Michael Lewis (book)

Juno (movie, 2007)

"Superman" comic book series

Stop Signs Optional

Lectionary Texts For
June 3, 2018 (Proper 4 (9) Second Sunday after Pentecost)

Texts in Brief
My dog ate my Bible!

FIRST READING
1 Samuel 3:1–10 (11–20)

Samuel hears God call him and he approaches Eli, thinking he called him. Finally, the fourth time, Eli responds to God who tells him to inform Eli that he will punish his family for all time because his sons have been disobedient to God. Eli accepts whatever judgment God hands down, and from then on, Samuel is known as a great prophet.

and

Deuteronomy 5:12–15

As part of the Ten Commandments, this passage outlines the requirement of sabbath; all Jews must reserve every seventh day for rest and worship. The God who delivered them from slavery in Egypt requires as much.

Psalm
Psalm 139:1–6, 13–18

The author refers to God knowing them so well that their words are known before they are spoken, and it speaks of being crafted since conception. Finally, the psalmist expresses wonder at the depth and breadth of God's wisdom and knowledge.

and

Psalm 81:1–10

A psalm reminding the audience to maintain a sabbath day for worship and, when worshiping, to worship only the God of Israel and no other.

Second Reading
2 Corinthians 4:5–12

Paul offers words of encouragement for the Christians in Corinth, whose way has evidently become treacherous and difficult. He reminds them to submit in action and will to Jesus and reminds them that, though they feel beaten down, they're not defeated. Finally, he extolls the glory of martyrdom in service to the gospel, as it leads beyond immediate death to eternal life.

Mark 2:23–3:6

Jesus pulls a piece of grain up on the Sabbath and the Pharisees accuse him of violating Sabbath by "working." He reminds them that, though they are serving the laws, those laws were put in place to serve people. Then he heals a man with a crippled hand, which led the Pharisees to go to King Herod's people and talk about ways of getting rid of him.

Bible, Decoded

Breaking down scripture in plain language

Herodians – Herodians were a particular Jewish group, highly influenced by Hellenistic culture from Greece. More than a religious sect, they were more of a political movement, whose primary aim was to help Herod become the king of Judea again. Given that they saw Jesus as a direct enemy or threat to that, they tended to engage him in confrontational ways.

Pharisees – Pharisees were a sort of ascetic group within the Jewish community and were considered experts on Mosaic law. Their primary identity was that they were strict in their adherence to Jewish law, and are portrayed in scripture as considering themselves to be set apart from—even superior to—the general Jewish populace.

Points to Ponder

First Thoughts

From one point of view, it makes sense that the tradition of Sabbath is first recorded in the creation story in Genesis where God rests on the seventh day after spending six creating all of the material universe. If God rested, and we are to imitate God in how we live, then it stands to reason to structure the story as such.

But also consider the other implications of the story. It seems like God gets tuckered out from all that creating. God's energy and potential, then, would be finite. How we approach such a story, especially if we take it literally, says a lot about our understanding of God.

Further, it says something about us and our need to see ourselves in the Divine if we require God to have rested in order to be able to justify it for ourselves. There's vanity in a need to be more like God. Maybe, like the Pharisees, we want to feel set apart from "those people" who just don't seem to get it, or to gain favored status in God's eyes.

Just as significant—or maybe even more important— as what we do, if we consider Jesus's response to the Pharisees in the Gospel text, is *why* we do what we do.

Digging Deeper

Mining for what really matters . . . and gold

This is hardly the only time that the Pharisees tried to catch Jesus in some sort of trap to get him in trouble with the authorities. Previously they had asked him his position on divorce, knowing full well that there are apparently contradictory texts to support either argument in Jewish scripture (Deuteronomy offers steps for how divorce is executed, while Malachi and Genesis seem to disallow it altogether). In some instances, Jesus offers a subversive third-way response to such binary right-or-wrong challenges. But in other cases such as this, he seems to take them on more head-on.

Of course he recognizes their hidden agenda, as it's not the first time they've tried it. But also, he flips the script on them, so to speak. While they are trying to set him up in a sort of "Who are you to snub our laws?" kind of situation, he's turning that back around, questioning on whose authority they are using the law—believed to be given to humanity as a gift from God for better, fuller living—to justify violence and to further a selfish agenda.

And really, his response is a reprise of his core message that he has shared before and will offer again: one that Paul too reiterates time and again throughout his letters. Though we have some laws to help keep us safe and help maintain a social order, and while others help bring us closer to God's intended way of life, in a perfect world we wouldn't need explicitly stated rules and laws at all.

A moral compass and the capacity for deep compassion are inborn in us and don't need stating aloud to be known. Laws generally serve more as reminders of what we sense as true and right already. They have their place, just as taxes and government do (which Jesus also affirms), but these are not the endgame.

And when such tools are used as devices of violence or oppression against our fellow human beings, we're not only justified, but expected, as followers of Jesus to confront and challenge such laws, despite potential consequence.

Heads Up

Connecting the text to our world

I was a devious younger guy sometimes, and I couldn't help myself when I felt the urge to pull a fast one on a friend. One of my buddies, who had only recently gotten his license, was driving us through the parking lot of a local mall when he pulled up to a stop sign and—as one might expect—he stopped.

"You know," I said, "you don't actually have to stop at that one." He asked why, and I explained that any stop sign with a white border around the perimeter was a conditional, optional stop. It only had to be observed if you really felt it was needed and saw other cars present or nearby. It was only after he rolled through three or four stop signs that my evil snickers got loud enough for him to realize he had been played.

I'm pretty sure that was followed by several shoulder punches, as he finally noticed that *all stop signs* have white borders around them.

But honestly, sometimes laws just make no sense, given the situation. My wife Amy gets mad at me sometimes when I stop and wait at a red light at night when the whole intersection is empty. Likewise, I get annoyed when she slows to twenty miles an hour in school zones, even when it's a national holiday and no classes are in session.

Some laws make sense some of the time, and at other times, they're just dumb and out of date. For example, there's a law in Massachusetts that mourners aren't allowed to eat more than three finger sandwiches at a wake. In Spokane, it's illegal to kneel on a pedestrian crosswalk. And in Quitman, GA, it's against the law for a chicken to cross the road.

Sometimes we have to know when to lean on the spirit of the law rather than its literal letter. Other times, there are more pressing needs at hand. Would we forgo crossing a street where there's no crosswalk to help someone who fell in front of an oncoming car? We can even get to the point where legalism is more about controlling people—even keeping them oppressed or in their place—than it is about the greater good or common safety. In the case of Jesus, he rejects such abuses of legalism and instead urges us to recognize the importance of the rule of law, while also not being beholden to it like it was a false God.

Laws aren't inherently good or bad; they're tools put in place for a reason. Blindly following them can be as bad as rejecting them out of hand simply because we don't like being told what to do. We're afforded wisdom and discernment for a reason.

Prayer for the Week

God, help me see more clearly when I'm serving the ways of the world rather than your ways. Sometimes it's easier to fall into a thoughtless, lazy pattern of dependence on our systems rather than doing the hard work of personal discernment. Afford to me the patience and clarity to know and do what is right.

Popping Off

Art/music/video and other cool stuff that relate to the text

"I don't like my job and I don't think I'm going to go anymore" scene from *Office Space* (movie, 1999) https://www.youtube.com/watch?v=jKYivs6ZLZk

Liar, Liar (movie, 1997)

A Matter of Priorities

Lectionary Texts For
June 10, 2018 (Proper 5 (10) Third Sunday after Pentecost)

Texts in Brief
My dog ate my Bible!

FIRST READING
1 Samuel 8:4–11 (12–15), 16–20 (11:14–15)

The Israelites complain that they want a king like other nations have. After prayer, Samuel conveys a warning to them from God that a king will lead to their oppression and exploitation. He reminds them that they need no other ruler aside from God. Still, they insist. So Samuel and the Jews go to Gilgal and consecrate Saul as their king, to whom they perform offerings.

Genesis 3:8–15

Adam and Eve hide from God in Eden because they are ashamed of their newly discovered nakedness. When

God asks Adam if he ate from the forbidden Tree of Knowledge, he blames Eve for enticing him to do it. When God asks her, she blames the serpent for tricking her. So God punishes the serpent by condemning it to a life slithering on the ground, and to be eternal enemies with human beings.

Psalm
Psalm 130
David prays for mercy and forgiveness for past wrongs, both for himself and on behalf of the people of Israel. It ends with a gesture of hopefulness that God will, indeed, offer such grace.

and

Psalm 138
The psalm proclaims God as king over all other earthly kings, and asserts that God not only looks on the lowly with favor, but also judges those who are filled with pride.

Second Reading
2 Corinthians 4:13–5:1
A message of assurance to those in the Christian community in Corinth. They are encouraged not to lose faith and focus on doing all that they do to glorify God when things get difficult. Paul reminds them that no present suffering compares to the ecstasy awaiting them in perfect union with God.

GOSPEL

Mark 3:20–35

Jesus, casting out evil spirits from people, draws a substantial crowd. His critics accuse him of calling on forces of darkness to do this, which he claims is absurd. In fact, he accuses them of blaspheming God, which according to Jesus is the only unforgivable sin. The crowd then tells Jesus that his family is outside, trying to get to him, to which he responds that those already in his presence are his true family.

Bible, Decoded

Breaking down scripture in plain language

Gilgal – There are several references to a place called Gilgal throughout the Bible, many of which could actually be different places. The name itself means "circle of standing stones," which often represented the identification of holy sites. So the Jews would have gone here to consecrate Saul as king because they saw it as a religious ritual to be performed in the presence of God. A place called Gilgal is referenced more than three dozen times throughout the Hebrew Bible.

Saul – Held in high regard by the Israelites for leading an army, successfully defeating the Ammonites who wanted to enslave them, Saul also had previously been anointed by Samuel as one chosen by God as a leader of his people. While some historians believe Saul reigned for about two decades, there are suggestions in the New Testament that he ruled twice as long. His reign ended when he killed himself to avoid being captured by the Philistines during a siege. He led many other successful military campaigns on behalf of the Jewish people.

Points to Ponder

First Thoughts

I often have a hard time with talk of God or Jesus as Lord or King. But when considered in the context of these sorts of texts, it starts to make more sense. There were three states of existence the Israelites knew: enslavement, living under outside occupation, or under the rule of their own monarch. Given these options (bearing in mind there was no such thing as representative democracy back then), the monarchy from within was by far the most appealing.

So a Jewish king would have been seen as a protector against outside threats and as an essential advocate and symbol of strength in a particularly volatile and dangerous region. Perhaps more important, the king was one of their own, who knew them, their values, and their needs. So to consider God as Lord or King likely would evoke images of comfort, protection, and deep love for their own, whereas we tend to think of kings today as despotic, exploitative, or oppressive.

In this way, God as King can be considered differently.

Digging Deeper

Mining for what really matters . . . and gold

Let's take the ideas above and dig a little deeper with them. The Israelites had, indeed, had leaders in the past. Moses was one, followed by Joshua, but these men didn't rule as kings. Rather, the culture was structured more as an egalitarian tribal society. And although this may sound appealing to many of us today, it was seen as the cause of much of the dangerous instability they had experienced for a long time.

In the period when Saul served either as a military leader and/or as king of the Israelites, he led campaigns against a half dozen outside forces, threatening to take over their land or enslave their people. And this was no short-lived concern: such conflicts spanned generations.

And like us, when things are uncertain or on a downturn, the response tends to be that we need change. So although they have subsisted on a leadership of tribal priesthood (who answered to the God of Israel), the other nations around them seemed stronger and more desirable in many ways. So it was decided among them that the solution to their problems was to turn away from more of a spiritually guided leadership system to one of political and military strength.

And who represented such power and the prospect of victory—if not at least safety—more than the most successful "general" they had in Saul? So they willingly placed their hopes and aspirations on him, pressing Samuel to bless this new governing structure, though he warned them it was not what God wanted for them.

It's curious that human beings are in such a state of constant turmoil and conflict to begin with. We struggle to achieve the prophetic vision of no longer needing our weapons of war anymore, turning them instead into tools for yielding and sustaining life. If we look at the Genesis text, we can try to blame Adam and Eve, claiming it's in our originally sinful nature to fight and conquer. But we can just as easily look to any time in history, from the Garden of Eden until today, and see what's at the heart of why:

Whatever we have today simply is not enough.

What's more, we have a remarkable tendency to idealize what someone else has and determine that, if only we have that, we'll finally achieve the peace, safety, and happiness we seek. With regard to the Christians in Corinth, Paul encourages them to remain steadfast in the face of threats posed to them by the Roman powers under which they're operating. But it might be that the subtext here is that they might just as readily get lured by the affluence and power that Corinth represented, as the region's capital and economic hub.

It's not that having any trust in, or even dependence on, a human led government is inherently evil. But once we afford such faith and obedience to anything of human hands, we break the covenant with God to place no others at the center of our lives.

Heads Up

Connecting the text to our world

How many times has a politician run as the "change candidate"? And how many times have we been let down? If both numbers are (inevitably) the same, then one has to wonder why we keep expecting it to work.

It's said that insanity is defined as doing the same thing, over and over, while expecting a different result. And we don't just behave this way with respect to government; faith in all large institutions, from religion to education and corporations, is at an apparent all-time low.

For some, the answer is that we have gotten weak, and the answer therefore is to choose leaders who represent the kind of strength and power we've been lacking. We've gone soft, let our defenses down, lost sight of the need for our dominance on the world stage. And so tyrannical forces emerge, promising once again to embody the solution to all of our woes, taking us back to the days of greatness when all was well, we were respected, and people were happy, secure, and certain.

Never mind that such a time never existed, especially not for those not sitting in the seat of privilege.

But such dissolution of confidence in human-made systems is the sign of a new emergence, laying the groundwork for a new awakening into something new. Perhaps we've venerated our religion, government, and businesses to the point that they are the false idols that have come between us and God.

This has happened before. It's why, in some respect, Jesus prophesied the destruction of the great temple of Jerusalem. It wasn't that the temple itself was evil; rather, it had become a false God, leading people away from their God-intended potential and seekers of the spirit. More temples may have to crumble before we wake up. But if we hold on too tightly as they do, we risk being crushed under the weight of them crashing down, revealing them as the fragile edifices they were all along.

Prayer for the Week

God, I put lots of things before you from time to time, depending on my present desires and apparent needs. Help us get over ourselves, recognizing where the real power and peace lie.

Popping Off

Art/music/video and other cool stuff that relate to the text

The Last King of Scotland (movie, 2006)

Triumph of the Will (movie, 1935)

Thicker Than Blood

Lectionary Texts For
June 17, 2018 (Proper 6 (11) Fourth Sunday after Pentecost)

Texts in Brief
My dog ate my Bible!

FIRST READING
1 Samuel 15:34–16:13

Samuel is beset with regret over blessing Saul as king. Before Samuel's death, God sends him to Bethlehem to meet with Jesse and his sons. God tell Samuel one of Jesse's sons is chosen to be the God-anointed king of Israel. Seven of Jesse's sons come before Samuel but none is the one God chose. Finally, Jesse sends for David, who is tending the family's sheep. God tells Samuel that David is the one, and Samuel anoints him with a horn full of oil, after which David was filled with a sense of God's presence in him.

and

Ezekiel 17:22–24

A curious allegorical text (as many in Ezekiel are) about God taking a small branch from the top of a cedar tree and planting it on a mountaintop above Israel. This will grow into a great tree in its own right, serving as a protector and sustainer of all who dwell beneath it

PSALM

Psalm 20

A psalm to God's people, reminding them that God is both protector and provider. Though others find value in their material possessions, they are only to find value in the more lasting favor of God.

and

Psalm 92:1–4, 12–15

A call to praise God for all of God's people is at the beginning of the text, followed by a metaphor about cedars of Lebanon that suggests all that prospers in our lives is credited to God's care for us.

SECOND READING

2 Corinthians 5:6–10 (11–13), 14–17

Paul paints a picture of the dynamic between body and spirit, and how holding closely to one draws us further from the other. Though we did not know God in the physical sense before, now we do because of Jesus's presence among us. And given that he and we are all part of one greater body, when he died and was raised, so was all of humanity. And since through this miracle God in spirit has been revealed in a new way, now we can and should see people from the same perspective, not as physical beings, but as creatures of spirit.

GOSPEL
Mark 4:26–34

Jesus, speaking to a crowd, compares the kingdom of God first to a field of grain sprouting from the earth, maturing and then being harvested. Then he compares it to a minuscule mustard seed which, once planted in rich soil, produces a great tree, filled with life. Though he continued to speak in parables to the public, he only explained all of these to his disciples in private.

Bible, Decoded
Breaking down scripture in plain language

Jesse – Jesse is of particular importance in the Bible because he is the father of David. Aside from being an important king and the author of scores of psalms, David is of particular significance to Christians since prophets told of the messiah coming from the line of David.

Mustard seed – Most of us are familiar with what's known as the parable of the mustard seed, but mustard seeds are actually referred to five different times in the gospels. Primarily, the illustration is used because they were considered to be the smallest seeds known at the time, while also yielding a much larger plant than most herbs did. Also, they were familiar to anyone from the region, so they knew what was being talked about as much as we would be familiar with apples or oranges.

Kingdom of God — The understandings of what the phrase means are wide-ranging. As far back as a few centuries after Jesus's death, it was suggested that, perhaps, the kingdom of God was a reference to Jesus, while another understanding was that it meant the presence of the larger church and its faithful. Of course, a more common way of thinking is that it refers to an expression of God's reign in a future period following the fulfillment of the scriptures. Interestingly, though the phrase seems to come from references to God as king, the actual phrase "kingdom of God" doesn't appear until Jesus introduces it in the New Testament.

Points to Ponder

First Thoughts

It's worth noting that the mustard tree described in the Mark text is very similar to the description of the cedar tree in the Ezekiel text. It's likely that the author did this with intention, drawing a connection between the two passages. This is very common, especially between gospel texts and those of the prophets, in part to suggest that these prophecies described previously are now fulfilled.

Texts like the one in 2 Corinthians have contributed to a sort of dualistic thinking about the physical versus the spiritual world, considering them as commingled and yet separate. This contributes to the notion that our bodies are simply houses for a spiritual presence, dwelling inside us. But others understand our spiritual side to be more intimately interwoven with physical creation. There also can be risks in seeing physical creation as little more than a temporary residence for the soul in the reverence with which we approach and care for nature and our bodies.

Digging Deeper

Mining for what really matters . . . and gold

It's helpful to understand some backstory for this short and confusing passage from Ezekiel. It comes after two much longer allegories describing the problems brought to the Judahites by the king of Babylon and by Zedekiah, the last king of Judah, who served as a stooge of Babylon. Some believe the new branch planted over Judah was predicting the coming of another great king, more in line with David, whose reign at this point has ended. Others believe it's a prophecy about Jesus, tracing him back to the line of David.

It can also be seen as a sign that, despite the trials the Jews continue to undergo, God will renew them and cause them to prosper in the long run. Others see such an allegory as a prophecy of the later emergence of the Christian church. Such is the risk of stories that depend on metaphor, rather than stating more directly what is meant. We see much the same thing taking place when Jesus talks about the kingdom of God here in Mark. Though he is more explicit in his teaching behind closed doors with his small group of disciples, he is more intentional about not explaining himself further when speaking to a larger audience.

Teaching in this way was very common in the Jewish tradition. They were not quite as hung up on didactic instruction with clear, conclusive meanings to be drawn from every lesson. This is more of a byproduct of contemporary western thought. This is not to say that nothing was ever taught explicitly or directly at the time, but it was standard practice to speak in this way when conveying more abstract ideas.

For one, our brains are hardwired to connect with story. Though we may not remember too many scientific principles or specific historic dates, it tends to be much easier to remember stories. From there, we can delve deeper to mine multiple layers of meaning. This, as we've talked about before, is central to the *midrashic* tradition of teaching and wisdom, in which there is more than one exclusive, absolute truth in any one story. In fact, it would demonstrate a lack of intellectual and scholarly rigor to arrive at only one conclusion for such a parable.

Also, Jesus says at one point that his teaching is meant to meet people where they are. He teaches in more depth to his disciples because they have invested their lives in him and his message. For others who may be encountering him and his ideas for the first time, or who are unsure of how bought-in they really are, a full explication on the kingdom of God might be a little overwhelming. And so in the spirit of pitching a broad tent under which all can find a place, his teaching has multiple points of access.

Heads Up

Connecting the text to our world

We in the west have a love-hate relationship with the idea of royalty. On the one hand, we seem never to get enough stories about royalty in other countries, and the notion of a tradition being passed down through a single bloodline is intriguing, to say the least. But these kinds of dynamics just don't mesh well with democracy, where anyone and everyone is meant—at least in theory—to have a chance to lead and have a voice. We even have anti-nepotism laws to keep people in power from affording special favor to someone, only because they are related. We value the idea of a meritocracy over an aristocracy.

Clearly, though, they are very important in the times when the books of the Bible were written. While more than one Gospel takes pains to trace Jesus's bloodline back to David, it's interesting that Mark follows his family tree through Joseph and not Mary. (Side note: You'll also notice in Mark, which is considered the first gospel account written, that there is no telling of a virgin birth.) These connections were made because it would have been important to establish his legitimacy among people at the time.

Much like Jesus speaking in parables, the biblical stories attempt to speak in the ways and norms that would have connected with the people hearing—and later, reading—them. As a result, though, we struggle sometimes to understand the big picture thousands of years later. I'm guessing that you, like me, don't happen to have some mustard seeds, hyssop, or nard lying around.

But while the biblical stories connect with these ancient cultural values, there's a constant tension at the same time to break loose of the power these traditions and norms have over us. As far back as Ezekiel, Samuel is trying to tell the people of Israel that they don't need a king, simply because everyone else does it. Likewise, we're not to defer to a leader, simply because of who they are or who their parents were. The risk of giving too much power and credibility to any traditional norms, religious traditions, or political or religious leaders is that we place our trust and faith in something other than God.

Jesus didn't call us to chaos and destruction of all we know and care about. He was intent, however, on reordering things, setting God at the head of our list of priorities, rather than human systems or titles. So how do we know when we're trusting too much—or maybe even too little—in our modern-day lords, be they people, institutions, or human laws? Jesus likely would have directed us to one of his many parables on the matter, trusting that those who invest ourselves fully enough in them will come away with exactly what we need.

Prayer for the Week

God, it's easy for me to fall back on old beliefs and practices rather than doing the hard work of reordering my life around you. Help shake me loose of those habits when I need it.

Popping Off

Art/music/video and other cool stuff that relate to the text
The Giving Tree, by Shel Silverstein (book, 1964)

But Why, God?

Lectionary Texts For
June 24, 2018 (Proper 67 (12) Fifth Sunday after Pentecost)

Texts in Brief
My dog ate my Bible!

First Reading
1 Samuel 17:(1a, 4–11, 19–23), 32–49

The full account of Goliath, a Philistine, and David, a Jewish shepherd under King Saul. Goliath is a huge armed man who strikes fear into the Jewish army. He defies them to send someone who can beat him in combat, promising that the Philistines will be their servants if he's defeated. Only once he's convinced God has commissioned David to do this does Saul agree. David, unarmed except for a sling and a handful of smooth stones, runs toward Goliath and hurls a stone, hitting him in the forehead and killing him.

and

Job 38:1–11

God lashes out at Job after he questions God's actions toward him. God is offended by being second-guessed, somewhat sarcastically asking Job if he was around when all of creation was set in its place, and if he understands its ways. This is one of the clearest examples of God's outrage and very human-like traits and emotions.

PSALM

Psalm 9:9–20

David, at a low point in his reign as king, turns to God for solace and protection. He notes that other nations are suffering by their own hand and their own devices, which he sees as execution of God's judgment. And while he is struggling as well, he vows not to forget those who suffer. Finally, he beseeches God to put people back in their proper place, reminding them that they're only human beings, and not God.

and

Psalm 107:1–3, 23–32

David offers a poem or song of praise to God by painting an image of people on rough seas, battered by storm and waves. The men are freaking out, until they call out to God and find courage. Then God calms the waters and they are safe.

SECOND READING
2 Corinthians 6:1–13

The Christians in Corinth seem to be struggling with their ministry. Although they are apparently threatened by local authorities, Paul assures them that they are doing God's work, and will not encounter hindrance provided that they call on God for the necessary courage and help. He counters every likely hardship they face by suggesting a virtue with which God "arms" them. And whereas their own capacity to love God is limited, God's capacity for loving them is not.

GOSPEL
Mark 4:35–41

Jesus is traveling across the Galilean sea with the disciples when a big storm hits. They look for Jesus to help but he's asleep. He wakes to find them in a panic, and chastises them for not having enough faith to trust they would be okay. He orders the storm to be still, then shows his disappointment that they don't yet believe he is who he says he is. And even after this, they are in wonder, asking each other what kind of a person can perform such a miracle.

Bible, Decoded?
Breaking down scripture in plain language

Sheol – The Jewish resting place for the dead until they are called to be with God. Both the good and the evil go there after death, and it is not a place of suffering or punishment, not what we think of as hell.

Higgaion – This Hebrew word is tricky to define precisely, but is believed to be a note for a musician playing along with the psalm to offer an instrumental interlude, during which the listeners should pause in silence (*selah*) to imagine and contemplate the words that have been shared.

Philistines – In colloquial terms, the word is intended to refer to a person or people who are lowbrow, and do not appreciate the refinements of culture. They would be brutish and anti-intellectual and show disdain for arts and music. The etymology of the word in Hebrew is debated, as is the origin of the people referred to throughout scripture as Philistines. Some scholars believe they were from Crete, while others argue against that theory. Regardless, it's likely they were from the Aegean Sea region.

Points to Ponder

First Thoughts

It's interesting to consider the different relationships between faith and hardship in these stories. In Job, it's important to remember that he has undergone these problems because God is testing him as part of a bet between God and Lucifer about the resolve of human faith. In the story about David, hardship faces his people, and he is called on as the only one with the strength to face the threat and to save them. With the disciples, the threat is nature-borne, and Jesus saves them in spite of the fragility of their faith. And finally in 2 Corinthians, the Christians are being persecuted and are suffering because of their faith.

Although God is the savior from hardship in all of the other stories, the God portrayed in Job seems (in my view) petty, sarcastic, cruel, and prone to being manipulated. If anything in all of this would challenge my own faith in God's goodness and provision, it's the book of Job. Granted, later his fortunes were restored, but what about the children he lost? And the collateral damage of their dying in order to test Job is even worse.

This is one reason why I think we have to consider the implications of what we say before we offer comments to people who are struggling, like "Everything happens for a reason," "God is in control," or "God has a plan."

Digging Deeper

Mining for what really matters . . . and gold

It seems appropriate to focus on the connection made by the author of the story in Mark to the comments within God's reprimand to Job. It could even be traced back to the very beginning when, in the first creation story of Genesis, God brings order to chaos, and only then introduces humanity to it.

I'm going to throw out a big fifty-cent God-nerd word here and suggest that we consider all of these *eschatologically*. Eschatology is the study of things to come toward the culmination of history, at which time God sets things right, restores order to the chaos, and delivers humanity from it to be reconciled with God for all eternity. If we consider this, there's a sort of pattern of chaos, order, and deliverance. And the idea in recognizing patterns in our past experience or previous history is that we have an opportunity to learn from them and gain wisdom.

Whether faced with knuckle-dragging barbarians, natural disasters, or a series of life-altering events, we're called, time and again, to turn back to God. We're not promised the end of hardship or the solution of all our problems if we simply pray hard enough. What we are afforded, given an open heart and an orientation of trust, is delivery and perseverance.

Heads Up
Connecting the text to our world

When I was a kid, I remember losing my wallet with twenty dollars in it. Doesn't seem like much now, but it took me forever to earn that money. I felt hot and panicked all over, probably about how David felt, facing down an armed, knuckle-dragging giant (hey, I said it was important). So I got on my knees next to my bed and prayed to God to help me find it. Sure enough, a few minutes later I did. And for days I was convinced God had helped me find my wallet. Thanks, God!

But then something else bad happened. I don't even remember now what it was, but it got me thinking. If God was the one who found my blue canvas velcro wallet, then God might also have been the one who caused this terrible thing to happen. I wondered: Does God pick and choose when to do bad or good things to us? Could the source of all creation be so arbitrary? And frankly, why would God care about my wallet either way?

It was the first time as a young guy that I started to wrestle with the implications of my theology. God was always hands-on; all good things were rewards and the bad stuff was punishment. But then it occurred to me that tragedies struck all manner of people all the time, and some really cruel folks sat in positions of tremendous wealth and power.

At the risk of mixing pop culture metaphors, I suddenly felt like a character in *The Truman Show*, trapped inside a bubble world, performing to please and entertain while some Montgomery Burns–like divinity oversaw it all with the occasional "Eeeeexcellent!"

As I got older, I decided that sometimes really bad things happen just because. Sure, there are consequences to our actions, and sometimes they're proportionate to what the world tells us is fair and just. But sometimes it's not. Babies die, poor people's villages get wiped out in minutes, and I bet a few virtuous people have lost wallets, never to find them again.

What I take from these passages isn't that prayer is ineffective. But God also isn't a slot machine, doling out the occasional jackpot and sometimes taking all we have. What I hear is that we are, indeed, to turn to God and pray in those hard times in particular. But rather than asking for results, we're to find our comfort in prayers for faithfulness itself, and for courage to endure, even when the crappy stuff seems to be followed up by nothing other than more crap.

I don't believe God plays games with our lives, nor does God test us every once in a while with the unexpected pop quiz of tragedy. In the good times, we give prayers of thanks; in bad times, we pray for endurance. But the answer of what to do remains the same, regardless of the why.

Prayer for the Week

God, it's easy enough for my faith to get shaken when things are hard. Meet me where I am, and give me the strength to pray, even when I'm not sure what I believe.

Popping Off

Art/music/video and other cool stuff that relate to the text

When Bad Things Happen to Good People, by Harold Kushner (book, 2004)

The Simpsons Movie (movie, 2007)

The Truman Show (movie, 1998)

Life-and-Death Decisions

Lectionary Texts For
July 1, 2018 (Proper 8 (13) Sixth Sunday after Pentecost)

Texts in Brief
My dog ate my Bible!

FIRST READING
2 Samuel 1:1, 17–27

After defeating the Amalekites on behalf of King Saul and the Israelites, David offers a song of mourning on behalf of the people over Saul's death and his son, Jonathan's. He notes how intimately close Saul and Jonathan were and decries the loss of God's blessing over Saul's reign. Finally, he asks that the enemies of Israel (the Philistines) would not be blessed with continued victory in Saul's absence.

Psalm

Psalm 130

David writes a prayer to God from a place of shame over his own sins. Though he recognizes that no one would stand up to God's scrutiny if God kept score of our transgressions, justification for praise of God is, rather, in God's evidence of abundant forgiveness and mercy, rather than punitive judgment. In this, David embraces confidence that God will be the rescuer of Israel from their fall from a position of sovereignty and power in the region.

and

Psalm 30

This is a poem of resurrection of sorts, revealing how God's inclination toward mercy over judgment is life-giving. In times of hardship and trial—perceived as periods of God's distance, absence, or disapproval—though there is despair, God always renews hope through renewal of life, courage, and hope.

Second Reading

2 Corinthians 8:7–15

Paul seems to detect a flagging of the Corinthian Christians' passion for the work they've been given. He is careful not to order them, but to offer wise advice. He wants to make sure they don't just perform their duties out of a sense of obligation, but because they're passionate about it and believe in it wholeheartedly. Though it's easy to rest in the comfort that they have come into the spiritual inheritance the gospel offered them, he wants them to be as on fire about giving that to others as they were when they themselves accepted it. In that way, he assures them, they are living as Jesus did.

GOSPEL

Mark 5:21–43

Two miracles take place in this passage. First, a woman who has long suffered from "an issue of blood" touches Jesus's garment from within a big crowd. Immediately her bleeding stops, and Jesus tell her it is her own faith that healed her. Then he goes to the house of a synagogue leader whose daughter has died. He takes only Peter, James, and John in with him. There they find the family in mourning, and he asks them why they're grieving since she's not dead, but sleeping. They're incredulous, but he goes into her bedroom and resurrects her anyway. He then tells those present not to tell anyone what he did.

Bible, Decoded

Breaking down scripture in plain language

Book of Jasher – This is referred to several times in the Bible, but has never been discovered. It's believed, based on the references to it, that it's a collection of poems about the victories of Jewish leaders, similar to many of the psalms already in scripture. It's believed it may even have been a volume including several smaller books. Translated, it means "the book of the righteous man" or "book of the just man."

Amalekites – Amalek was the grandson of Esau, so he was a direct descendant of Abraham. The Amalekites were believed to have been a nomadic tribe, bent on gaining wealth and power by plundering others, much like the Vikings. So it's written more than once in early scripture that God called for their destruction. They were longtime enemies of the Israelites and were considered an ongoing threat.

Jonathan – Son of King Saul, he was admired as a fierce and courageous warrior. Though he and his father had conflicts (he occasionally defied Saul's orders), he was greatly loved both by Saul and by the soldiers he led). He, his brothers, and father all died at the hands of the Amalekites at the Battle of Gilboa.

Points to Ponder
First Thoughts

These passages are studies in contrasts, of the capacity of God for both judgment and forgiveness, as well as the human capacity either for fear and grief or for faith.

More important, they show that God's capacity for love and forgiveness is inexhaustible. Such a capacity is inherent and not dependent on what we do or don't do. And as David puts it in so many words in the psalm, thank God for that.

Digging Deeper
Mining for what really matters . . . and gold

The choices we're presented here can be framed as "life and death." Not that all of these decisions are potentially life-threatening, but rather that one choice comes from a life-giving place and the other does not. Or to put it more in gospel terms, we choose either a path leading to life or to death.

We can also frame these as matters of perspective or orientation. On the one hand, these choices are all "external," meaning that they are more framed as responses or reactions to external factors. The one option emerges from inside, and the other from outside.

In Samuel, the author begins in a state of great mourning, but resolves the passage with a tone of hope, seeking God's renewal despite present circumstances. In the Psalms, David offers effusive gratitude for the fact that, despite an abundance of justification for the condemnation for all of humanity, God looks "inward," offering inexhaustible forgiveness instead. This grace is not justified by obvious evidence; it's only due to a fundamental attribute of God.

In advising the Corinthian Christians, he recognizes that their initial honeymoon phase likely has ended, and that their desire to continue fulfilling their work isn't only because they feel like they have to. He wisely realizes that we can only be motivated externally so long, and that we have to find the proverbial "fire within" to keep us going.

Finally, the gospel text is a perfect example of a study in contrasts. First, the bleeding woman reaches out on her own, against the power of the crowd and without permission (fairly scandalous in itself) just to touch Jesus's clothes. It's notable that Jesus doesn't know who did this, not because he's mad at her for being inappropriate, but because it's important for us to know that *Jesus had no idea* this was happening until it was already done. This woman had every reason to have already lost hope. Doctors had failed her, and it's likely that she had been deemed cursed by God and irredeemable in human eyes.

But in Jesus she saw something the leader of the synagogue did not: hope. She had faith in spite of all evidence to the contrary. And the reason it is significant that Jesus didn't know this was happening is because the act was entirely inborn from her. He says in no uncertain terms, too, that he isn't the one who healed her, but rather her own faith that did.

The prestigious religious leader saw the present circumstances and despaired. He gave in to death, losing all hope to it. But Jesus—and the bleeding woman—saw something else. They looked beyond what was, to what could be. And in this, we find the life Jesus seeks for us, and that God offers.

Heads Up

Connecting the text to our world

John D. Rockefeller was asked, after already amassing an immense fortune, how much money would be "enough" for him. His answer was, "just a little bit more." Though this seems clever and savvy on the surface, it actually reveals a desperate sort of hopelessness, just beneath the surface. Rockefeller was addicted to the chase itself, never satisfied with where he was or what he had. He seemed to live in a state of constant restless dissatisfaction, seeing what was possible and discontented because it could always be a little bit better, in his mind.

In talks I've done before about generosity, I've said we have two methods to try and get rich. One is to make and get more; the other is to want less. No matter what we have, we can always find reasons to despair, worry, or be unhappy with it. We compare ourselves to others or imagine something that's just barely out of reach. We take this inherent restlessness of the human condition and resolve that the silver bullet to quash that restlessness is "out there" somewhere.

On the other hand, we have a sense of gratitude, plenty, and the peace that comes only from within. This, in a nutshell, is at the heart of what betrays the gospel call in the so-called "prosperity gospel." This twisting of Jesus's call to hope despite present situations trades this instead for a false promise that what God wants for us is more. What's more, we'll know we're really blessed by the evidence of material abundance.

But ultimately this yields nothing but more want, more restlessness, more discontentment and despair. Any orientation that leans on a mantra of "If only I had _____," or "If only _____ happens, then I'll be happy" points us in the wrong direction. It leads us down a lifelong path that results in nothing but more want. What God offers, and what Jesus models, is the way out of this death-cycle, and into a life that really is *alive*.

Prayer for the Week

God, sometimes it's hard for me to see beyond what is to what could be. Instead of indulging what I think I want, grant me the vision I need to see a way out.

Popping Off

Art/music/video and other cool stuff that relate to the text

Seven Years in Tibet (movie, 1997)

Wall Street (movie, 1987)

Chasing the Dragon

Lectionary Texts For
July 8, 2018 (Proper 9 (14) Seventh Sunday after Pentecost)

Texts in Brief
My dog ate my Bible!

FIRST READING
2 Samuel 5:1–5, 9–10

Leaders from the twelve tribes of Israel come together and conduct a ceremony to empower David as their king. He was thirty then, and ruled until he was seventy.

and

Ezekiel 2:1–5

God tells the prophet Ezekiel that the Israelites are rebelling against God. So he is sent to warn them and tell them to change their course. Though they may not listen, says God, at least they'll know the one who told them was speaking on God's behalf.

PSALM
Psalm 48

A song of praise and admiration of God, having guided the leaders of the twelve tribes to gather in the capital city of Israel on top of Mount Zion, presumably when they anointed David as king. The psalm further asserts that God's ordaining of their acts was wise and in the best interests of God's people.

and

Psalm 123

A prayer of humble supplication, asking God to remove punishments from the people of Israel for their transgressions, begging instead for mercy.

SECOND READING
2 Corinthians 12:2–10

Paul tells of a man who had either a literal or out-of-body experience with heaven. This man, he says, has a story worth talking about, but not his own. He remains humble, in part because of a self-described "thorn in my side" he has asked to overcome but has been unable to. But then he finds a sense of peace with his own real-life struggles, as they remind him he is still utterly human, which puts him in a proper place to be obedient and open to Jesus.

GOSPEL

Mark 6:1–13

Jesus went to the synagogue in his hometown to teach, but people were incredulous, knowing his social status and parentage. Resigned, he realized they could not be open to his wisdom, so he and the disciples left for other villages in the area where they could make an impact. He sent the disciples to various places in pairs, empowering them with the gifts of healing and exorcism. They were to take nothing with them, but rather would depend on the hospitality of the strangers they met

Bible, Decoded

Breaking down scripture in plain language

Twelve Tribes of Israel – Jacob, near death, blessed each of his twelve sons (Benjamin, Asher, Dan, Judah, Levi, Simeon, Reuben, Gad, Joseph, Zebulun, Naphtali, and Issachar) as the future patriarch of what would become known as the twelve tribes of Israel. There is *midrashic* significance in the number, whether he literally had twelve sons or not. It was a significant number in numerology, considered to be perfect, and symbolic of God's power and authority. So with the twelve tribes, like the twelve disciples, it would be an indication that this was a byproduct of God's work.

Third Heaven – This is understood differently by various groups within Islam, Judaism, and Christian traditions. Some believe that heaven has seven levels to it, and so the third heaven would be a lower, likely less honorable or less close-to-God level. For others, third heaven is believed to be the level where God resides.

Points to Ponder

First Thoughts

It's interesting that the passages in 2 Samuel and the Gospel text are paired this week, not just because of their numeric parallels. Given the explanation of the number's importance above, it's worth noting that in 2 Samuel, God convenes the twelve together, whereas in Mark, God disperses the twelve. Everything in its time, I suppose.

We tend to glorify martyrdom sometimes, almost "humble bragging" about our acts of service. But what Paul is talking about isn't just serving the poor or even living with them; he's talking about a mental state, keeping in perspective our own frailties, shortcomings, and limitations. Again, this isn't so we can feel good about self-hatred or disdain, but rather because once we accept our utter humanity and all the faults that come with it, we're open and ready to be filled with something entirely new.

Digging Deeper

Mining for what really matters . . . and gold

It's helpful to know why Paul is talking so much about the idea of becoming humble and lowly, as this is only part of a larger passage known commonly as the "fool's speech." He's gotten word that some of the apostles in Corinth are trying to use their status and authority to assert their claims and persuade the Corinthian people.

But, as Paul warns, this ends up putting ourselves ahead of God, which actually blinds both us and our audience to the true point of our claims.

So in a way, by telling of this man who experienced heaven first-person, contrasted with his own story of humility (one might argue, humiliation), it's his gentle way of reminding them, "You're not so special." After all, if their patriarch, Paul, finds no room to boast about himself and his accomplishments, who in the world are they to?

Then we find Jesus in his own town of origin, trying to share wisdom and being looked down on for "only" being a carpenter's son. But instead of stomping his feet and yelling "Don't you know who I am?!?!" he quietly and humbly moves on. Then he goes a step further by empowering his disciples with much of the same power and authority he has, but to go out and share this authority basically as beggars. The reason: then they have to depend on others and be humbled by their hospitality.

David actually had evidently been doing "king's work" for many years while Saul still held the throne, but without the credit. Maybe he remembered his humble roots as a shepherd, or that he wasn't even the first-born son in his family (something that was very closely correlated with social status). Or maybe he felt more compelled to fulfill the work God had called him to do, rather than by the admiration and wealth that normally come with it.

Later, David supplicates himself like a servant before God on behalf of his people. We've seen in other psalms that, despite his many faults, David seems to keep a fairly healthy perspective on the reality that he doesn't deserve the abundance of grace and forgiveness God continues to bless him with.

Throughout scripture we see God meeting people most intimately in moments of humble brokenness, and not just out of pity. It is when we are broken down and all pretense and title are stripped away that we're left just with us alone. We're struck by our own smallness and finiteness—a state necessary to help us really be open to that still, small voice of God that beckons, but never demands.

God is not impressed by our titles, social standing, wealth, or accomplishments. What God desires from us is openness, service, and humble obedience, as much as we hate that word. But in that obedience we find the liberation of true perspective and a sense of belonging that surpasses the whims and fickleness of the world. It's when, as Paul writes, we catch a glimpse of a sense of peace that surpasses understanding.

Heads Up

Connecting the text to our world

A few years ago I was at what I would call now, looking back, the height of my writing career. My agent had landed a big book deal for me with a major publisher, a booking manager was making plans for an extensive tour to follow its release, media plans were being developed, and my visibility was at its height. There were times when certain articles I published would reach readers numbering six figures. It was intoxicating.

I started realizing that, to borrow a phrase from drug culture, I was "chasing the dragon." This refers to what happens after the first ecstatic high wears off from heroin use, and the user becomes consumed with nothing but getting that next high. Each subsequent high feels a little less amazing, though, and it takes more and more over time just to get back up to normal.

The first time I had a blog post hit big, it was as intoxicating as I imagine a heroin user feeling. It was almost an out-of-body experience. The heart races, adrenaline courses, and you feel invincible. But not long after, you want more. But just repeating your past success isn't enough; you have to up the ante. It has to be bigger, better, and more in order to feel something similar to that first rush.

My wife Amy recognized my obsession as I checked my blog stats and online book sales rankings several times throughout every day. She worried, but I insisted (like any good junkie would) that the pursuit of some imagined ideal of success didn't have a hold on me.

And then reality hit. My book came out in the middle of an Amazon boycott of titles from my publisher. Not long after, the imprint I was with got cut off and plans were made to shutter it. The book effectively tanked and all of the other big publishers who had been courting me suddenly seemed to have lost my number. I started to lose heart, trying to no avail to boost sales with a tour so rigorous I literally made myself sick.

For a while, I wrote next to nothing. I sat with my sense of crippling smallness and near invisibility. I'm still not nearly at the same level of production as I was before, but when I produce something, it's different. It's because I really feel like I have something to say, and that I'm moved to speak about something that matters not for my career, but for the world beyond me.

I still fight the urge to chase that dragon again, especially when I see friends and peers land the deals I wish I had or go on the trips I covet. But my consolation is that I'm trying to do the humble work of a servant and a half-blind prophet now, rather than as a public figure.

Prayer for the Week

God, help me get over myself. Remind me (gently if possible) that I'm not so special, but I am loved and cherished, regardless.

Popping Off

Art/music/video and other cool stuff that relate to the text

Do the Right Thing (movie, 1989)

Can't Buy Me Love (movie, 1987)

The Mighty Have Fallen

Lectionary Texts For

July 15, 2018 (Proper 10 (15) Eighth Sunday after Pentecost)

Texts in Brief

My dog ate my Bible!

FIRST READING

2 Samuel 6:1–5, 12b–19

Uzzah, a regional leader where the ark of God was previously located, dies and David secures the region under his throne. So both as an act of refocusing the kingdom around God, but also as a conquering act of power, David moves the ark to Jerusalem. Along the way, he dances in worshipful ecstasy in a loincloth, making sacrifices as he goes.

and

Amos 7:7–15

In a time when Jeroboam is king of Israel, Amos has a vision that God will defeat him and that the Israelites will be forced off their land. A priest tells Jeroboam about this treasonous vision, then tells Amos to go leave Israel.

PSALM
Psalm 24

A song of praise to God and also a reference to "the hill of the Lord," and what is required to ascend it. David, believed to be the psalmist, noted that only those whose hearts and works are pure are fit for such a task.

and

Psalm 85:8–13

A passage beckoning people to righteousness, ensuring that those who are faithful to God are protected, provided for, and given a clear path forward in their lives, individually and collectively.

SECOND READING
Ephesians 1:3–14

Paul is offering a beckoning or reminder similar to the one offered in Psalm 85, but here to the Christians in Ephesus. Just as God gave life to Jesus as a son born in love, so are we adopted as children of God in the same manner through that same act. As such, we owe our spiritual—if not physical—lives to such a gesture of love, and should invest ourselves wholeheartedly in giving such love back in kind through our daily life and spiritual practice.

Gospel

Mark 6:14–29

King Herod is getting word of Jesus's miracles, and wonders if Jesus is John the Baptist, raised from the dead. The remainder of the passage tells of why Herod had John jailed and beheaded. Though he didn't like being judged by John for marrying Herodias, his brother's wife, he was afraid of John and God's wrath if he did anything to him. Herodias hates John, though, so her daughter performs an erotic dance for Herod and his dinner guests on his birthday. Herod is so "moved" that he promises her anything she wants. Herodias advises her daughter to ask for John's head, so Herod has him beheaded.

Bible, Decoded

Breaking down scripture in plain language

House of David – Under the rule of King Saul, much of the Israelite kingdom has strayed from its fidelity both to their king and to God. Part of David's ascent to power as a king was to recapture the errant regions and bring them back into alignment under his rule. Once David conquered the Jebusite fortress of Jerusalem, it was thereafter known as the City of David.

Ark of God – Also called the "ark of the testimony," it is described in the book of Exodus as a gilded container that holds the stone tablets on which the Ten Commandments were believed to have been written.

Plumb Line – The wall referred to in Amos is believed to have some metallic quality, as the original words can be interpreted as "tin wall." The "plumb line" is usually a string tied to a lead weight that hangs vertically and helps builders make a wall straight, but the Hebrew *hā'eben habbedil* is translated both as "plummet" (AKA plumb line) but more directly as "stone of tin." So here it's likely symbolic for the defenses and self-glorifying architecture that betrays what has become the true "god" for the citizens and leaders of Jerusalem.

Points to Ponder
First Thoughts

As an editorial aside, sometimes I think the creators of the lectionary text combinations are sadists. Just saying.

It seems the most prevailing theme here, which takes some digging since it's often only implied, is the conflict of earthly desires or priorities, with what God desires. And as we will consider in the following section, through humanity's inclinations toward reverting to selfish ways, we seem to see an evolution of sorts in how God responds to it, or at least in our understanding of how God does.

Finally, this is one of those weeks in which leaning on exegesis (mining deeper into the cultural symbolism, original language, and historical/cultural context) is very helpful in really grasping what is going on.

Digging Deeper
Mining for what really matters . . . and gold

There are layers to consider in the Samuel text. On the one hand, we can see it as David fixing what was broken under Saul's rule, and Saul's faithlessness being punished proportionate to David's blessings for his faithfulness. However, there's more to David's acts than simply doing right by his people and honoring God. Moving the ark also is an act of power, as was taking Jerusalem to be his kingdom's capital. Jerusalem was not owned by any particular one of the twelve tribes at the time, so it was seen as a remarkable act of might to bring it back into the fold. It's also quite a powerful statement to reclaim the ark, one of the holiest relics of the Israelite faith, and dovetail it as symbolic with his reign.

Then he goes on in the first psalm to venerate Moses (albeit indirectly) as pure of heart and deed, and one of only a few worthy of ascending "the hill of the Lord" to speak with God and convey God's words to the people. And yet David has taken the remarkable step of moving the ark to a place of his choosing, and on top of that, he has staked his claim (and therefore placed the ark) in Jerusalem, located on Mount Zion.

If David is implying he's worthy, on a level like Moses, it begs the question of whether he's guilty of pride, ironically causing him not to achieve such a state of purity.

Paul beautifully beckons the Ephesian Christians back into a parent-child level of intimacy with God, placing their egos aside and replacing them with God's will, first and foremost. And we know Paul speaks often of humility and boasting, and how we're only supposed to boast of the power of God by way of Jesus within us. But we also know he struggles with a constant "thorn in his side." Though there is much debate as to what this is, it's quite possible his thorn is, like David's, pride.

As for Herod, he is restrained at first by his respect of, or fear of, God/John; however, he is ultimately subsumed by physical desire. And in doing so, he is giving his power and good judgment away, wholesale.

The best of intentions, what we say, or even how we see ourselves, only takes us so far. And sometimes it's curious how Paul talks about being lifted up by making ourselves lowly. But perhaps he's onto something; we do compromise much when giving into our baser nature. We give away so much in exchange for a quick fix of self-gratification, pleasure, or the illusion that we are better than we are. What's worse, we can often do it in a way that the world affirms as right and good, or even godly.

In the end, these small, incremental compromises are what pull us from the path that God desires for us. And on that path, though it requires setting aside our egos and wants, we are opened to the true nature and fullest potential of what we are meant to be.

Heads Up

Connecting the text to our world

A February 2, 2017, article on Raw Story talks about "why so many brilliant, talented people are so unhappy and dissatisfied." It posits that part of the issue has to do with expectation. In order to be successful, we often have to set unrealistic goals for ourselves. And though the world may admire our accomplishments, there's often still an ideal in our minds we never quite live up to.

Also, it turns out that the pain of failure affects us far more profoundly than does the pleasure of success. And as another article on the greatest fears of the wealthy notes, one of the things they worry about the most is losing what they have. That fear, in itself, diminishes the positive experience of having whatever we want. We have a pathological tendency to compare ourselves to others too, no matter how much we have achieved or amassed and, inevitably, there is someone who has more or who has done more.

We fear that those around us don't really like or admire us for who we are, but presume their attention and affection may be driven by ulterior motives. Plus, as the movie *Happiness* points out, even on a national level material prosperity and innovation don't correlate well to our sense of well-being.

All of these are true, and it may even be easy enough to try and convince ourselves that the praise we get from others is legitimately earned. However, when we do succumb to the illusion that we are what we have or what we do, and if we've devoted ourselves single-mindedly to such a level of status, there's a part of us that knows we've done so at the cost of worshiping a false god, one that ultimately gives nothing in return.

So we seek even further distraction from the pain of inevitable loss and the consuming fear that we're not actually good enough. We know the narrative we've tried to tell ourselves—that we are our success, our power, our money—rings hollow. Yet we keep chasing, yearning to fill the chasm with . . . anything else.

"How the mighty have fallen," says the prophet in 2 Samuel. The question isn't whether the fall will come, but rather what, if anything, will be there to catch us when it does.

Prayer for the Week

God, help me not to fool myself, even when I've convinced others that I'm something I'm really not.

Popping Off

Art/music/video and other cool stuff that relate to the text

Happiness (movie, 1998)

"Why so many brilliant, talented people are so unhappy and dissatisfied" from Raw Story (article, February 2, 2017) http://www.rawstory.com /2017/02/why-so-many-brilliant-talented-people -are-so-unhappy-and-dissatisfied/

"Secret fears of the super-rich" from *The Atlantic* (article, April 2011) https://www.theatlantic.com/magazine /archive/2011/04/secret-fears-of-the-super-rich /308419/

"I" and "Other"

Lectionary Texts For
July 22, 2018 (Proper 11 (16) Ninth Sunday after Pentecost)

Texts in Brief
My dog ate my Bible!

FIRST READING
2 Samuel 7:1–14a

David seems to feel restless, wondering if being settled in behind fortified walls is where he belongs. After all, God is not contained by such confines, so why should he? Then his advisor, the prophet Nathan, has a dream in which God tells him that God is with David and the Israelites wherever they are. He was with David in the sheep fields, and with them as they wandered the desert. But now God intends for them to have roots and a sense of place, and for David's bloodline and legacy to grow over generations.

and

Jeremiah 23:1–6

Jeremiah's prophecy from God, decrying the incompetence of former leaders of Israel, likening them to enemies of the Jews, destroying them, but this time from within. The prophecy continues that the "sheep" of Israel need a new Shepherd, whom they will find in David, an actual shepherd by trade. Under him, Jeremiah says on God's behalf, they will live safely and prosperously.

Psalm

Psalm 89:20–37

A poem foretelling, again, of God's anointing of David as the future king of Israel, and greatest among kings. Those who stand against him and his people will fall. God makes a loving covenant of faithfulness to David throughout his reign, which will continue on beyond his own life. Nothing will break God's promise to David and his people, and they will endure for all time.

and

Psalm 23

One of the best-known passages in the Bible, this is a poem of comfort for those afflicted or lost. Though they may feel surrounded by darkness and utterly alone, God does not abandon them.

Second Reading
Ephesians 2:11–22

Paul writes that those who are "born gentile" (aka, not Jewish) but who come to embrace the teaching of Jesus are no longer any different from God's chosen people. This, he says, is God's wish, despite what any law, human boundary, or other distinction might indicate. This covenant between humanity and God, which Paul says men formalize through the ritual act of circumcision, embodies God's intended path to peace for humanity.

Gospel
Mark 6:30–34, 53–56

After the disciples return from their appointed ministries in the surrounding villages, Jesus takes them in a boat to "foreign territory" across the Sea of Galilee for some privacy. Still, people find and follow them, bringing the ill and afflicted in search of healing.

Bible, Decoded
Breaking down scripture in plain language

Circumcision – The Jewish act of circumcision is a religious ritual that removes part of the foreskin of the penis during infancy. It was done as well as a consecrating act for adults in the time of Paul (and, in some cases, since then) to adults claiming the Christian faith to show their belonging. While some also believe it is hygienically beneficial, others feel it is unnecessary and unreasonably painful. Some countries even practice ritual female circumcision, in which the girl's clitoris is removed before puberty. While some cultures believe it helps a woman remain faithful to her future husband, many argue it is a fundamental abuse of human rights.

Nathan – A trusted spiritual advisor who not only shared affirming visions from God with David, but also words of condemnation for his errant ways. In addition to being a court prophet, Nathan was believed to be behind many of the writings in 1 and 2 Chronicles, telling of the rule of both David and Solomon.

Points to Ponder

First Thoughts

The Samuel text is frequently the source of controversy in the Middle East, since the proclamation of God, by way of Nathan, that the Jews should forever have a place and not be moved, lies at the heart of what some believe is Israel's divine right to their territory.

Another risk in these sorts of texts is that it suggests that true leaders are appointed as such by God. We hear this today, even in twenty-first-century American politics, where one group or another asserts that their choice for a leader is the only divinely sanctioned heir. This is one reason, among many, why Jefferson was so vocal about maintaining a "wall of separation" between church and state.

It's worth noting that, while Jesus maintains he never came to abolish religious law, but rather to fulfill it, here Paul says that God does indeed abolish human law, replacing it with divine sacrament and covenant.

Digging Deeper

Mining for what really matters . . . and gold

Every time I read about circumcision, I think about a cartoon in a book by Mark Russell and Shannon Wheeler called "God Is Disappointed in You," where a guy standing next to a chopping block mumbles "oops." the line of victims waiting to be circumcised behind him are beset with expressions of terror, covering their privates with both hands as they stand in the line. There are debates about whether the physical act of circumcision is necessary in order to be in God's good graces, or if it's more of a metaphor for personal transformation and a sacrament (sacred ritual) binding us to God through a promise.

I wonder, too, if such debates are at the heart of the West Bank debate between Israel and Palestine, in a way. Orthodox Jews in Israel believe God gave them this land through an irrevocable covenantal contract, whereas the Palestinians maintain that not only would such boundaries bar them from having access to many of their own Muslim holy sites; some even argue that the land is being stolen from them. David struggles too with this idea of place, and whether he's betraying God by staying in one spot. God assures him, however, that no matter where he goes, there God is.

When Jesus and his disciples go across Galilee into outsider territory, they're mobbed by gentiles. Interestingly, while the disciples and other Jewish leaders have fussed about Jesus's reaching out to non-Jews, the gentiles couldn't seem to care less where he's from or what faith he claims. They are drawn to him because in him they find something far more important than the sum total of all of their differences: they see the promise of hope, healing, and renewal.

So while we get hung up on who's in and who's out of our particular religious circle, or who should be on which side of a wall, God's longing for us is revealed in Psalm 23, Jeremiah, and in Ephesians. Rather than running and seeking God elsewhere, or trying to outrun our immediate problems, all we have to do is be present to God's ever-present longing for hope, healing, and renewal for us. And not just *me*, but *all of us*.

Whether we're in the valley of the shadow of death, across oceans, behind walls, or divided by lines of class, orientation, race, or otherwise, God meets us. But this is only the first step. Then it's placed in our hands to be the hands of reconciliation for the rest of the world, not to fortify walls and defend our territories, traditions, or ideologies, but to go beyond them, even working to eliminate such difference and distinction altogether.

Such is God's dream for us, and such is our mandate as partners in that covenant to live out such a dream.

Heads Up

Connecting the text to our world

I was born in downtown Dallas, where my parents had an apartment. Then, over the years into my teens, we moved further and further out of the center of the city. The reason I always heard was because property was cheaper out north, and that we could get more home for our money. But what I didn't know was that we were a part of what would later be known as "white flight." This was the phenomenon (still is in some places) of white people growing restless about the cultural diversity (read: too many people of color) in their communities, opting instead to migrate outward where the neighborhoods were more homogenous.

Over time of course, diversity found those neighborhoods too, and man, did we hear the complaints about "those people" moving into "our neighborhood." I'd overhear neighbors whispering about their Jamaican neighbor or the Chinese family who lived across the alley. Though some were quietly tolerant, or even openly hospitable, others were happy not to hide their disdain. Of course, few people ever confess to being racists. Usually I heard broader, apparently more benign phrases like the quality of life being compromised, or property values being negatively impacted. But make no mistake; it was racism.

Today, it's more common to see gentrification, where people of means (often predominantly white professionals) move back into urban settings into high-dollar homes and apartments built on the former sites of older structures. With them naturally come the businesses to accommodate their needs and wants, along with higher taxes, increased cost of living and skyrocketing rental costs. Though it's not necessarily explicitly or intentionally done, those who lived there before (usually those left behind when white flight happened in the first place) are forced out because they can't afford to live there anymore.

Sometimes our marginalization of the other is overt and aggressive. More often, particularly these days, it's more subtle. Some of us may be so unaware of it that we assume the neighborhood improvements are good for everyone. Perhaps, but it's only good if everyone can afford to be there.

Whether our divisions are formed intentionally or incidentally, God calls us to reconciliation. It's well and good to speak out against racism or homophobia when it's obvious, but followers of Jesus's way are called to do more. Every dollar we spend, every choice we make, even everything we choose not to do or even neglect through inaction, has an impact on others, the world, and ultimately, ourselves.

Loving others isn't just something we are called to say; it's something we're called to say and do with everything from our mouths and hands to our wallets. When we do, we find God, waiting.

Prayer for the Week

God, despite my own efforts, I still frame the world too often in terms of "I" and "other." Help me find compassion greater than my need to draw and defend lines of difference.

Popping Off

Art/music/video and other cool stuff that relate to the text

God Is Disappointed in You, written by Mark Russell, cartoons by Shannon Wheeler (book, 2016)

Gran Torino (movie, 2008)

Cube (movie, 1997)

Give and Take

Lectionary Texts For

July 29, 2018 (Proper 12 (17) Tenth Sunday after Pentecost)

Texts in Brief

My dog ate my Bible!

First Reading

2 Samuel 11:1–15

While his troops were off at war, David stayed in Jerusalem. From the roof of his house, he sees Bathsheba, Uriah's wife, bathing. He summons her, sleeps with her, and she gets pregnant. So David sends for Uriah, and tries to send him home to sleep with Bathsheba to justify her pregnancy, but Uriah stays with his troops. So David sends Uriah to the front lines of a dangerous battle to die.

and

2 Kings 4:42–44

A man brings a sacrifice of his farming yields to the prophet Elisha, who tells him to give it to the crowd of a hundred or more people present. Though the man protests there isn't enough, Elisha orders him again to do it. When he does, the crowd eats and there is food left over.

Psalm

Psalm 14

A text filled with disdain from David about what he sees as the ungodly opposition to his people all around them. In his eyes, there is not a grain of good in any of them. He longs for God to exact judgment on them so that the Israelites would stand sovereign again and live in peace.

and

Psalm 145:10–18

A song celebrating God as sustainer, provider, protector, and righteous judge over all.

Second Reading

Ephesians 3:14–21

Paul prays for the Christians in Ephesus that God might fill them from the inside out, and that from God's presence in them they might find all they need to sustain them.

GOSPEL
John 6:1–21

Jesus goes up a mountain to meet his disciples and is followed by a huge crowd. He asks Philip how to feed them and Philip worries that a half-year's wages wouldn't buy enough. So he asks for the five pieces of bread and two fish a boy brought, prays over it, and hands it out. Not only is everyone fed, but there are a dozen baskets of food left over. Then when Jesus senses the crowd wants to make him king, he retreats to a mountain by himself. The disciples begin to cross the sea without him, the waters get rough, and they see Jesus coming toward them, walking on the water. They invite him into the boat, and suddenly they're on the other side of the sea.

Bible, Decoded
Breaking down scripture in plain language

Wash his feet – This is one of several euphemisms for having sex in the Bible. Though we have to be careful not to assume every time someone washes their feet in the Bible, it means they're sleeping with someone. Sometimes foot-washing is just foot-washing!

Passover – Passover is a big Jewish holiday that takes place in the spring. It lasts about a week, and is a remembrance of the Exodus event, when God ordered them to wash their doorways with lamb's blood, which protected their firstborn children from the coming angel of death.

Points to Ponder

First Thoughts

It's worth noting that when Uriah refers to "My lord," he's not talking about David, but rather Joab, who is a fierce military commander. So though David may have been concerned about getting caught for impregnating Uriah's wife, it's also possible that he saw Joab, especially with the influence of such an officer as Uriah, as a possible threat to his rule.

If we know the gospel stories at all, we see echoes of the story of Jesus feeding the multitudes in this excerpt from 2 Kings. As I've said before, this is an intentional device called *midrash*, which helps indicate that it is God working through these people to provide this. It also helps reinforce that both Jesus and Elisha are men of God.

Digging Deeper

Mining for what really matters . . . and gold

In this story, timing is everything in a sense. If you notice, not only does the sequence with David and Bathsheba happen in spring, but so does the story of Jesus feeding the multitudes around Passover. And the same goes with the passage in 2 Kings when the man is offering a sacrifice of "first fruits" of his yield, which would have been in the spring as well, most likely.

This is the time every year when things are in bloom, food is plentiful, and we are surrounded by life. This is also why we find Easter, the celebration of new life, in spring. It actually is based on the ancient pagan calendar, which has the annual fertility celebration around the same time. This helps explain why we have eggs, bunnies, and other fertility-related symbols attached to Easter.

So it is a time when most of us aren't worried about having enough. Of course, in the highly interconnected world we live in, we don't think much about the note-worthiness of walking into a store in February to buy blueberries. But back then, many people often didn't survive the times of want, when drought hit or even just during a particularly harsh winter. So spring was a time to breathe a sigh of relief that we made it. And now we enjoy the fruits.

And yet, we worry. We want more. We can't see beyond what is to what will be, though we live in the midst of miraculous cycles of renewal and provision all the time. David has everything he could ever need and so much more, and yet he takes from someone who not only has far less, but who sacrifices his own life while David is safe behind fortified walls. We see the need and see what we have and immediately assume there can't be enough.

But God is patient, lets us work through it and fig-ure out that, just like it has before, it usually works out. God doesn't force us into sharing what we have either; God invites, asks for a bit of trust and to loosen our grip on what we have so that everyone would have more than enough.

Release leads to life; taking what we want but don't need or holding all we have close, to death. To have such power in our hands places a big responsibility on us, and in every decision we make, from what we consume and buy to who we welcome in or exclude. Give and take, it turns out, is a life-and-death choice.

Heads Up

Connecting the text to our world

I wonder sometimes in these feeding stories where the real miracle lives in them. Maybe it's in Elisha and Jesus, and their divinely given power, or in the thanks given over the offering, or in the offering itself, in one case from a small child. After all, without the farmer and child both agreeing to hand over what they have, there is no miracle.

Sometimes we get caught up in thinking that miracles are either relegated to an ancient past, or that they have to be some magical phenomenon in which we have no active part, except to "ooh" and "ahh" over. But maybe more miracles today lie in wait, until they are realized through our own acts of selflessness.

There's a woman in our church who made a comfortable living in the professional world before deciding that just earning a good living, and clocking in and out every day, wasn't fulfilling enough. So instead, she cashed in her retirement early, sold her home in town and moved out onto a semi-rural property with several run-down old residences on it.

She lived in one of the houses while also remodeling it to make it more livable. Others from the community, coming from everywhere from halfway houses to the same kind of urban life where she had been, could live there rent-free as long as they worked instead. A small group planted and expanded a community garden, shared meals and living quarters together until one home was complete. Then they would all start on another. Everyone cooks, cleans, gardens, and builds; they pay what they can when they can to keep the place going; and, miraculously, they've always had enough. This has been going on for years now, and the woman has no intention of changing her ways.

She has a niece who needed intensive heart surgeries and therapy in the Portland area, so the woman let her come to live there too. We had a couple at church who suddenly had no work, so she welcomed them in too. Later, when the group needed transportation, another congregant was inspired to donate one of his cars for them to share. They continue to grow most of the food they eat, and they share everything.

It's not always that easy. It's hard daily work that includes discomfort and sacrifice. And yet there is always enough. What's more, the woman seems to be more at peace and more in tune with her life, living out what she believes more than nearly anyone I know. It's both inspiring but also intimidating, to see someone so fully invested in her faith in real time. And yet it works.

That is a miracle.

Prayer for the Week

God, help me let go more easily and to take more slowly.

Popping Off

Art/music/video and other cool stuff that relate to the text

Pay It Forward (movie, 2000)

House of Cards (Netflix original series, 2013–)

Love vs. Desire

———————∿∿∿∿———————

Lectionary Texts For
August 5, 2018 (Proper 13 (18) Eleventh Sunday after Pentecost)

Texts in Brief
My dog ate my Bible!

FIRST READING
2 Samuel 11:26–12:13a

David takes Bathsheba in as a wife after she mourns Uriah's death. The prophet Nathan tells David a story of a rich man who takes a poor shepherd's only sheep, to which David says this man should be judged and make right his wrongs. Nathan says the story is about him and that, because of his sins, God will allow David's wives to stray from him publicly so he is humiliated.

and

Exodus 16:2–4, 9–15

The Israelites complain to Aaron and Moses that it would have been better to die in Egyptian captivity than to wander the desert hungry. God hears them and sends birds and bread for them to eat every day.

PSALM

Psalm 51:1–12

David laments his transgressions against God. He prays desperately to be made clean again, for God to forgive his sinful ways, not to abandon him for his greed, and to renew a right spirit within him.

and

Psalm 78:23–29

A song about the blessings described in the Exodus passage, given to the Israelites by God.

SECOND READING

Ephesians 4:1–16

Paul urges his audience to put group unity and peace ahead of personal ambition or desires. He likens our bond to God to being a captive in prison. He goes on to say that, through resurrection, Jesus demonstrated a power greater than all earthly bondage, including the prison of death itself. To be self-interested is childish, so we should "grow up" in our faith life and embrace what it means to follow Jesus in all parts of life and with our whole selves.

GOSPEL

John 6:24–35

After the multitudes had eaten their fill, they sailed across Galilee to Capernaum to look for Jesus and his disciples. Jesus notes that they hungered for him only after their physical hunger was satisfied. But he wants them to change their priorities, so their spiritual hunger comes ahead of all else. Referring back to the story above in Exodus, Jesus reminds them that the Israelites were not nourished by a man (Moses), but rather by God.

Bible, Decoded

Breaking down scripture in plain language

Aaron – Moses's older brother who was his companion and advisor as Moses led the Israelites through the desert.

Manna – Though it has traditionally been taught that the manna described in the Exodus text was bread like we think of today (or more specifically, unleavened bread), some historians believe the word came from a description of the hardened resin from tamarisk trees, which were plentiful in the region. Later in scripture, manna is described more like a coriander seed but paler in color, which could align it with the theory that it was this sort of honeydew that indeed would have been left behind and would have hardened after the morning dew lifted.

Capernaum – A fishing village on the north edge of the Sea of Galilee where the prophet Nahum was believed to have lived. Several disciples, including Matthew,

Simon Peter, Andrew, James, and John all were thought to have been born in Capernaum.

Points to Ponder

First Thoughts

Paul's comparison of faithfulness to being a prisoner is strange, given that he is so concerned in general about free will, and since a prisoner doesn't generally have any choice about their captivity.

It's strange to consider that David is the antecedent to so many leaders after him who, despite apparently having the world at their feet, find ways to desire more. And like them, in pursuing it, they end up kicking their own ass. We humans sure seem to come with a built-in self-destruct button.

Digging Deeper

Mining for what really matters . . . and gold

It's easy in the 2 Samuel passage to focus on David, the flawed nature of so many of God's chosen, or the eventual consequences of sin. But we shouldn't overlook the courage of Nathan in standing before the king and condemning him on behalf of God. Now, he doesn't start out by casting judgment; rather he takes an approach more like Jesus would later in the gospels by offering a parable. Thus David arrives at his own condemnation by suggesting that a man who would take a man's only sheep while having so much for himself is, in so many words, a jerk.

But in the end, Nathan nails him. Clearly he doesn't do this for his own health, as challenging a king to his face is a sure way to shorten one's lifespan. He does it for a couple of reasons: first, he is compelled by the voice of God to speak prophetically to David, and second, he knows what sort of discord such behavior from a leader can bring upon his people. So this is an act of prophetic compassion, of sorts. And although his truth stings David, he also is telling David what he *needs* to hear rather than what he might *want to hear*. He tells the truth because he loves David.

This is what Paul means in the Ephesians passage when he tells his fellow Christians to speak the truth in love. Sometimes we may mistake being nice as being loving, but that's not always the case. After all, Jesus was radically loving, and he was hardly nice all the time. On the other hand, we may feel it's best to tell it like it is at all times, but if it's not done from a place of compassion for the one to whom we're speaking, we're likely to hurt far more than help.

Truth and love are necessary companions. Love without truth is incomplete. Truth without love can easily become a weapon. We have to practice both in concert to realize the personal peace and communal harmony God longs for within and among us.

Heads Up

Connecting the text to our world

It's not hard to find examples of rich, powerful, and (at least according to conventional standards) successful people sabotaging their own success. From Kennedy to Clinton, and from Charlie Sheen to Lindsay Lohan, we can start to wonder what's the matter with people who seem to have so much and yet, inexplicably, find some way to blow it.

In reality, we are all our own worst enemies sometimes. It's just more remarkable when someone who apparently has everything does it. *If I had everything they had,* we mistakenly think, *I'd never want for another thing in my whole life.*

But we are creatures driven by desire. Anyone who took a Psych 101 class remembers Maslow's Hierarchy of Needs, placing more basic necessities like food and shelter at the base and self-actualization at the top of the pyramid. But this says little about the limitless potential of desire, irrespective of what we need or even already have.

Desire is inexhaustible, a black hole that longs to be fed without ever being satisfied. We tend to set benchmarks for ourselves, despite this reality, at which point we'll have enough that the desire will go away. But it never does. Peter Rollins calls this eternal longing "the Gap," but in my book *PostChristian: What's left? Can we fix it? Do we care?,* I call this "The Hunger." Desire is a basic driver that motivates us.

Jesus recognizes that the crowd only seeks him and is open to his teaching after the rumbling in their bellies is satisfied. God answers the complaints of the Israelites who would rather be back in the prison of Egyptian slavery than to starve. And yet, if we remember, later they complain that the food is boring, and crave something else. David arguably has more than any other Israelite, and yet he fixes his desire so intensely on Bathsheba that he wreaks destruction in his path.

Paul wisely recognizes that this human tendency to be consumed by our desire is like an inescapable prison, which likely is why he finally likens our faithfulness to God to being held captive. We'll be beholden to something, be it to God or our own desire. And as history shows, the latter leads to chaos, division, and worse. So if we're to be beholden to anything or anyone, says Paul, make it God.

We're not to ignore the inevitability of human desire. It's more a matter of orientation, directing that longing toward unity with the Divine. And in doing so, we achieve greater unity among ourselves and greater peace within. This is why Jesus is the "bread of life," or the "water of life" after which we will no longer be enslaved by our own physical needs and wants.

It's a path to freedom.

Prayer for the Week

God, help me act more out of love, and less out of desire. Help my words first be informed by that love, so that my truth always comes from the right place.

Popping Off

Art/music/video and other cool stuff that relate to the text

The Wolf of Wall Street (movie, 2013)

"Still Haven't Found What I'm Looking For" by U2 (song, 1987)

Lolita, by Vladimir Nabokov (book, 1955)

Feeding the Beast

Lectionary Texts For

August 12, 2018 (Proper 14 (19) Twelfth Sunday after Pentecost)

Texts in Brief

My dog ate my Bible!

FIRST READING

2 Samuel 18:5–9, 15, 31–33

Absalom, David's son, has rebelled against him and his troops. So David orders them into battle with him and his rebel cohort, but entreating his soldiers to go easy on Absalom. Twenty thousand men die in that battle, including Absalom at the hands of David's men, which greatly grieves David.

and

1 Kings 19:4–8

Elijah is alone in the woods when he lies down to rest. An angel awakes him twice, leaving behind food and water for him. After being awoken to eat twice, he ventures into the desert and to Mount Sinai alone for forty days, not having to eat or drink again during the journey.

PSALM

Psalm 130

The author grieves the ways in which they fall short of God's expectations, begging for mercy, and extolling the preciousness of God's gift of apparently inexhaustible love as expressed through forgiveness and a "short memory" of our shortfalls.

and

Psalm 34:1–8

David offers a poem of reassurance, likely for himself and his audience, that God is sure to deliver those who seek God's help in times of despair. He also begins in a tone that we see often later on in Paul's letters, when he claims his only justification for boasting is in his witness of God's goodness.

SECOND READING

Ephesians 4:25–5:2

Paul warns the Christians in Ephesus that, while they may witness sin all around them, it's no justification for talking down to others or speaking negatively about them among themselves. The locals may seem corrupt, but the Christians are reminded to look at them with the kind of grace and love with which God sees them, rather than with contempt or hate.

GOSPEL

John 6:35, 41–51

Jesus claims to be the bread of life, sent from heaven, which throws the Jewish people listening to him for a loop. They start talking negatively about him, which he nips in the bud. Instead of backing down and being intimidated, he calls them out for not believing him and talking trash. He doubles down on his claims, asserting that he is the way to knowing God, which they claim to want.

Bible, Decoded

Breaking down scripture in plain language

Absalom – The son of David, he is faithful to his father until his pride begins to take over. Rather than serving his father he starts to talk divisively to the people in his own region of Hebron, claiming he is more fit to hear their needs than David. After a few years of this, and gathering an army of support behind him, he finally believes his own hype enough to lead a revolt against David, claiming autonomy from the kingdom until David sends his military in to reclaim the region.

Bread of Life – Jesus speaks often about the apparently unending cycle of seeking nourishment—or "bread"— and yet being hungry again later. He uses this phrase, "bread of life," not to suggest that people who follow him never have to eat real food again; rather, his message is that we can break free of the futile cycles of seeking and trying to use solutions from the world to end our persistent needs—whatever they may be—turning instead to a spiritual wellspring that he claims is the only ultimate way to quench these yearnings.

Points to Ponder
First Thoughts
We tend to assume that, if our outside circumstances change (better job, happier relationship, more money), then we'll finally be happy. And yet we see in the stories of Elijah and David that even when all goes right, everything can still feel wrong. Happiness, then, must be more of an inner orientation than a circumstantial thing.

Maybe that's why Jesus's words related to this appear back in Mark, echoed again in Matthew and Luke:

What good is it for someone to gain the whole world, and yet lose their soul?

Digging Deeper
Mining for what really matters . . . and gold
It's helpful to know a bit more backstory to help connect both the Samuel and Kings texts. Though it's clear that David goes into battle (and emerges victorious), what we don't see in the 1 Kings text is that Elijah is coming off of an encounter with prophets for other gods, Baal and Asherah. He comes out of that encounter having demonstrated the primacy of the God of

Israel, but for some not entirely known reason, he's deeply troubled.

For David, we know why he's grieving; he has lost his son, and at the hands of his own men at that. Why Elijah is ashamed after carrying out God's work is unclear. Maybe the conflict resulted in what he saw as an unnecessary loss of life. Maybe his depression is more existential, dealing with a sense of superiority or pride. But regardless, we see two men who stand as ambassadors on God's behalf, and who come out on top.

And yet they're deeply troubled.

Maybe Paul's warnings in the Ephesians passage give us a clue. Given that, in that case, the Ephesian Christians are carrying out what they believe to be God's work, they seem to have been getting derailed by negative personal feelings toward those around them. So maybe part of David's grief isn't just in the loss of his son, but that he ordered the battle against Absalom and his soldiers from a place of anger or self-righteous contempt.

And we know by now that Elijah, while a devoted prophet of God willing to do anything asked of him, also is a man of tremendous passion. Maybe in God's prevailing over the Baalite deities, Elijah felt a rush of arrogance, like an "I told you so" moment. Maybe he even did a little happy dance inside upon seeing them humiliated and even killed.

Jesus claims to the Jewish audience before him that he is the bread of life, sent to them from heaven. They seem incredulous at this, experiencing a sort of "who does he think he is?" moment. And though he does address their doubts, asserting that they can't truly come to know God without seeing God through him, his primary concern is their complaining about what they see as his heresy or, at the very least, his confounding claims.

We've heard of the phrase "don't feed your anger," or something to that effect. That's because these resentments, wrath, or contemptuous feelings we have toward others actually take from us. *They feed off of us.* Elijah is finally depleted and overwrought from feeding his own wrath, and his renewal comes in the form of bread and drink as God's gift. This bread that sustains him is what Jesus claims to be. It may not be something we feast on at a meal and immediately satisfies our pangs, but a spiritual nourishment that gives to us, rather than taking away.

Heads Up

Connecting the text to our world

It's a little bit ironic that I'm writing about this week's passages today, given the morning I had. I went round and round with a company that provides an essential service for my company, and yet continues to disappoint. If I had an option to change services, I would in a second, but they have a relative monopoly. I begin to wonder, as this trend of underperforming persists, if they are all too aware of their clients' lack of options and, as such, don't bother to do a better job since there's little to compel them to.

Why do more than the bare minimum, after all, if you suffer no loss by skating by? Why invest more money or effort if it won't change the outcome for their bottom line?

Then I started to question their basic competency, marveling that they have become such a big contender in this market with so many apparently unqualified people running their operations. Actually, I think the phrase I used was "parade of idiots."

By the time lunch came around, I was seething. The argument with them inside my own head—and my own sense of self-righteousness—reached overheated levels. I could feel the prickles along the back of my neck and a knot growing in my stomach.

What the hell am I doing? I finally told myself. *You're tearing yourself up from the inside about something over which you have no control, and yet they could not care less.*

Because I was so convinced they weren't doing their job, and because I felt out of control of the results, I took it out on myself. *Well, that was pretty stupid,* I came to realize.

The whole miniature tirade I played out in my head changed nothing except taking from my own serenity and happiness. So finally I focused on my breathing, calming myself down, and on letting the whole thing go. I would do what I could from a productive standpoint on my end; the rest I simply had to surrender to God. It was almost like I imagined myself tottering in with a messy mountain of paperwork, dumped it in God's in-basket, and God said "I got this."

No, I don't expect God to make them finally do a better job, or to develop a newfound empathy for how their efforts affect my own business. But I do feel a little bit better now, as though I have some perspective. Some of it is just out of my hands. And if I interacted with them when I was feeling the way I did, nothing good would come from it.

And if nothing else comes from it, I feel better right now. A little humiliated after writing this down, yes, but hey; maybe a little dose of humility was what I needed to knock me off my high horse.

Prayer for the Week

I suck at letting go of hard feelings, judgment, and a sense of self-righteousness. God, help pry my heart loose of these soul-killing thoughts and feelings when I can't seem to do it on my own.

Popping Off

Art/music/video and other cool stuff that relate to the text

Power, Ambition, Glory: The Stunning Parallels between Great Leaders of the Ancient World and Today and the Lessons You Can Learn, by Steve Forbes and John Prevas (book, 2009)

"The Price of Arrogance," from *Forbes* (article, June 18, 2009) http://www.forbes.com/2009/06/18/alexander -great-hubris-leadership-power.html

"When Pride Goes Wrong," from *The Sport Journal* (article, August 19, 2011) http://thesportjournal .org/article/when-pride-goes-wrong/

Smart vs Wise

Lectionary Texts For
August 19, 2018 (Proper 15 (20) Thirteenth Sunday after Pentecost)

Texts in Brief
My dog ate my Bible!

First Reading
1 Kings 2:10–12; 3:3–14
King David dies after serving as king for forty years, which puts his young son, Solomon, on the throne. The boy feels overwhelmed and asks God for guidance. Because he asked out of concern for his people and not himself, God grants him wisdom and guidance, promising to give him a long, prosperous life if he remains faithful.

and

Proverbs 9:1–6

Wisdom is personified as a hostess at a feast, inviting those without wisdom to take their fill and to set aside old, childish thoughts and habits.

PSALM

Psalm 111

This is a song of jubilation about God's provision and steadfast faithfulness to those who are faithful to God. It ends by claiming that the seeds of wisdom first are planted in the fertile soil of respect for God, and that in living a more disciplined life informed by this respect for God, we gain understanding.

and

Psalm 34:9–14

A poem about how the key to the alleviation of endless want and suffering is having respect for God and God's desires for our lives.

SECOND READING

Ephesians 5:15–20

Paul offers advice on how to live wisely, which primarily focuses on healthy balance rather than self-indulgence. Such self-discipline leads us to greater wisdom. The intent seems to be on presence and mindfulness about whatever we are doing in the moment, and to do it, whatever it is, with our whole heart and strength.

GOSPEL

John 6:51–58

Jesus continues to speak about himself as the Bread of Heaven and speaks of the "word becoming flesh" that begins the Gospel of John. People are baffled, since they're taking him literally. They wonder how and why it is that they're supposed to eat his flesh. He alludes again to the blessings of the manna for the Israelites in the desert, reminding him that the "Word become" flesh and blood to which he is referring is an act of truly taking in the word and spirit of God until it is an inextricable part of who they are.

Bible, Decoded

Breaking down scripture in plain language

Solomon – The son of David who lived for about eighty years, around 1,000 years before Jesus's life. He was considered to be a great king, succeeding David after his death, and his wealth and wisdom were renowned. He was believed to have overseen construction of the first temple in Jerusalem and, despite being admired and loved by God, did stray from a faithful path later in life. This fall from God's graces was believed to be the beginning of the division that led to his kingdom splitting under the later rule of his son Rehoboam.

Gibeon – An ancient city in the northern region of Judah. It was the center of a lot of conflict, governed for some time by the Canaanites under the pretense of a questionable and possibly deceptively executed treaty with the Jews. Saul later wreaks violence on the Gibeonites, which leads to a famine in Jerusalem as God's punishment. It was where David killed Goliath, and the territory, then under Philistine rule, was rejoined with the Israelite kingdom. It was considered a holy site in the time of Solomon.

Points to Ponder

First Thoughts

Though David may well have reigned literally for forty years, it's a literary nod to the number used throughout scripture to indicate a time when a person or people are closely connected or blessed by God. So in stating this, the idea is that, despite his shortcomings, his rule was divinely directed.

It's interesting, maybe even ironic, that the issue in the Gospel seems to be that people are mistakenly interpreting Jesus's words literally rather than understanding the deeper wisdom within them. Sounds a lot like the fights we have about scripture today. Sorry God, but maybe we'll get it right some day!

Digging Deeper

Mining for what really matters . . . and gold

In a study of this 1 Kings text, Garrett Calvin notes that the word "heart" appears three times, each translated from a different Hebrew word. This is not unlike how we see three different words for love in the ancient Greek. Too often, when we hear the Bible referring to our hearts, we mistakenly fall into the contemporary western culture trap of thinking this has more to do with feeling than with wisdom.

We've co-opted the symbol of the heart for greetings cards on so-called Hallmark holidays, and have even reduced it to an emoticon on our phones. But our hearts are not just a metaphor for feelings, any more than love always means the same thing.

Solomon is trusted and empowered by God because he has a wise heart. It's not that he's always mushy-gushy, sending valentines out to his people. Here, it's more of an orientation or lens through which he sees the world, and in particular, his father who ruled before him. Solomon is all too aware of the stumbles and flaws from which David suffered, and he's not willfully blind to them. He doesn't just brush those aside so he can focus on the warm, fuzzy stuff. But he doesn't let David's shortcomings blind him to the goodness—even greatness—in him.

What's more, he is able to take his understanding of this greatness and learn from it, even internalize it as part of his own practice. So in a sense, his ability to see the past clearly, particularly with regard to what makes a leader great, helps inform his and his people's future with richer wisdom.

Paul does likewise, urging his fellow Jesus-people to forgo the easy distractions of indulging the wants of the heart and body, opting instead for focus on a more nourishing source—that spiritual discipline and wisdom they can find in remaining in God's presence and heeding God's call. Sure, it may be less fun in the short term, but his vision—and the vision he wants for them—is broader and longer term.

Solomon, David, and Paul each find the basis for wisdom foremost in deference to the desires of God over their own. And what does God desire? Jesus's response to his fellow Jews is that he has the answer to that ever-nagging question. But as the hostess in Proverbs sets the table and prepares a feast of wisdom and spiritual gifts for those who seek it, the offer always is a standing invitation, rather than a mandate.

Come, see, accept, know, live, and understand. The invitation only asks for a response of yes.

Heads Up

Connecting the text to our world

If I had a nickel for every time I had either been told, or later told my own son, "for a smart kid, you do a lot of dumb things," I'd have retired years ago. As a kid, I tended to conflate intelligence with wisdom, assuming that if you're smart, you're automatically wise. Only later—much later—did I really start to understand the difference.

One example I used to illustrate the distinction with my son had to do with money. For whatever reasons, he has a real fascination with currency. And I mean how it's made, the evolution of currencies, different types from around the world, and even our eventual departure from the gold standard. He knows more facts about money at the age of twelve than most people learn in a lifetime, or want to know, for that matter.

However, despite that vast repository of factual knowledge, he's terrible with managing it. He's forever upside-down with his allowance, and I have to check his laundry sometimes to see if he's developed gaping holes in the bottom of his pockets. Meanwhile, his younger sister, five years his junior, is still learning exactly what the abstractions of money represent. Yet she is more radically generous and prudent with what she has than many adults.

Whenever there is a fundraiser at school or church, she gives a surprising amount away. She spends some on herself occasionally after weighing the decision, and still always has more money in her piggy bank (yes, it's literally a ceramic pig) than any of us ever has on hand. In fact when I'm low on bills she always offers to spot me, which I graciously decline.

When we think and act from a place of wisdom, a mentality of—and it seems, even the reality of—abundance inevitably follows. And while in scripture they draw parallels with God giving more to the wise, I'm not sure it's as much of a hands-on divine intervention as it is an orientation of our hearts and the way we see the world.

Scripture also correlates age with wisdom. Generally when someone is described as having lived a ridiculous number of years, the point is that they're remarkably wise. And yet age in itself doesn't guarantee wisdom. Presence, mindfulness, self-discipline, and patience are the foundation. For some of us, the architecture of wisdom takes longer to build. In Solomon's case, his wisdom as a young boy impresses God.

Likewise, living from a practice of wisdom doesn't guarantee longevity or material success. But it certainly doesn't seem to hurt our chances.

Prayer for the Week

I don't mind being self-disciplined and operating from a place of wisdom when it's convenient. God, help me stick to it even when it isn't.

Popping Off

Art/music/video and other cool stuff that relate to the text

Last Days in the Desert (movie, 2015)

"You Don't Get to Say 'I'm bored'" clip, from "Louie" Season 2, Episode 5 (TV series, 2010–) https://vimeo .com/98267560

Tent City

Lectionary Texts For

August 26, 2018 (Proper 16 (21) Fourteenth Sunday after Pentecost)

Texts in Brief

My dog ate my Bible!

FIRST READING

1 Kings 8:(1, 6, 10–11), 22–30, 41–43

Solomon convenes leaders of the twelve tribes of Israel, and he orders the ark of the covenant from the city to the inner sanctuary of the temple in Jerusalem. When placed there, a cloud from God's presence fills the temple, and Solomon prays before all in attendance. He asks for God to be with him and the people of Israel and to protect and guide them. He asks that those who come from elsewhere would be equally inspired and would take word of God's greatness to all corners of the earth.

and

Joshua 24:1–2a, 14–18
Joshua calls together leaders of the twelve tribes of Israel and urges them to cling to the God of Israel alone, leaving behind all other god figures from their past, or adopted from foreign cultures.

PSALM
Psalm 84
A prayer of gratitude for finding sanctuary, belonging, and a sense of home in God's presence.

and

Psalm 34:15–22
A poem of assurance that all who seek sanctuary and confidence in God will be cared for, renewed, and will not suffer at the hands of those who do not follow God.

SECOND READING
Ephesians 6:10–20
Paul compares depending on God to protect us from evil in the world to arming ourselves for battle. He describes truth as a belt, righteousness as a breastplate, and faith as a shield. Finally, he describes the word of God as a sword and salvation as a helmet. So when we are acting and thinking from a place of faith, truth, and righteousness as informed by God's teaching, we are armed against evil.

GOSPEL

John 6:56–69

Jesus's followers seem troubled and even doubtful about his teachings regarding the need to eat and drink of him in order to find real life. So he calls them out for it, saying that if this seems too hard or questionable to them, they're welcome to leave. After many do, he presses the remaining twelve if they wish to go too. But Simon Peter says there is nowhere else for them to go since he is the very source of life, as they see it.

Bible, Decoded

Breaking down scripture in plain language

Cherubim – Originally the job of the Cherubim, who serve God, was to protect the Garden of Eden. They're named more than ninety times in the Bible, though they are attributed varying forms and, in some cases, no form at all. Their roles vary too, and some believe their origins predate Judaism, stemming from early spiritual notions of supernatural animal hybrids, like a mix of lions and eagles.

Lord of Hosts – The Hebrew for this phrase, *Adonai Tzavaot*, can be most directly translated as "Lord of Armies." Though it is used to describe God more than 200 times in the Bible, here it is likely used as a title to affirm that God is the sole God over all twelve of the tribes and armed forces within the nation of Israel.

Amorites – A somewhat nomadic group that had taken up residence in the areas of modern Palestine and Syria. According to scripture, God helped Israelite forces to drive them out of the land as part of the effort to reconcile the previous territory recognized as part of the land of Israel.

Points to Ponder

First Thoughts

Throughout the books of Kings and Samuel there are many accounts of God driving non-Jews off the land to make room for the intended nation of Israel. While I can see the people correlating their own faithfulness with military might and success, it presents a dangerous logic when applied similarly today. We've seen everything from the Crusades to Manifest Destiny and other examples where violence was justified because it was believed to be ordained by God.

In hanging onto such an ideology, I think we have to be very mindful of the kind of God we're presenting to the world, and it's incumbent on us to question whether we're using "God's will" to justify what we already really want anyway.

Digging Deeper

Mining for what really matters . . . and gold

In the earlier texts of the Bible, and really throughout scripture, the notion of place is very important. The spiritual ancestors of the Jews assure them that God intends for a specific region to be there to live on forever, and they take this very seriously. But as these areas were highly tribal and many of the competing groups did not necessarily stay in one place or recognize particular sovereignty of one group over a claimed piece of land, there was great conflict about who belonged and who didn't. So we see from the leadership of Joshua and through the reigns of Saul and David, this fierce effort to hold together the Israelite nation, which itself is made up of a dozen different tribal groups.

Consider that in the country of Iraq there are far fewer tribal factions, and yet the region is rife with territorial disputes, and cultural and ideological conflicts. The resulting violence is seemingly unending. And even with respect to Israel and Palestine, the struggle for land rights and national recognition continue.

But God wants more for us. We're not divinely endowed with a given place to live, resources to possess and use, or the mandate for others take heed of our spiritual right to such things. God doesn't require such a place either, as if to hide in the innermost sanctuaries of our churches and holy places. It's not that God is not there, or that God doesn't necessarily bless our sense of place or community identity. But God is far more than just that.

In the epistle, Paul compares God more to a suit of armor rather than a fortress or domicile. This is important because armor goes with the person wherever they go. This means that the protection and comfort offered us by God is not restricted necessarily to a particular place, beyond which God abandons us. Rather, God is more of a companion in our journey, alongside us in good times and bad.

And then Jesus, as he was known to do, took the idea a step further. He challenges his followers to the point that many are disturbed to the point of giving up. Rather than wrestling with the complexity and ambiguity of the claims before them, or perhaps because they saw such teaching leading them down a path directly in opposition to the governing forces of the time, they opted for the comforts of their homes instead of taking the chance.

Fine, says Jesus, *if this journey is only one you intend on sticking with when it's easy, it's best to give up before it really gets hard.* He even invites the remaining disciples to go back home if they feel the same, but Simon Peter responds on their behalf. He tells Jesus that although they may have houses and families they left behind, those are no longer their homes. Their residence, their identities, their very lives are interwoven with Jesus now. So the idea of going back is not an option to them. Where he goes, they follow. Where he rests, they call home. And when he says to press forward, so will they.

Their belonging is no longer tied down and place-specific. Their sense of home is in the presence of God, wherever that takes them.

Heads Up

Connecting the text to our world

Portland is known to be friendlier than most American cities toward people living outside, or those who others may call homeless. But they would contest the use of that word. A man named Ibrahim who lives outdoors has been delegated as a public advocate and vocal representative of the community in both the media and when engaging figures in government. In a recent interview on a local radio station, he explained that, rather than homeless, his community consider themselves to be houseless.

It may seem a simple matter of splitting semantic hairs to some of us, but to them, the distinction is important. Ibrahim's point in the interview was that, although he and his neighbors may not have a place where they live that conforms to the traditional notion of what a house is, they consider their own community of people, albeit an outdoor community, to be their home.

As for where they live, that is a consistent point of contention for many. Anyone visiting Portland, especially in the winter months, will notice tents and makeshift dwellings on highway medians, under bridges and along sidewalks where there are vacant lots. Many of them congregate in public plazas and parks in the daytime, and there are even neighborhoods, like the one where Ibrahim lives, where many come together to form a sense of community.

One example is Tent City off of Burnside, in the northern part of downtown. Their camp includes electricity, a communal water supply, and toilets, and they even have their own community rules and neighborhood watch. However, it is not without its problems. For one, it lacks the typical aesthetic appeal of what many of us expect when we think of a neighborhood. Local businesses complain from time to time that Tent City's presence brings inordinate levels of crime and drugs to the neighborhood, though many in the houseless community suggest a lot of this is hype, created to justify an existing desire to make them go away.

Finally, the local government buckled and now has a plan to dismantle Tent City. There are some vague discussions about relocation, though the residents in the camp are realistic that it will happen again, regardless of where they're moved. Some will disperse, at least for a time, but like anyone else, they need somewhere to sleep and claim as a sense of place. While there are temporary shelters, many won't accept adult men, and they tend to be over capacity on any given day, especially when weather turns hostile. So they move, and move again, resisting and calling for support, while also recognizing that their life inevitably is somewhat nomadic by circumstance, if not by choice.

Regardless of all of this, they claim a collective identity as a cohort, a community that, while it may be relocated and broken up, time after time, find each other and grow whatever roots they can to connect, share what they have, and reclaim their sense of home and belonging. It begs the question, while those with power and resources may continue to claim particular places as their own, even to the detriment of others, some will still be home, wherever they are.

Prayer for the Week

Help me find a sense of home, God, wherever I am and with whomever I find myself. Remind me to make room for others as well, especially the "others."

Popping Off

Art/music/video and other cool stuff that relate to the text

The Soloist (movie, 2009)

Streetwise (movie, 1984)

Set Apart

Lectionary Texts For
September 2, 2018 (Proper 17 (22) Fifteenth Sunday after Pentecost)

Texts in Brief
My dog ate my Bible!

FIRST READING
Song of Solomon 2:8–13

In this poem of romance and longing, a woman antici-pates the return of her lover after a long winter apart. Just as everything else is in plentiful bloom, her heart feels similarly full, to the point of overflowing.

and

Deuteronomy 4:1–2, 6–9

A call by Moses to Israelites to learn and closely follow the laws given to them through him. This is not only for the sake of upholding their covenant with God, but also because they are being held to a uniquely higher standard, from which others will find inspiration and respect, perhaps even coming to know God.

PSALM

Psalm 45:1–2, 6–9

A poem of admiration, affection, and awe about the king. The author describes him as majestic and handsome; he even smells great! His reign is seen as righteous and sure to endure, as it has been specially blessed by God. He and the queen are held in the highest esteem, and they deserve the respect of other royalty, at home and abroad.

and

Psalm 15

The author stakes a claim about who is and is not worthy to be in the presence of God (and more specifically, into the holiest parts of the temple). Such a privilege should be for those who follow God's commandments faithfully and who live out a holy life in all ways.

SECOND READING

James 1:17–27

Human beings are specially beloved by God, above all the rest of creation, and are held to a higher standard because of it. It is not enough just for us to read and know God's law intellectually; we have to embody them as daily practices, day in and day out. Just being part of religious rituals, studies, and knowing all the right prayers is not what is expected, but rather purity of heart, mind, and body, as well as acts of compassion for those in need.

GOSPEL

Mark 7:1–8, 14–15, 21–23

The temple leaders complain to Jesus, asking why his disciples do not follow Jewish purity laws before eating. Jesus, however, says that purity of one's hands is not what matters, but rather purity of one's heart.

Bible, Decoded

Breaking down scripture in plain language

Ophir – This was believed to be a name of one of the sons of Joktan from the book of Genesis, but in this case it refers to a place. King Solomon commissioned an expedition to Ophir, which is believed to have been in the area of modern India or Sri Lanka. They brought back large amounts of gold with them, which was made into special items, like jewelry for royalty.

Cassia – This was likely referring to the aromatic bark from evergreen trees located in far-east Asia. As such, its scent would have been very special and rare in Jerusalem, again reserved for royalty or other special people.

Holy Hill – Mount Sinai, where Moses received the Ten Commandments, and Mount Zion, where Solomon constructed the temple of Jerusalem. This was considered the holiest site in Jewish culture, as it was where God resided and where the arc of the covenant was housed.

Points to Ponder

First Thoughts

To the contemporary mind, all this talk of who is the greatest, highest, and who is included or worthy is quite a turn-off. It's a remarkable shift from the current desire to draw those who may or may not know what they believe or who have checkered pasts (or maybe even checkered presents) into our communities of faith. And based on Jesus's teachings here and elsewhere, such admiration and special status for those obsessed with religious legalism were missing the point he wanted them to get.

Conversely, we are to be careful in simply throwing out everything religion and our spiritual history presents us in exchange for just being a good person. Commandments can be good, when placed in their proper context. It's when they become the velvet rope test that keeps some on the outside, or makes us think that just checking off a list of rules is enough that we are at risk of straying from Jesus's desired path.

Song of Solomon is one of—if not *the*—most sexually oriented books in the Bible. Think a woman calling her man a stag is steamy? Wait till he tells her that her breasts are like towers! You're welcome for that visual.

Digging Deeper

Mining for what really matters . . . and gold

There are different reasons for various Jewish purity laws. The ritual *mikvah* bath was similar to our modern baptism ritual, symbolizing being washed clean of past sins and emerging from the waters refreshed and worthy once again of God's presence. Washing another's feet was an act of hospitality and humble service by those offering the washing. Others, like washing one's hands, avoiding pork, abstaining from certain cuts of meat, and slaughtering animals in specific ways, had more to do with basic sanitation and health.

However, human beings tend to turn these into a symbol of particular piety, a reason to feel superior to the great unwashed who don't know or do any better.

There is another purity law that specifically was meant to set people—namely women—apart. A practice known as *niddah* required women to leave their home and live in a tent or separate dwelling while menstruating. They were considered to be unclean and therefore should be set aside until they were fit to be with men again.

On the face of it, one might think Jesus was advocating being sloppy, or didn't care about their health. On the contrary, he says very clearly that the body is to be cared for like a temple. He sees, as he often does, the intent in the hearts of the pharisees and scribes behind their challenge. First of all, they would love nothing more than to trip him up on a technicality and have reason to turn him over to the authorities for willingly flouting Jewish law. But also, they like the idea of being special and set apart. They take great pride in their knowledge of the scriptures, their place in the religious and political hierarchy, and the sense that they are better than ordinary people.

But Jesus cuts to the heart of it, in a manner of speaking. After all, he notes in his usual subversive way, what good is it to have clean hands and external fineries that dazzle if the heart is contaminated with pride, self-righteousness, and ill intent? Like a truly vibrant temple, the façade is far less important than the spirit filling the dwelling from within.

Heads Up
Connecting the text to our world

Amy and I aren't big gamblers, but we do enjoy quick getaways to Las Vegas when we feel the need to be adult children for a weekend. Mostly we enjoy the food, spectacle, time together, and the shows. One thing that always has intrigued me about Vegas is the lengths to which places will go to make people feel special. Equally fascinating is how much people will pay to take part in the charade.

There are some clubs around town where you can get in for a reasonable cover charge (reasonable in Vegas terms, anyway), but then there are tiers of access for those who care to indulge. Out of a sort of morbid curiosity, I guess, I picked up the information about the velvet-rope amenities a particular club offered in its VIP section.

Whereas others either had to stand or wait for a chair at the bar or tables, the section behind the velvet rope offered couches. The package also came with a chiller containing a bottle of spirits that would normally go for about $40 in the store. You got a server who would come by a few times an hour and offer to sell you some little trinkets like a pair of champagne flutes. The section was placed in a highly visible spot from anywhere in the club, and was even put up on a slightly raised platform so everyone could walk by and wish they were you.

The cost for this privilege: $1,500. Oh, and you had to buy a minimum number of other drinks (at a premium) and a 20 percent tip was not included, though mandatory.

It's a curious—and often exploited—part of our social identity that lures us to pay out so much money, just to sit alone behind a red rope and drink the same stuff everyone else is drinking. If nothing else, it points to the value of feeling special and set apart, if only as a sort of game, and if only for a few hours.

Jesus recognizes this in us and responds in a typically radical way. Though being special, set apart, and more important than the rest, he realizes it's not what we need. In fact, if we consider his many words and deeds in this regard, it's the kind of thing he came to dismantle. When he wants to cross the Sea of Galilee to be with, and minister to, non-Jews, the disciples object. They want to remind him that they, the ones on this side of the water, are the special ones. We're chosen and particularly beloved! Scripture even says so.

Even among themselves, his faithful bicker about who will inherit particular positions of honor in heaven. Jesus's response, however, is that their desires are misdirected. Rather than elevating them above others and set apart, the gospel calls them down into the trenches, into the mud and mulch of the common people. It's there, he says, that people will truly find him and, perhaps once and for all, get it.

We don't follow a velvet-rope messiah.

Prayer for the Week

Help me remember that I don't need to be special to be loved, and that my place isn't set apart, but in the midst of messy, beloved community, like everyone else.

Popping Off

Art/music/video and other cool stuff that relate to the text

The Red Tent, by Anita Diamant (book, 1990)

Gandhi (movie, 1982)

Was Jesus a Jerk?

~~~~~~~~~~~~/\/\/\~~~~~~~~~

Lectionary Texts For

September 9, 2018 (Proper 18 (23) Sixteenth Sunday after Pentecost)

Texts in Brief

My dog ate my Bible!

FIRST READING

Proverbs 22:1–2, 8–9, 22–23

A piece of wisdom on the basis for generosity and mercy (especially toward the poor and marginalized'). The favor we gain in God's eyes, after all, is worth far more than any status or wealth to be attained on earth.

and

Isaiah 35:4–7a

The prophet offers a vision of hope, restoration, and of all wrongs being made right. This is an excerpt from a larger prophecy that follows on the heels of a portrayal of bleakness, despair, and absence from God.

PSALM
Psalm 125

This psalm compares those who are faithful to God to Mount Zion, a most holy site in the Jewish tradition. Faith in God means one will be protected and will be as immovable as the mountain itself. This is a message of particular appeal to a people who have been repeatedly displaced and without a home.

and

Psalm 146

A psalm espousing the many virtues of God as creator, protector, provider, and sustainer, beyond the bounds of mortal life. This is contrasted against the temporary authority of earthly leaders, whose power and status die with them.

SECOND READING
James 2:1–10 (11–13), 14–17

This passage questions where the faith lies of those who pander to the wealthy. Aside from questioning an apparent misplacement of adoration and respect that should be given to God instead, the author challenges their deference to the very people who oppress them. He notes that following the law in part is not enough, and that adherence to God's law is the key to their freedom. It ends with a reprimand also for those who are kind in word, but who do not follow through in deed.

GOSPEL

Mark 7:24–37

A non-Jewish woman seeks healing for her daughter from Jesus, as she is overcome by evil spirits. He rebuffs her, basically calling her a dog, to which she answers that even the lowly among them deserve mercy when they seek it. At this he concedes and heals her daughter. Then he goes to another town and encounters a deaf man with a speech impediment who he is also asked to heal. He does so in private, beseeching the handful who are present to tell no one. But they talk about it anyway, telling everyone about his miraculous work.

Bible, Decoded

Breaking down scripture in plain language

Tyre – A city in what is now Lebanon, mentioned many times by the prophets and other texts in the Hebrew Bible. King Hiram of Tyre ruled around the same time as Solomon and David. The prophets predicted the city's destruction primarily because its inhabitants were seen as godless and beyond redemption.

Syrophoenician – This was a term used to refer to people from the area between the cities of Tyre and Sidon. It was primarily a Greek territory, but the word derives from Syrian and Phoenician, meaning someone who likely was of mixed descent.

Dog – The original word Jesus uses, usually translated as "dog," is *kuon*, which means "wild cur." So in using this word, he is calling her a mongrel, and he is referring to her afflicted daughter as such too. This was apparently a term used frequently at the time by Jews for those considered to be absent of God's spirit. Such an address would have been socially acceptable in the place and time where Jesus was, as those who were not Jewish were considered to be unclean and less than. It would not have sounded any more shocking to his peers than a white person using the N-word sixty years ago in the U.S.

Points to Ponder

First Thoughts

Psalm 146 is particularly interesting with its focus on directing our faith away from princes and toward God, especially since so many of the psalms are written by David, arguably the most well-known king figure in the Bible.

Some who want to keep from seeing Jesus's response as unpleasant or even cruel suggest that the root word he used in referring to the woman actually means "puppy," as if it was a term of endearment. But personally I've never met a woman who finds being called any iteration of dog to be endearing. It's also been suggested that this is just a test of faith for the woman, and that Jesus didn't really mean it. We'll address the implications of this below.

Digging Deeper

Mining for what really matters . . . and gold

This text in Mark is both one of the most interesting and challenging in the Gospels, particularly because it presses us to decide which Jesus we see in this story. The two most obvious options to choose from is one where Jesus sets the woman up for a test of faith, contrasted with another where Jesus refuses a woman her request (at first), even casting an insult toward her and her ailing child.

Growing up, the argument I heard was the former; Jesus wanted to make sure she really, really wanted it and would not easily give up on her request before granting it. And while there is evidence that Jesus may have challenged people from time to time to discern whether their conviction matched their words, this perspective is problematic, for more than one reason.

First, we have to keep in mind that Mark is believed to be the oldest and, therefore, first of the Gospels. And though Jesus may have tested people elsewhere, there is no other evidence of him doing this anywhere else in Mark. In addition, the author makes a point of noting that Jesus is far from home, meaning he has traveled a long way and likely is road weary. He may also be suffering from what we call compassion fatigue today.

Sometimes even the biggest hearts among us need a break and feel drained by the apparently endless needs around us. And while Jesus was more than human in our traditional understanding, he also was, as is asserted more than once, entirely human at the same time. We see him get short-tempered and even lash out at times. We even see other times when he seeks to withdraw from the crowds, or even from his own inner circle.

However, it's the only instance on record when he both refuses someone the help they ask for and calls them a name. And further, it's the only time when he insults a child, in this case one who is suffering.

Ouch.

So maybe he is road-weary, compassion-fatigued and, in a moment of complete humanity, he succumbs to the reaction nearly anyone from his culture would have had toward the woman. The difference, however, is that he catches himself upon her insistence and makes it right. In a way, it's not dissimilar from examples throughout scripture when God changes God's mind. Time and again, when it happens, it's to fall on the side of mercy.

Perhaps as compelling—or even more so—is our resistance to allowing Jesus even one moment of human fallibility. It seems to be beyond the scope of some of our Christian imaginations to continue to have faith in a messiah who occasionally is wrong, or who makes mistakes. But if he never was wrong or never screwed up, it seems like there would be a huge part of human nature missing from this messiah who was supposed to be entirely human.

Heads Up
Connecting the text to our world

All parents use moments when their kids fall short of expectation as an opportunity for learning and growth from time to time. But every once in a while it's the parents who become the object lesson. This was one of those times.

My son got five bucks from his uncle Joe back when he was a kindergartner for being irresistibly sweet and cute. I offered to carry it for him and he let me for a bit before asking for it back. We talked about responsibility and how, once some things are gone, that's it. In other words, there's no insurance for negligence.

That night after I read him a bedtime story, he asked for his money, to which I responded that I had already given it to him. I proved it by reaching into my pocket and coming out empty-handed. His look of indignation grew almost instantly as he snapped that, yes, I *did* have his money, and if it wasn't there anymore, it's because I had lost it. I reminded him of when he asked me to give it back, but he was dead-set. I had the money and he wanted it, period.

After some de-escalation, he regained his emotional center, smiling at me through his subsiding tears. "Dad," he said, "I forgive you."

I thanked him, but asked if he really knew what forgiveness was. He said he wasn't sure, so I explained it's when someone does something wrong, but you don't stay angry at them. "Okay then," he smiled. "I forgive you."

He offered me a hug, and of course I was not going to refuse. And even if it is a little misguided, who am I to shoot a kid down for trying to extend a little grace?

Later when I was getting ready for bed, I was emptying my pockets and felt something tucked in a crease inside. Out came the five. My shame was crushing. The next day, I explained what happened to him, and he smiled and hugged me again. "Dad, I forgive you again." I kept waiting for a rooster to crow after this third act of mercy, but no luck. "But," he said, pulling back and looking me in the eye, "we will not forget this. Every Christmas as long as we live, you will remember this."

It's not Christmas, but he's right. Sometimes it takes someone else's worst to bring out another person's best.

I certainly never meant to hurt him or mislead him, but he taught me something far more valuable than whatever he ended up buying with that five dollars, now forever immortalized in our family as a symbol that, sometimes, kids teach parents a thing or two.

Prayer for the Week

I'm so human sometimes and I even disappoint myself. God, help me always to err on the side of mercy and compassion, even when I don't really feel like it.

Popping Off

Art/music/video and other cool stuff that relate to the text

Process Theology: An Introductory Exposition, by John Cobb and David Ray Griffin (book, 1996)

A Christmas Carol (movie, 1984)

All You Can Tweet

Lectionary Texts For
September 16, 2018 (Proper 19 (24) Seventeenth Sunday after Pentecost)

Texts in Brief
My dog ate my Bible!

First Reading
Proverbs 1:20–33

Wisdom calls out to its audience to take heed and receive her, not just when disaster and crisis strike, but because it is a matter of choice. If we only seek wisdom when we're already in trouble, we won't find it. Instead it has to be internalized as a regular practice so that we can avoid getting into such crises that foolishness and carelessness lead us into in the first place.

and

Isaiah 50:4–9a

The prophet Isaiah considers his ability to convey wisdom and knowledge to be a gift from God. Even when he was persecuted for the things he taught, he remained faithful in honoring this gift, as he was sure that God could make things right in the end. And, he asks, if God is on his side, how can such persecution ultimately stand?

PSALM

Psalm 19

Creation itself is a testament to God's incredible work, speaking of God's power and beauty without words. God's wisdom, which permeates all of creation, is available to all, and is to be treasured more than any material possession. Such wisdom helps keep us on a God-inspired path, which then informs our daily words and deeds.

and

Psalm 116:1–9

A prayer reaching out to God in longing to be saved from the death-dealing ways of the world that lead to suffering. It is a call for help, but also a gesture of gratitude for God's mercy on all who seek it.

SECOND READING

James 3:1–12

A word of caution to those who teach others because, although we all make mistakes, it's those who misdirect others who will be held to greater account because they take on the responsibility for others in teaching them. It goes on to elaborate on the power and potential dangers of reckless speech, as it is one of the few "untamed" things in our world that we can't seem to control. Just as any tainted source can't yield good fruit, evil speech doesn't lead to anything good.

GOSPEL
Mark 8:27–38

Jesus asks his disciples who others say he is, and they respond that people see him as a prophet or others described in scriptures. He asks them who they think he is, and they affirm him as the "chosen one." He orders them not to tell others this. Then he foretells of the path he is on and where it leads in the end. Finally, he says plainly that following him will result in a similar fate for them, but asks what good it would do just to save their skin if the price is giving up their principles and what they say they really hold as important.

Bible, Decoded
Breaking down scripture in plain language

Set my face like flint – To take on a countenance of fierce determination, as flint is a hard stone, in earlier times used for making knives, arrowheads, and spearheads.

Brackish water – A term for water that has been contaminated, particularly by salt. It's not referring specifically to seawater, but rather otherwise fresh water that has mixed with salt water (maybe at the mouth of a river or the like) to the point that it is not suitable for drinking or irrigation.

Get behind me, Satan – On the surface, it's easy to assume Jesus is calling Peter the devil here, but that's not really the case. If we look at the root of the word, *satan* is Hebrew for "adversary, obstruction, or opponent." And in the context of the previous text this week, which suggests that evil works through the foolishness of people, it's also possible that Jesus is speaking more to the evil he sees behind Peter's words, well intended as they likely were.

Points to Ponder

First Thoughts

These passages as a collection remind me of the old saying, "idle hands are the devil's playground," except in this case the playground would be the tongues of fools.

In the Gospel text, all it tells us is that Peter rebukes Jesus. But given their exchange, especially after what Jesus just told the disciples, it's fair to assume that Peter was trying to talk Jesus out of taking this path to inevitable martyrdom. We know that he loved Jesus, so he was probably concerned for his well-being, but he could also have not been able to see past the importance his own feelings or limited understanding, especially as they pertained to the fulfillment of scripture for the prophesied messiah. Maybe he tried to convince Jesus to run away, or that he could do far more alive than he could as a dead man. In either case, Peter's shortfall was one either of well-meaning concern or a lack of broader vision.

Digging Deeper

Mining for what really matters . . . and gold

Though the one overarching theme in these passages is fairly straightforward, adding the passage from Mark enriches the perspectives we can take on this a great deal, while also letting us witness the simplicity or foolishness described in the other scriptures play out.

With Mark, we can get a look at events past, present, and future. We see that Jesus really believes this messiah stuff, and as such, he understands why the early prophets predicted what they did for him. Even when we push back against this idea that Jesus had to die in order to achieve human salvation in God's eyes, he saw as clearly as the prophets that someone preaching the things he was offering to his people was such an interrupt to the status quo and the powers-that-be, that they would seek to destroy it.

We also see an example of what is called the Messianic Secret, which we see a few times in Mark. This is when Jesus tells his disciples and other witnesses not to try to convince people of who he is, but rather to allow them to see it for themselves, and to arrive at their own conclusion about him as messiah. And if recent events serve as any precedent, we know they won't listen.

Jumping back to the first chapter of Mark, Peter's urging Jesus not to go through with the culmination of his ministry at the cross is eerily reminiscent of when Jesus was tempted in the desert. Now as then, no one would have blamed Jesus for deciding to take the deal and not choose the hard road. In fact, they would likely welcome it as Peter would, keeping him there among them, perhaps eventually convincing him to become the king they wanted. And it's not as if God treats faithful kings so badly—I'd trade Jesus's situation for that of Solomon or David any day.

Consider Peter (again, poor guy), who denies Jesus at his moment of greatest personal danger, opting for the self-saving route he wanted Jesus to take as well. And yes, he survives the moment, but we have to wonder if, when the rooster crowed after his third denial, Jesus's words that day echoed in his head, over and again. . . .

For what will it profit them to gain the whole world and forfeit their life?

It doesn't mean that, because of his foolishness, God will forever turn away from Peter. On the contrary, Jesus promises to build the future of the church on him. I suppose, then, we shouldn't be surprised when organized religion acts much as Peter did, and as he wants to do, sacrificing so much of what it claims to hold sacred to live another day.

But the weight of such choices is haunting and heavy. Jesus, on the other hand, resolves to live in the lightness of an unburdened soul, even if it means his days will be numbered fewer. It's the age-old quality-versus-quantity debate. But the wise choice often is made contrary to impulse and desires at hand. It requires seeing beyond the impulse to the deliverance on the other side of it.

Truth illuminates the path of wisdom, but does not force us to walk along it.

Heads Up

Connecting the text to our world

There are four words in our contemporary culture that may as well be those of Satan. You know them well, and they may even have tempted you with their seductiveness, emblazoned before you, beckoning like a temptress, promising a beautiful destruction:

ALL YOU CAN EAT

So maybe I'm being a little bit hyperbolic to make a point, but hey, if Jesus can do it, why not me, right?

All blasphemous humor aside, we do live in an all-you-can-eat reality today. Pay a flat rate and fill ourselves until our eyes bulge and our waistband yelps for mercy. We can buy an entire meal through a window for less than five bucks, and the giant vat of popcorn at the theater comes, of course, with endless refills. Because, you know, who can really stop at one cubic foot of snacks?

We're emerging into an equally impulsive all-you-can-tweet reality. As communication has been liberated from otherwise confining media, we have become increasingly cavalier with the content itself.

But reckless consumption—be it of food, alcohol, or other commodities—can have as much damage on ourselves as reckless words can have toward others. Then we witness an increasing ideological schism among us, along with spikes in hate speech and the crimes that accompany them. Opinions and facts are conflated, and the slow, careful discipline of wisdom gives way to the immediacy of seemingly infinite information, fact-based or not.

When the moments of decision face us, the burden is on us to look back at past experience and learning and, at the same time, look ahead to the implications of the present decision before it's made. The result may be a less satisfying result in the immediate term, but it's the only way to keep moving forward in life, rather than living in circles.

Prayer for the Week

Sometimes, God, my mouth gets ahead of my better judgment. Help me have the self-control to look backward and forward, rather than just at what's in front of me.

Popping Off

Art/music/video and other cool stuff that relate to the text

Sliding Doors (movie, 1998)

My Dinner with Andre (movie, 1991)

Worst Job Descriptions Ever

Lectionary Texts For
September 23, 2018 (Proper 20 (25) Eighteenth Sunday after Pentecost)

Texts in Brief
My dog ate my Bible!

First Reading
Proverbs 31:10–31

The text offers an extensive list of attributes one should look for in a wife. They should have physical strength for diligent work in the fields, they will wake up to find food and cook before dawn, and they will work after sunset. They will be tireless in providing for their family, while also producing fineries to sell. They are honest, wise, and kind, and merit their children's respect and husband's praise. Beauty and charm are not as important, it concludes.

and

Jeremiah 11:18–20

The prophet learns from God of a plot to kill him, apparently because his speeches against the corruption of the government and its people are considered treasonous. He claims to be blameless, though accusations are made against him because he is God's servant. He then asks God to exact vengeance on those who seek to do him harm.

PSALM

Psalm 1

The book of Psalms opens with a word of advice, noting that we don't find happiness in taking advice from those who are evil, but rather in living by God's laws. While the righteous will stand firm and flourish like bountiful trees, the wicked will die and be blown away by the wind.

and

Psalm 54

David is under threats against his life from his enemies. He calls on God both to protect him and also to strike down those who oppose him and wish him harm. He offers a sacrifice for this request, remembering that God has helped him emerge in victory over his opponents before.

Second Reading

James 3:13–4:3, 7–8a

The author stakes a claim that those who are pure of heart should live a life that expresses as much outwardly. He warns against bragging that we are good when we know better, and not to be proud in claiming wisdom about earthly ways. Rather, we should be intent on gaining wisdom from the divine, which yields a disposition of gentleness, kindness, and honesty. He wisely points out that the root of much of our inner and interpersonal conflict emerges from desire and is motivated by selfishness, rather than by a desire to obey God.

Gospel

Mark 9:30–37

Jesus continues to try and explain his role in the fulfillment of the prophecies about the Messiah, but they are still not getting it. Meanwhile as they travel together, the disciples argue about who is best and most favored among them, to which Jesus responds that they have it backwards. They should seek to overcome their desires and egos, and seek only to serve God and neighbor.

Bible, Decoded

Breaking down scripture in plain language

Distaff/spindle – Tools used together for spinning raw fibers (often flax) into yarn for knitting or weaving.

Chaff – Generally, chaff refers to the husks on corn or other grain that are light and scatter in the wind. It can also refer to dried, cut grass used as hay for animals, or anything considered to be worthless or garbage.

Points to Ponder
First Thoughts

To all the male pastors surely eager to tackle that Proverbs text this week from the pulpit, good luck. Oh, and learn to duck really fast.

We can start to see why Jeremiah is known as the Weeping Prophet. He is a man of great passion, faith, and conviction, and certainly doesn't shy away from confrontation. But it does seem to take an emotional toll on him quite often.

Though the principles in these passages are firmly at the heart of the Jewish and Christian traditions, they also resonate closely with the notions in Buddhism that the root of human suffering is desire, and that true enlightenment can only be achieved once we are able to overcome—even destroy—our egos.

Digging Deeper
Mining for what really matters . . . and gold

I suggest we look at several of these texts as responses. I think it will help us consider them differently.

Jeremiah learns of plans to kill him, at least by citizens, but likely in coordination with the government of his own land. His sermons are tantamount to treason, and he's starting to feel the full weight of his responsibility press down on him.

Though his followers still haven't wrapped their hearts and minds around it, Jesus has accepted his calling as the Son of Man, and given how well he knows the Torah and the prophets, he sees what's ahead as he continues forward to his ministry's grim conclusion. David certainly had his moments of glory, wealth, and fame, but there comes a moment that he knows if he didn't have the walls of Jerusalem to protect him, even from his own people, he'd be a dead man.

And the women described in the Proverbs text get about as much say as most women get in the Bible.

It reframes our entire perspective of ourselves when we commit to a life of unglamorous labor, conflict, and even personal danger. It can profoundly affect how we live when faced so imminently with the prospect of death. Joy becomes precious to the point of sacredness when all that seems good is stripped away from us.

The recipe is right there, in the words. We have to die to our desires, to the illusions that our achievements and titles matter, and to the breathless pursuit of empty ambitions. Only once these die to us first can we see clearly the kind of life that Jesus talks about, and the life to which God invites us.

Want to live? First you have to die.

Heads Up

Connecting the text to our world

Write up any of the calls in these texts as job descriptions and see which one you want:

Seeking woman to work eighteen to twenty hours a day. Needs to make clothes, clean clothes, care for children, grow food, prepare food, and provide sufficient crafts to sell at market for extra income. Pay (offered in the form of praise) is according to how few hours of sleep she is willing to live on.

Wanted: King to reconcile twelve splintered, and often warring, tribal factions. Must be a natural-born slingshot assassin, world traveler, reconciler, warrior, and poet, willing to dance naked in public. Remuneration guaranteed to be in the form of death threats and widespread disdain.

Needed: Prophet to go from town to town to tell people how much they suck and how they're all going to die unless they shape up. Must weep and gnash teeth convincingly. Uniform of sackcloth and ashes provided. Must be willing to deal with regular assassination attempts.

Want to move up? Get low! Come be a part of a winning team that wins by losing, rules through service, and must be comfortable working with IRS auditors, lepers, and prostitutes. Full vesting in beheading program after three years, guaranteed.

I didn't think so.

God's call often stands in direct opposition to what the world says we should want and work for. The values are completely up-ended. This is why people like Jeremiah, Jesus, and sometimes David get the stink eye from so many detractors, and sometimes even from their closest allies. Their ideas are challenging, their ways are hard, and the promises are doubtful.

Let's just say there's not exactly a 401(k) plan involved.

Like it or not, what's right and what's convenient, pleasurable, or rewarding (at least on the surface) often don't get along. This isn't to say that our faithfulness to God is measured by how miserable we are. But money, fame, and status are fleeting, snatched from us like chaff, blown away with the slightest breeze. And yet, we put so much of our lives into sustaining these illusions.

I think it's because, as hard as it may be, the prospect of going all-in with what God desires scares the hell out of us.

I know it scares me. I test the waters from time to time: I give enough to charity to keep the guilt of my privilege at arm's length, and I try to use my gifts for good (while also being more than happy to take a paycheck with it). The call isn't glamorous and, if we're recognized at all for it, chances are good that people will hate that we stand for something other than what they want to believe is important.

We don't all have to be martyrs or fire-breathing prophets. But there's a theme in these jobs for a reason: because even though it's been God's invitation for thousands of years, we still work actively a lot of the time at not getting it or, at the very least, not living it out. And yet the invitation continues, never insisting but always beckoning.

Prayer for the Week

God, my ego and desire to satisfy my desires first, then serve later are strong. Help me get past them and do real servant's work.

Popping Off

Art/music/video and other cool stuff that relate to the text

Worst Jobs in History (TV series, 2004–)

Dirty Jobs (TV series, 2005–2012)

Civil Disobedience, by Henry David Thoreau (essay/ book, 1849)

Do the Right Thing

—/\/\—

Lectionary Texts For

September 30, 2018 (Proper 21 (26) Nineteenth Sunday after Pentecost)

Texts in Brief

My dog ate my Bible!

First Reading

Esther 7:1–6, 9–10; 9:20–22

Esther, queen of Persia (who also is Jewish and orphaned) is offered a wish by her husband, King Ahasuerus. She asks for her life and that of her Jewish people to be spared from Haman, the king's "vice president," who has a plot to kill her and the rest of the Jews. So the king put Haman to death and sent word to the Jews that they were no longer under threat and should recognize this day going forward.

and

Numbers 11:4–6, 10–16, 24–29

The Israelites, in the desert with Moses, weep over having no meat to eat after so much time and petition Moses to help them. He protests to God to either help him not bear the load of their suffering alone, or to let him die. So God fills other leaders in the camp with a prophetic spirit to help Moses in his leadership.

Psalm

Psalm 124

A corporate prayer for the people to remind them that, had God not been on their side, their enemies would have long since killed them all.

and

Psalm 19:7–14

The psalm reminds its audience that God and God's laws are perfect and good, and that respect for them and for God leads us to a good life. The psalm ends by praying on the people's behalf that they might hold fast to the virtues that God desires for them.

Second Reading

James 5:13–20

All things warrant prayer, both good and bad. In addition, the author compels listeners to be bound together in community by prayer for one another, and in seeking what is best for the other and for the group as a whole. It holds up the value of mutual accountability to each other, and not letting someone fall away from the path of virtue and right living.

Gospel
Mark 9:38–50

The disciples told Jesus that they saw someone casting out demons in his name who wasn't a part of their group. But Jesus says they should leave him to his mission, so long as it is done in his name. The group they hang out with is not as important as the spirit in which they conduct themselves. In fact, he offers them a grave warning if they try to stop anyone from acting in his name; he names it as a terrible sin. He ends with his hyperbolic example of removing any part of the body that causes us to stumble.

Bible, Decoded
Breaking down scripture in plain language

Haman – The primary antagonist in the Book of Esther, he is effectively the vice president to King Ahasuerus, who also is known historically as Xerxes I. Haman has a plot to kill the Jewish people, but after Queen Esther reveals his plot, the king has Haman put to death.

Esther – Born Jewish, she was married to the Persian king during his rule of formerly Babylonian territory. Because she is said to have revealed the plot to have her fellow Jews killed, she is considered a hero, and is at the center of the story commemorated by the Jewish holiday, Purim.

Salt – Salt is referenced many times throughout scripture, particularly by Jesus. It is considered to be an essential ingredient in food, used as a preservative, and also to disinfect wounds. In this passage in Mark, it is alluded to as an important ingredient in community and relationships, representing covenant, goodwill, and compassion.

Points to Ponder
First Thoughts
Fun fact #1 – I named a principal antagonist in my *Blood Doctrine* novel series after Haman, the main "bad guy" in Esther.

Fun fact #2 – Also, Esther is the only book in the Bible that does not explicitly mention God.

Fun fact #3 – The Jewish festival of Purim is the religious holiday observed to remember when King Ahasuerus spared Esther's and the other Jews' lives from Haman's plot to kill them.

Digging Deeper
Mining for what really matters . . . and gold
Let's hold three words or phrases in tension together: deliverance, intercession, and redemptive violence. First, deliverance.

The story of the Jewish people, throughout scripture, is one of exile, occupation, and bloodshed. Those under any illusion that being among God's chosen equals a life of privilege and comfort only need to look anywhere from Exodus to Revelation for evidence to the contrary. And yet, time and again, God offers deliverance, sometimes in rather unexpected ways.

First, God delivers them out of the hands of Egyptian rule and into the desert. From there, they are delivered to the promised land after four decades in exile. What follows is a series of occupations by everyone from the Persians to Babylon and Rome. Clearly, their road is not easy. But God does respond, if not in the time they always prefer, delivering them from their oppressors.

In the stories here in Esther and again in Numbers, we see leaders interceding on behalf of their people to ask God to deliver them. These are selfless acts, though there is at least some awareness, it seems, that help for the whole also benefits the self in some ways. Esther asks for her fellow Jews to be spared from Haman; Moses files a grievance with God to help give him a way to share the burden of leadership. David prays for those under his rule on their behalf; James exhorts all to pray for each other in their community, and finally; others outside of the tight-knit group of disciples perform acts of healing and exorcism in Jesus's name.

The disciples seem to think they know the right and wrong way to do this, though they are reprimanded for their particular thinking by Jesus, who says that anyone doing for others in his name are duly blessed in their efforts, no matter who they are. Esther asks her husband, the king, to deal with Haman, who ends up being hanged. Though later Jesus would push back against this ancient notion that violence against some leads to peace for others, the themes of intercession and deliverance remain consistent, be it from the threat of death, hunger, or illness.

This does lend support for the notion of the necessity of intercessory prayer. Though we're told elsewhere in scripture that we can go straight to God with our needs and grievances, we often opt instead for an appointed representative to take our needs to God for us. Jesus's lesson to the disciples suggests just the opposite, and yet, we don't see an every-person-for-themselves attitude about prayer or actions either.

Consider Jesus's response when asked how we should pray, which I think we can safely assume also informs how we should act from day to day. Notice in the Lord's prayer that there is no mention of the self in first person anywhere: only you and we/us. Perhaps my favorite phrase offered by Jesus—one from which we should take great wisdom—comes when he is faced with sacrificing all he has. Just before his crucifixion he does ask if perhaps he can skip the whole torture-and-death thing, but concludes with respectful, humble deference:

Not my will, but Thine be done.

Heads Up

Connecting the text to our world

I'm not much of a prayer guy. I prefer quiet meditation and contemplative silence without words, which I guess could be considered prayer, though not in the traditional sense. So when my wife Amy told me our church in Colorado was going to spend the entire summer in small prayer groups together, I got a knot in my stomach.

My solution: create a group for the "prayer-averse" among us. Turns out there were a good number of folks like me who bristled at the idea of praying aloud, especially in front of other people. So while some groups gathered and spent more than an hour in tag-team prayer, we talked, shared a drink, and visualized our prayers in silence together.

I came to realize over the weeks that *how* we prayed in terms of the words we did or didn't use, or even whether we were sure what we believed, had been baptized or joined the church, was the intention behind our time and our acts. We were listening more deeply to each other, our stories, joys, struggles, and values. And though we were given a sort of thematic framework to work within, there wasn't a right or wrong way to be together.

The most explicit part was how we were to spend the last fifteen minutes or so of each session. Again, we didn't have to pray aloud, speak in tongues, or whatever, though it wasn't discouraged either. Most important was that we addressed several levels of intention: to pray for each other individually and as a group, to pray for the church, to pray for our community, our nation, and our world.

The one notable absence, which was very intentional, was to "pray for yourself." Why, after all, bother with such a selfish orientation when so many others are holding your heart before God for you? It was both unfamiliar and comforting at the same time, and it took some time to get used to. But it got easier over time, and we noticed a distinct shift in the spirit of the church family after the summer was over. So we did it all again the next summer, and the one after that. After a few years, people couldn't wait for the small groups to rejoin, continuing various iterations of the groups year-round.

And that was when we knew the church was working. It doesn't mean all the leaks in the roof and toilets were stopped, or that we never had disagreements again. But through it all we had a mutual love that surpassed the sum total of our struggles and differences, which meant all the hard stuff was worth it.

Prayer for the Week

Give us this day our daily bread, and deliver us from evil.

Popping Off

Art/music/video and other cool stuff that relate to the text

Seven Pounds (movie, 2008)

Schindler's List (movie, 1993)

The Giving Tree, by Shel Silverstein (book, 1964)

Walking Dust

Lectionary Texts For

October 7, 2018 (Proper 22 (27) Twentieth Sunday after Pentecost)

Texts in Brief

My dog ate my Bible!

FIRST READING

Job 1:1, 2:1–10

God remarks on Job's faithfulness regardless of his circumstances to satan, who scoffs at the idea. He says if Job is put through enough he'll turn on God like all others would. So God lets satan infest him with sores. Job's wife entreats him to reject God and accept death, to which Job says we have to take what comes to us under God, both good and bad.

and

Genesis 2:18–24

God decides Adam shouldn't be alone, so animals are created to keep him company. Then God creates Eve from Adam's rib and intends them to join together as if they were one body.

PSALM

Psalm 26

King David asks for God's protection, grace, and vindication since he has remained faithful to God at all times. While some have fallen away, he has remained faithful, and as such, should gain God's favor.

and

Psalm 8

A song of praise not just because God has given human beings life, but because they are the most beloved among all creatures, given dominion over all else on earth.

SECOND READING

Hebrews 1:1–4, 2:5–12

Jesus is held up as the source through which all creation comes and from whom we can see the manifestation of what God's glory is like. This shift in status of Jesus from being placed among other humans "just below the angels" to being at God's right hand above the angels after death is an allusion to both the intermingling of his humanity and divinity, as well as the importance of God to express grace in a form understandable to humanity, in the life, suffering, acts of mercy, and death of Jesus.

GOSPEL
Mark 10:2–16

First the Pharisees, and then the disciples, ask Jesus about divorce, which is allowed under Jewish law in certain circumstances. To the Pharisees, Jesus cites the Genesis text in which God intends man and woman to be one flesh and not to be separated. To his disciples, he is more direct, saying that to divorce and remarry is adultery. Then when parents show up with their children to be touched by Jesus and the disciples shoo them away, Jesus calls them out. He suggests that the innocence of a child is necessary to get it, after which he blesses the children brought to him.

Bible, Decoded
Breaking down scripture in plain language

Potsherd – A fragment of pottery, which presumably would have a sharp edge. It might also be used explicitly to imply the brokenness of Job's spirit, though not of his faithfulness.

Ashes – Another symbol used to indicate Job feels used up, worthless, perhaps even abandoned or, at the least, neglected by God. This and the potsherd represent hopelessness.

Satan – In Hebrew the word *satan* means "adversary," or "prosecutor." So the character of satan here is acting almost like a plaintiff in a trial. At this point in scripture, satan is not seen as some lord of the underworld who claims souls of the unrighteous to torture for eternity.

One flesh – The idea of this speaks to the sacredness of the union between two people in covenant together. They are to be joined on all levels, not only physically/sexually, but spiritually, emotionally, intellectually, financially, and with respect to mutual property.

Points to Ponder

First Thoughts

If we take the story of Job at face value, consider what it says about God. Not only is God somewhat petty in feeling the need to sort of make a wager with satan; God also allows satan to subject Job to all manner of horrible things, despite not having warranted it, simply as a test. This seems unreasonably cruel unless we consider it from a less literal place like, why bad stuff happens to us sometimes even when we're good.

Digging Deeper

Mining for what really matters . . . and gold

Sometimes the best way to understand ourselves is to understand the language we develop to frame, understand, and communicate our experience of life. Consider the word *human*. Though the etymology of the word just means person, it also is a close cousin to the word *humus*, which means dirt. Put another way, as my wife Amy explained to our eight-year-old daughter Zoe when her fish died recently, we are all stardust. We come from it and ultimately return to union with the stuff of stars.

Also, think about the words *Adam* and *Eve*. Translated from their root meanings, these mean "person" and "life," much the same as "human being," or "animated dirt" to put it less poetically. But to consider ourselves as walking dust bunnies feels diminishing somehow, even denigrating. I'm not saying we aren't any more than that, but for me, starting there offers a healthy, sometimes necessary, dose of humility.

Interestingly too, if we dig into the original language of the Genesis text, Adam is not differentiated as a man until woman is formed. After all, what point is gender if there is no other? And while this opposite is good in God's eyes, it's also when the trouble starts. In some more traditional interpretations, we get the sense that the fall of humanity in the garden is woman's fault, which has fed into much patriarchal sexism.

But the problem of humanity actually preceded the encounter between Eve and the serpent. The true Original Sin was recognizing difference, and therefore, developing the concept of "other-ness."

Philosophy teaches that suffering comes from the notion of "I and thou," in recognizing the separation, differentiation, and therefore the opportunity to compare, to order, rank, and be better than. It's a sort of paradox, because we long both for deep connection, to the point that we are one flesh, while also wanting to differentiate ourselves from others and from the rest of creation. We seek both union and transcendence. But the two aren't easily reconciled.

Fast forward to Jesus's chiding of the disciples for having a "how dare they" attitude toward the outsiders performing miracles in his name. Jesus understands, more profoundly than the others, that we want both this perfect union but also differentiation and superiority, but knows we can't have both. So at the heart of the gospel we find the path to work through that most difficult choice.

What Jesus wants for us, for them, for all, is what we really need. What it requires—which is the part we resist—is giving up on the idea of what we think we really want.

Heads Up
Connecting the text to our world

One of my favorite authors is Oliver Sacks. He's best known for writing the book *Awakenings* about his work with Alzheimer's (he was a neurologist and psychiatrist), but he's done lots of fascinating work with people who experience pretty unique cognitive and neurological phenomena. One story he told about a patient with long-term memory loss was particularly chilling to me, for whatever reason. This person lived entirely in the present since she couldn't remember anything from more than a minute before, but Sacks's observation and the way he described it was what really struck me.

Sacks said it was as if someone had "scooped out her soul." She was just sort of this Skinner Box of an organism, responding to her outside environment from one isolated moment to another, but she was trapped in that present. She couldn't form any lasting relationships. She couldn't experience love. She had no sense of being herself because she had no point of reference in relation to the rest of the world to give her a sense of who we are.

Just imagining that sensation was what terrified me. We talk of this idea of a soul, and many consider it to be something personal and uniquely human. But the soul is void of purpose without the capacity to know love. There is no self without connection to others. Without love and connection we are animated corpses, walking dead, soulless zombies.

Or maybe she's perfectly at peace. After all, she has no anxieties about what comes next, and no recollection of past pain or resentments. She just . . . is.

Jesus doesn't ask us to abandon all sense of self and difference. He doesn't pull the Stephen Colbert "I don't see color" act, nor does he want us to be blind to what makes us distinct or special. What he does require of us is not to let that awareness become the definition of our worth, or that of others. When distinctions lead to value judgments or keep us from working toward reconciliation or living into radical compassion, then it's problematic.

We're entreated to love ourselves. We're just not allowed to stop there.

Prayer for the Week

Help me remember that getting what I need and getting what I want aren't always the same thing, and help me let go of my wants.

Popping Off

Art/music/video and other cool stuff that relate to the text

When Bad Things Happen to Good People, by Harold Kushner (book, 2004)

"You Can't Always Get What You Want," by the Rolling Stones (song, 1969)

Life without "What If?"

Lectionary Texts For
October 14, 2018 (Proper 23 (28) Twenty-first Sunday after Pentecost)

Texts in Brief
My dog ate my Bible!

FIRST READING
Job 23:1–9, 16–17

Job has undergone tremendous hardships, to the point that he feels God has abandoned him. He longs to grieve to God for his suffering, and to petition for mercy, but feels God isn't there. Without the chance to have God hear him, the only alternative he sees for himself is to disappear and become nothing. Yet he does not curse or abandon his search for God.

and

Amos 5:6–7, 10–15

The prophet speaks of the dangers of people turning away from God and the harmful acts that inevitably follow. Aside from the damage they do in their godless acts, he warns of the punishment God will levy against them for it.

PSALM
Psalm 22:1–15

This psalm of despair holds the words famously believed to have been said by Jesus, just before his death: "My God, my God, why have you forsaken me?" The psalmist attributes the many hardships in his life to being abandoned by God. In this case, David fears the many threats from enemies on all sides that he worries will destroy him and all he has built.

and

Psalm 90:12–17

A petition to God on behalf of Moses for his people, who have been struggling through their decades of wandering in the wilderness. In last week's text, Moses sought support from God to get help from other leaders, and now, he seeks direct results from the people's efforts so they can see that God is still with them.

SECOND READING
Hebrews 4:12–16

God's word is piercing in its discernment of truth, cutting through a façade of actions or words to the heart of a person's true desires and intent. God, through Jesus's own human experience, deeply understands our own frailties, and yet doesn't buy excuses for missing the mark of what we're to be.

Gospel
Mark 10:17–31

A rich man calls Jesus "good teacher," which he rejects, because he says the only goodness is from God. The man goes on to ask how to inherit heaven's kingdom, to which Jesus responds that he should keep the commandments. After he says he has since childhood, Jesus recognizes what is really holding the man back: his wealth. So Jesus tells him to let go of it all and follow him, which the man can't do.

Bible, Decoded
Breaking down scripture in plain language

Bashan – A large territory where King Og stood against the Israelites as they entered the promised land, but was beaten. It was a vast region with rich natural resources, including the still-contested Golan Heights. Under Solomon's rule, the territory was broken up into four sub-regions to decrease its threat against his kingdom. But it was an area of ongoing contention and unrest adjacent to and, at times, within David's and Solomon's kingdoms.

Good Teacher – The exchange around the rich man addressing Jesus this way can be interpreted a couple of ways. From one perspective, we can see Jesus as simply demonstrating humility and deference to God.

From another view, maybe he is pressing the man to see how he really sees him. Maybe he's discerning whether the man thinks Jesus is simply a wise teacher, or does he see more?

Wormwood – A lot of biblical scholars look at the use of wormwood in scripture as a symbol of the evil or darkness prevailing on earth. Known for its bitterness, it was often an outward symbol of human bitterness or darkness of heart.

Points to Ponder
First Thoughts

Interestingly, Psalm 90 is believed to be the only psalm attributed to Moses.

Can't honestly say this series of texts presents a compelling sales pitch for those trying to get more people to become Christians. "Hey, come join us and have people persecute you, get sores all over your body, and then top it off by giving away all your stuff and wandering the earth until you die. Come on in!"

I've often thought that the last job in the world I'd want is to be President of the United States. But now, I'm thinking maybe being king of the Israelites was worse.

Digging Deeper
Mining for what really matters . . . and gold

It doesn't necessarily mean God is punishing us or turning away from us when things go badly. Anyone who has a sense of God has been there, in those moments when you're searching, but God just doesn't seem to be there. It's even been suggested by some that, when

Jesus quotes this well-known psalm text, he's experiencing a profound moment of atheism.

As we discussed previously, the God of Job seems a bit petty, making deals with the Adversary to see how much humanity really believes and holds fast in their faith. That, or God is outright cruel, or at the very least, arbitrary, picking and choosing when to come and go, regardless of whether we're living virtuous lives or not.

Even the man who can't entirely muster the fortitude to go all in when Jesus suggests he should gets to go home and live out his life in comfort. Why not take it all away, give it to the poor? Or maybe the disciples deserve a little. After all, they've done what Jesus is telling the rich man to do as well, but they're still poor and he's not.

If we let go for a moment of the ideas that God's presence in our lives ever includes active punishments, as well as the notion that misfortune equals God's negligence, we may get to the heart of something deeper here: the real cost of desire.

In each of these cases, from Job to Mark, there's a pattern of recognizing where we are and desiring something different. Job is reduced to his knees and longs for nothing more than annihilation to end it all. Moses sees his people suffering and desires mercy. David sees external threats and desires their neutralization. Even the wealthy man in the Gospel, who seems to have it all, clearly desires more. In his case, though, what he desires isn't circumstantial but existential.

He has everything the world tells us we should aspire to, and yet the longing persists. It haunts his dreams, keeps him restless, makes him painfully aware that all of his stuff doesn't offer him the peace he hoped it would. And yet, in a show of one of humanity's greatest collective ironies, the thing keeping us from what we really want is the one thing we can't let go of.

It is hard for us to release, be it our material possessions or simply our expectations of how things ought to be. Try shoving a camel through a keyhole; you'll have better luck with that.

Heads Up
Connecting the text to our world

I've mentioned elsewhere how language can reveal much about the structure of our consciousness and how we perceive the world. But sometimes, language itself returns the favor, forming our perspectives for us. An example of this—and I know this may sound boring at first, but stay with me—is the grammatical device known as the subjunctive mood.

In case you've forgotten your sentence-diagramming lessons in grade school, I'll offer an example as a refresher. In his TED Talk called "Grammar, Identity, and the Dark Side of the Subjunctive," Phuc Tran tells about a time when he tried to explain the subjunctive to his dad, who is not a native speaker of English.

"Dad," he says, "you can say 'If it hadn't rained, we could have gone to the beach.'" His dad's response: "That's stupid. Why would you want to waste your time talking about something that didn't happen?" The whole notion of how alternate conditions could have presented different outcomes seemed totally specious and foreign to him.

The subjunctive is concerned with what Tran calls "possibility, potentiality, and contra-factuality." It's not about what is, but looks at what is or was, and considers possible outcomes. But for someone who lacks this grammar, quite literally, there's no point in wasting our time creating false alternate narratives.

Yes, the subjunctive can help us reflect on the past and hopefully learn from it (if I hadn't touched that stove when the element was red, I would not have gotten burned), but it can also feed a sense of dissatisfaction with the present (if I had studied a different major in college, I would have gotten the job I really want).

It's not that any particular grammatical device is the source of our misery (if we hadn't invented the subjunctive mood, I would never consider other possible outcomes beyond my control, and I'd be a lot happier). But it does reveal something about our nature, both in our present cultural context, and also in the broader human experience.

Put another way, as my friend Angela's grandmother used to say, "Even if things were going good, you'd go hunt up something to worry about."

It's hard to accept things as they are, and even harder to accept how much is completely beyond our control. What's more, the key to the peace we want, though we may seek it in any number of other ways, seems to be in the hard, ongoing practice of acceptance and release. Only then do we find some perspective, the healthy humility Jesus expects, and the freedom from the chains we may even come to love.

Prayer for the Week

God, as hard as it may be, help me seek and see you in all things and all circumstances. Remind me that a faithful life isn't always about being comfortable or prosperous, but that faith is, in itself, its own reward.

Popping Off

Art/music/video and other cool stuff that relate to the text

"That's All I Need" scene from *The Jerk*, (movie, 1979) https://www.youtube.com/watch?v=rSWBuZws30g

"Grammar, Identity, and the Dark Side of the Subjunctive," by Phuc Tran (TEDxDirigo Talk, 2012) https://www.youtube.com/watch?v=zeSVMG4GkeQ

Suffering for Perfection

―――∿―

Lectionary Texts For
October 21, 2018 (Proper 24 (29) Twenty-second Sunday after Pentecost)

Texts in Brief
My dog ate my Bible!

FIRST READING
Job 38:1–7 (34–41)

God offers a poetic, if somewhat sarcastic, response to Job's grievances and his questioning. In effect, God asks Job who he is to question the one who is the source of all being, unless he claims such power himself. Essentially, he cannot possibly understand the mind of God.

and

Isaiah 53:4–12

Though this sounds much like something Paul might say about Jesus later in his letters, here, the suffering

353

servant is a personification of the entire nation/people of Israel, which now is in exile and under Babylonian rule. Isaiah speaks of the great injustice of their being displaced. He believes that the many trials the people of Israel are suffering are because God sees it as reasonable, even if for reasons they don't grasp. And still, they remain faithful, which surely will be rewarded in the future.

Psalm

Psalm 104:1–9, 24, 35c

An offering of awe for the wonders of all God has created. It is recounted in a style that is reminiscent of the first Genesis creation story.

and

Psalm 91:9–16

All who seek shelter in God's presence will find refuge, protection, rescue, and long life. Those who call on God will be answered.

Second Reading

Hebrews 5:1–10

Paul talks about the roles and responsibilities of being a spiritual high priest like Aaron and Jesus, and how one doesn't decide to become one, but is chosen by God. He explains that Jesus, from a long line of anointed high priests, was thoroughly formed (perfect) and perfectly obedient, and as such, and by learning his obedience through the suffering he underwent, he revealed a path to salvation from sin.

GOSPEL

Mark 10:35–45

James and John ask Jesus to assign them special status of honor with him in paradise. He replies that this isn't for him to decide, and that their priorities are distorted. Rather than thinking hierarchically like earthly rulers, they should aspire to humble service.

Bible, Decoded

Breaking down scripture in plain language

Waterskins of the heavens – Another phrase for clouds, seen as skins holding the water within them until turned down toward earth to pour out.

Melchizedek – Both a king and high priest in Salem, mentioned all the way back in Genesis. Most notably, he blesses Abram, who is renamed Abraham, forefather of the twelve tribes of Israel. It was believed that all anointed high priests were part of the lineage of Melchizedek. Jesus was known as the completion of that order, serving as the High Priest to all forever.

Points to Ponder

First Thoughts

Given the way we think of the phrase "high priest" today, it's an honorific, holding someone up who has authority and power over others. However, as Jesus points out, the role of an anointed high priest of God is to be humble in service to all. Notably, Melchizedek not only blessed Abram, but also fed him, like a servant.

It's interesting that we are fascinated not just with the sources and nature of suffering, but we also feel compelled to find an explanation for *why* we suffer, as if all suffering has to be somehow reasonable. See below for more on this.

It's fascinating to read Isaiah's description of Israel's suffering and the reasons why it must go through this, especially given how often we frame everything as leading up to Jesus's story. Yes, they're strikingly similar, but I think we have to consider how tying their then-contemporary stories (New Testament) to the past stories of their people was essential to credibility, a way to honor the past and to demonstrate the veracity of the teachings of their ancient prophets.

Digging Deeper

Mining for what really matters . . . and gold

The Jewish people could identify with a messiah both as a suffering servant and a king in some ways. As we see in this Isaiah text, and as we see throughout Paul's letters, they are no strangers to suffering and to service, albeit not by choice. If they weren't subjugated by tyrannical kings of Egypt, Babylon, or the like, they were struggling with internal tribal violence, famine, and threats from outside powers wanting to seize their tentatively knit kingdom.

In that context, we can imagine how the message from Jesus went over, that their apparent Messiah would have to suffer and die. Not only was he to undergo tremendous suffering, but they too were to take such a path to achieve union with the divine. They've known few times free from war, exile, and oppression since their conception as a people, and now they kneel under the heel of Roman rule. It's reasonable in light of this to hope for a King of kings who, following in the steps of David and Solomon, would fulfill the promises they believed were made to them centuries before.

How long, God? How long?

Few, if any, want to take a path into suffering willingly, but especially after knowing little besides suffering already. In a way, it's hard not to become defined by it after so much time, and it's part of human nature to try and make sense of it, to ask "why?" and "how much longer?"

Compared to the span of chronicled history, the story of the United States is only beginning, and we've known relative sovereignty and prosperity by comparison. Some might even argue that we are, in many ways, the new Rome. But a leader would be received very differently if their principal message was one of surrender, humility, service, and even chosen suffering. For crying out loud, Jimmy Carter was laughed out of office after telling people that part of the solution to the looming energy crisis was to lower their thermostats and put on a sweater.

As these and other texts reveal, any time we try to answer questions about why suffering happens or when it will stop for good, we're focusing our attention incorrectly. Suffering is part of the human condition. Granted, at times we give in to the illusion that we have enough control to be able to end it for good. That, ironically, leads to suffering. Clearly in the Job text, God bristles at such efforts either to question God's nature or to play God by trying to change the realities of the human condition.

What we can do is try to discern what good can come from it. This doesn't mean we have to believe God is doing these things to us, or lapse into the intellectual laziness and resignation of believing everything happens for a reason. But as we reflected in the previous study, wisdom is gained in overcoming the myopia of being fixated on the present, focusing instead on what brought us to this point and how it will inform our decision, actions, and even our character going forward. Will it burn us to ashes or forge our character, burning away our illusions about what we deserve, what makes us who we are, and what's more, whose we are.

Approaching suffering and hardship with humble acceptance and also with the desire to be made better in the process is not easy. It's highly counterintuitive and countercultural. But it is the path of the suffering servants, and one that leads us closer to God.

Heads Up

Connecting the text to our world

We are a culture obsessed with perfection. At the same time, we tend to glorify suffering. Consider how often we hear—or even say—something about how little sleep we got or what insane hours we work, almost as if it implies some notion of the nobility of self-imposed suffering. Actually, it's a sign of the normalization of imbalance and unhealthy practices in our daily routines.

The result of the perceived demand for perfection and the normalization of self-imposed suffering can be devastating, even fatal. The National Eating Disorders Association reports that, in the United States alone, 20 million women and 10 million men struggle with eating disorders. Meanwhile we celebrate fad diets that advocate for even more imbalance, and we hold up icons of celebrity who have been physically ravaged by the pressures on them to live up to some elusive and illusive concept of what perfection looks like.

It starts young, too. When Amy and I were youth pastors together in Texas, we anonymously surveyed the kids in our group about how many of them struggled with eating disorders and a distorted sense of body image. More than three-fourths of them said they did. Just last week my eight-year-old daughter, who is perfectly healthy, active, and lovely, asked us if she was fat. My heart broke for her and for the world she's growing up in.

It's important to consider in the Hebrews text the order in which the concepts of suffering and perfection come and how they relate to each other. Jesus's suffering wasn't what made him perfect. His suffering revealed wisdom, from which he learned and through which he was more perfectly made whole. He did not have to pile suffering on himself; his relentless pursuit to fulfill his vision for the world brought more than enough directly to him.

What in the world did Jesus have to learn from his struggles and suffering? He used the experience to become greater, and he invites us to do the same.

What curious clothing wisdom wears sometimes.

Prayer for the Week

God, help me experience every day, including the bad ones, with eyes wide open. Help me take what I can from each experience, good and bad, and use it to become more of what I was lovingly made to become.

Popping Off

Art/music/video and other cool stuff that relate to the text

"Perfectionism: A Psychological Dimension of Eating Disorder" scene from *Black Swan* (movie, 2010) https://www.youtube.com/watch?v=54tYgmVw1m4

"Get the Facts on Eating Disorder" from the National Eating Disorders Association (Article, 2016) https://www.nationaleatingdisorders.org/get-facts-eating-disorders

I Am No One

Lectionary Texts For
October 28, 2018 (Proper 25 (30) Twenty-third Sunday after Pentecost)

Texts in Brief
My dog ate my Bible!

FIRST READING
Job 42:1–6, 10–17

We reach the conclusion of the Book of Job when Job responds with humble apology and regret to God's reprimand for questioning God's motives. After Job prays for his friends, God sends his loved ones to him to offer help. What follows is a period of prosperity that surpasses his previous life, including many sons and daughters and a very long life.

and

Jeremiah 31:7–9

The prophet speaks of God bringing back together the people of Israel who have been dispersed far and wide, and who have suffered much.

Psalm

Psalm 34:1–8 (19–22)

A song of thanks and also an offering to listeners of an example of the value of humility and of prayers being answered. He notes that the righteous still suffer, but God doesn't ignore them and ultimately will offer relief.

and

Psalm 126

This psalm is a glance at past, present, and future. It reminds us of the restoration of the fortunes of Israel, as requested in the Jeremiah passage, then asks for a similar restoration again.

Second Reading

Hebrews 7:23–28

The author notes that intercession (stepping in on people's behalf between them and God to appeal for them) historically has fallen on priests to handle. But now that Jesus has come as the one who intercedes on behalf of everyone, and who does not succumb to the limitations of physical death, such human intercession is no longer required. As such, the sacrifices or love offerings made to God to appease God's anger over their sin is not necessary, since Jesus has provided sufficient sacrifice to end all sacrifices.

GOSPEL
Mark 10:46–52

As Jesus and the disciples are leaving Jericho, Bartimaeus, a blind beggar, calls out for his help. He's told to be quiet, but he just calls out louder. Jesus asks him what he wants, and he says he wants to see again. Jesus says his faith has made him well, and his vision is restored. So Bartimaeus gets up and follows Jesus.

Bible, Decoded
Breaking down scripture in plain language

Ephraim   The reference to Ephraim in Jeremiah can be a little confusing, but it helps to understand a little bit about Jacob's lineage, from which the twelve tribes of Israel were said to have descended. Jacob had several wives, one of whom was named Rachel. Her grandson was named Ephraim, who was considered to be the patriarch of one of those twelve tribes. More broadly, the name "Ephraim" refers to the Israelites distributed within the northern regions.

Negeb – This region, later called Negev, has suffered tremendous drought. So the psalmist asks that the parched soil of the region would be sufficiently watered by the tears of those who have suffered there so that it will yield abundance once again.

Points to Ponder
First Thoughts

For those of us who struggle with the idea of substitutionary atonement (the concept that Jesus had to die in order to save us from our own sinfulness), this Hebrews text can seem to present a real challenge on its face. But if we recognize that the focus is on getting people to release their old practices and preconceptions about having any agency over reconciling their own sins with God's grace, it's actually a liberating lesson in submission and letting go of the illusion of control.

It's nice to see Job get some relief after going through so much, but the text offers no resolution for his loved ones who died in the process of his suffering.

It's interesting in Psalm 126 that it doesn't just ask for relief and restoration for Israel. It seems to draw a sort of correlation between the degree of individual suffering and the amount of blessing they should receive in turn. It alludes to grief being the seeds of future prosperity, which will be watered by the tears of those who have wept. This doesn't mean that God wants us to undergo grief and suffering as a test of our faithfulness. Rather, it says more about humanity's need to justify why we suffer in the first place.

Digging Deeper
Mining for what really matters . . . and gold

If we gloss over this conclusion to Job and just summarize that he humbles himself before God, God restores his fortunes, and they all live happily ever after, we can miss some important parts. First, it doesn't say that God restores his fortunes after he shows humility and regret; his life is renewed beyond what it had previously been after praying for his friends. Given his state, this is a remarkable act of selflessness. Second, the text acknowledges that the evil brought on Job was brought by God. In the age-old debate about whether God is either all-loving or all-powerful (or maybe both, or neither), it's worth noting that God brings evil on one of God's beloved.

Next, the beginning of Job's restoration of his fortunes doesn't just magically fall out of the sky, but rather it comes in the form of help from others. It's reminiscent of the feeding miracle stories in the Gospels, where the divine miracles begin first with a human act of generosity. And finally, it's notable that Job offers an inheritance not just to his sons (which would have been most common culturally), but he also offers inheritances to his daughters. It's a remarkably empowering gesture, especially considering that most women were viewed as property rather than property-holders.

Several of these observations are both counterintuitive and countercultural. Similarly, so are the observations offered in Hebrews. Though we may consider (especially in the Protestant tradition) the lack of need for a priest to intercede on our behalf to God as normal, it was radical at the time. So was giving up the practice of offering sacrifices to God. This does not mean, of course, that we are to give up on the idea of sacrifice; rather, we're called to live sacrificially, which is more all consuming and is in imitation of Jesus's sacrificial path throughout his ministry.

Continuing the countercultural theme, Bartimaeus, unquestionably an other who is relegated to the outer boundaries of town given his worthlessness to the larger society, was considered way out of line in making a request of a famous prophet and teacher. But even as he is castigated for his impropriety, he calls out even more. This disruption of the social norms is what gets Jesus's attention. It moves him, figuratively and literally, to come to the man and help him.

Finally, though we like to think of Jesus as this powerful miracle worker (how he is described elsewhere in the Gospels), he is explicit here and elsewhere in stating that he is not the one making the man well. It is the man's own faith that is the source of his healing. If we circle back to Job, similarly there is no mention of any specific restoration of Job's fortune coming directly from God's hand. It begins first with his own act of selfless prayer for others and continues with his loved ones offering him gifts and gestures of compassion. Subsequently his estate is made to flourish, but it doesn't say that he sat back while God just zapped it all better.

Maybe the agency comes from within us the whole time. In this case, our relationship with God is a sort of silent partnership, with God working through us and others, but only—and paradoxically—once we release the misconception that we have any sort of control over the outcome to begin with. Like Jesus, we're required to lose ourselves in the act of healing and restoration, to throw our whole selves into it, which can come across like some sort of test we have to pass in order for God to finally give up the goods.

In releasing our own power, our expectations, and sense of what ought to be, we may finally channel the truly divinely inspired power that comes from being emptied out of all else. Maybe it's only then that there's enough room made for God's miraculous work to take place. For some it may take having all they hold dear burning to ashes. For others, it may depend on having their national and tribal identities stripped away. And for some, it may take being cast out, told you are nothing and no one, in order to make room in the emptiness for a presence that moves only when given room.

Once the space is made and a place is prepared, not with stunning ornamentation and impressive offerings, but with stripping away all that is not God, miracles begin their work.

Heads Up

Connecting the text to our world

I'm a huge *Game of Thrones* fan. In particular—heresy alert—I like the TV show, despite its many valid criticisms. But one thing I didn't care for, and in fact it ended up making me pretty mad, was the plotline about Arya Stark and the Hall of Faces.

In case you don't follow it, Arya is a young girl on the run who gets taken in by this Fagin-like character who rescues her from a dangerous encounter. She decides that she wants to learn his ways, and he proceeds to teach her that, to become part of the Hall of Faces network, she first has to become "no one." This proves to be no easy task, as she undergoes many painful and humiliating tasks over the course of two seasons under the pretense of releasing all ego and notions of self that she hangs onto. She is no longer a Stark, bloodline of royalty. She is not a girl who has suffered unfairly and seeks to reconcile with her family.

She is nothing.

Though this is interesting, the purpose of this process is disappointing. The Hall of Faces is a collection of façades of the dead which, once they become "no one," the members of the network can take on and walk through the world in complete disguise. From here they can steal and kill as assigned by their Master, whose greater purpose remains not entirely clear. It's a quasi-religious cult whose leader seems more intent on breaking people down for the purpose of his own selfish motives more than for some higher aim.

This is not the sort of ego-releasing selflessness God requires, either in the process by which it is achieved or for the ends portrayed by the Hall of Faces storyline. Selflessness is not a practice to then be turned into a weapon or a tool for personal gain. It is total submission to make room for something more, something mysterious and truly life-giving. It requires a level of submission—which sometimes comes from crushing external forces but not necessarily—that our cultural norms suggest is more than worthless; it is foolish and dangerous.

Maybe it *is* foolish and dangerous. It certainly seems to up-end much of what we think is normal and good. It's impossible to know what would happen if we really could let go this far, until the answer to that question no longer matters. Because No One is not concerned with answers and outcomes, so much, as submission for submission's sake.

Prayer for the Week

Help me become No One, so that I might be so much more.

Popping Off

Art/music/video and other cool stuff that relate to the text

"The Hall of Faces" scene from *Game of Thrones* Season 5, Episode 6 (TV series, 2011-) https://www.youtube.com/watch?v-_zQ3K-ylk 4

"Overcoming Our Ego: The 8 Crippling Manifestations," From *The Huffington Post* (Article, Nov. 5, 2014) http://www.huffingtonpost.com/thai-nguyen/overcoming-our-ego-the-8-_b_6104096.html

Counterculture

Lectionary Texts For

November 4, 2018 (Proper 26 (31) Twenty-fourth Sunday after Pentecost)

Texts in Brief

My dog ate my Bible!

First Reading

Ruth 1:1–18

The essence of this passage is about faithfulness to family in spite of devastating tragedy. Naomi, her husband (Elimelech), and two sons (Mahlon and Chilion) are trying to escape the drought in Bethlehem by traveling to Moab. A woman named Orpah marries Mahlon and Ruth marries Chilion. Then Elimelech dies, and not long after, so do the sons. Naomi decides to return to Bethlehem, so Orpah leaves her. But Ruth refuses, saying she will stay with Naomi until death.

and

Deuteronomy 6:1–9

Moses offers an extensive reproach to the Israelites before entering the promised land, which is occupied by other cultures with other religions. He warns sternly that they are not to put any other gods before the God of Israel, and that this is essential to their prosperity not just presently but for generations to come.

PSALM

Psalm 146

A psalm of praise to God that also echoes Moses's directive in Deuteronomy always to put the God of Israel first. While kings and princes die, God is eternal. Also, God can perform acts of provision, healing, and protection that even the mightiest earthly leaders can't give.

and

Psalm 119:1–8

David asks God to help him find the conviction and strength to stay faithful always to God. He recognizes that this is the path to peace and happiness, and away from shame.

SECOND READING

Hebrews 9:11–14

The author compares the inferiority of our attempts to equal Jesus's offering of himself with our own animal sacrifices (at least at the time, when it was religious tradition). Our acts don't come near the perfect selfless-ness that Jesus demonstrated, and the lengths to which he went in his love for others, even to the point of death.

GOSPEL

Mark 12:28–34

A scribe asks Jesus which is the greatest command-ment. Jesus offers a two-part response: love God with all you have and love others as you love yourself. The scribe agrees with Jesus, to which Jesus responds that he is near to the kingdom of God.

Bible, Decoded

Breaking down scripture in plain language

Ruth – Though the book primarily focuses on Ruth, the author of the text is unknown. Notable about Ruth is that she is David's great-grandmother, but also that she is a "Moabite," meaning she is not an Israelite. One rea-son this is significant is because marriage across tribal identities was a heated and controversial issue at the time this was believed to have been written (c. fifth cen-tury BCE). As such, its treatment of this issue is in some ways a response to the social climate of the time.

Naomi – The arc of Naomi's story can be seen through-out the book of Ruth, and is a demonstration of how God can render goodness and beauty from the most despairing and desolate situations.

Scribe – The primary job of scribes was to keep records and to function as both preservers and disseminators of important information. They served the dual purposes that today would be handled by libraries or archives and printing presses (or perhaps blogs). They would copy important documents like scriptures, letters from kings, and territorial decrees. Though they are mistakenly thought of sometimes as the authors of scriptures or these other texts rather than recorders, they also had power, as they could manipulate text at times to suit their own agenda.

Points to Ponder

First Thoughts

The ending of this passage in Deuteronomy is the basis for many symbols you see especially in orthodox Jewish communities. This is why we see enclosures on doorways that hold prayers, and why some Jews, especially pilgrims, will have little boxes affixed to their hands or foreheads. The boxes contain this commandment, so they're doing precisely what they believe they were commanded to do here in Deuteronomy.

Whereas Jesus often engages pharisees and scribes in a way that feels more confrontational and ultimately confounding, his exchange with this scribe in Mark feels different. It seems like he can sense the different orientation of this scribe's heart, and that he really wants to know the answer to his question for his own growth. On the other hand, the scribe's peers generally look for ways to undermine or condemn Jesus, which he recognizes despite their frequent flattery and feigned respect.

Digging Deeper
Mining for what really matters . . . and gold

The entirety of the Book of Ruth is countercultural. Though parts of it are sometimes read at weddings, as it has some beautiful language about beginning new lives together, that's not at the heart of Ruth's message.

For starters, it's atypical in scripture, as its two central figures, Naomi and Ruth, are women. To recognize how remarkable this is, we only have to look through the rest of the Bible, or even just at the names of the other books. It's a boys' club, by and large, so dedicating an entire book to two female figures is unusual, especially at the time this was written, centuries before Jesus.

Next, there's the fact that the story involves marriage of two people from different cultures. This was a hot-button issue when this was written, as cross-cultural marriage was taboo to many. So simply by putting this in a scroll to be studied and revered was a challenge to the status quo.

Finally, when Ruth's husband dies, her insistence on following her mother-in-law wherever she went was pretty significant. The author even points out that she parts ways with her own sister-in-law to stay at Naomi's side. This was not expected of her, as generally she would have returned to be with her family of origin, since her husband's brother had also died and couldn't marry her next (maybe weird to us now, but customary then).

So the storyline, the principal characters, and the book itself assert that, sometimes, there's something more important than going with the flow. There are occasions when there's something bigger at stake. As for what that is, at least in the case of these texts, it is faithfulness. For David and for Moses, the emphasis is about faithfulness to God. We could argue that this too is the case with the scribe in Mark, though it could be equally compelling to suggest that his faithfulness is to the true spirit, or to truth within the religious text. And of course for Ruth, her faithfulness is to Naomi.

Jesus was no stranger to bucking social convention. In fact, it was his disruptive presence in the social, religious, and political orders that caused so many to fear and hate him. They depended on things staying largely the same in order to maintain their positions of privilege, power, and comfort. His assertion that their faith was misplaced posed a direct challenge to the god they served.

However, as countercultural as Jesus was, he wasn't inherently anti-culture. He didn't dismiss the scribe outright because of his position in the present power structure. This is because for Jesus, his faithfulness to liberating people from oppressive and violent power structures always sat second chair to his commitment to reaching people's hearts. This runs against both those who seek to prop up broken or immoral power dynamics today (be they religious, economic, political, or social), and those who sometimes want to distill Jesus down to little more than an anarchic social radical.

He was messiah to and for all. And all, as Paul says, requires a pretty big tent.

Heads Up

Connecting the text to our world

In the fifteen-plus years my wife Amy and I have been involved in ministry together, it seems the one place where we keep encountering social and religious stigma involves the rights, inclusion, equality, and empowerment of LGBTQ people. When Amy was in seminary, we both worked at what many in town called "the gay church." We didn't know, first of all, that our church was a boy church. And little did we know that our boy church liked to have sex with other boy churches! News to us.

We've ministered, written, preached, and marched based on our conviction for inclusion and affirmation of LGBTQ people for much of our adult lives. We've paid for that position at times, but certainly nothing compared with the price so many pay for simply being who they are, in all their divinely made beauty. And for those who have dug into their biblical texts and, through prayer and study, still can't come around to similar positions, I can respect that, while not letting go of my own convictions.

But the people I meet with whom I take greatest issue are those who, privately at least, agree that full inclusion of all God's people is gospel-centered and just. However, they refuse to take public positions that express these feelings for fear of losing something: their jobs, congregations, friendships, book deals, or fan bases. And while I understand, and can empathize deeply with, this internal conflict, it doesn't justify their silence.

After all, if we're content to keep silent for the sake of our own survival or comfort, how can we ever claim

with any authority to have good news to share with anyone? Good news can't be good if it picks sides, chooses
winners and losers. We can do that just fine without
Jesus and the gospel to compel us. What makes it truly
good is that it's fully, sacrificially, and sometimes dan-
gerously inclusive.

Jesus was clear that our faith will not survive without sacrifice.

Prayer for the Week

*God, loosen my grip on all that holds me back from pro-
claiming all that is good news to—and for—all, despite
the cost.*

Popping Off

Art/music/video and other cool stuff that relate to the text

Selma (movie, 2014)

The Powers That Be: Theology for a New Millennium, by
Walter Wink (book, 1999)

More Than Jezebel

Lectionary Texts For
November 11, 2018 (Proper 27 (32) Twenty-fifth Sunday after Pentecost)

Texts in Brief
My dog ate my Bible!

First Reading
Ruth 3:1–5; 4:13–17

Naomi, Ruth's mother-in-law, wants Ruth to have more protection, so she directs her to sleep with Boaz, who then marries her. They have a son whom they name Obed, who is the father of Jesse and grandfather of David.

and

1 Kings 17:8–16

This passage introduces the prophet Elijah. He meets a poor woman at the edge of Zarephath and asks her for bread and water, to which she responds that she has almost nothing. He tells her that if she will do this (feed him first, then her son and herself), she'll not run out of grain and oil until the present drought is over. She does as he says and she doesn't run out.

PSALM
Psalm 127

All works should be done with God's blessing or they're worthless. And having many sons is not only a sign of honor; it is a blessing given by God.

SECOND READING
Hebrews 9:24–28

The author compares human attempts at equaling the significance of the acts of Jesus, calling human efforts a mere copy of Christ's. Our churches do not impress God, and neither do our sacrifices, which is why Jesus has taken on that role for us in God's presence.

GOSPEL
Mark 12:38–44

Jesus says that those who use their authority to exploit others, especially the vulnerable, will have a lot to answer for to God. He also celebrates the example set by a poor woman who gives all she has to God (in the form of a money offering) as the one who has given the most of all among them.

Bible, Decoded

Breaking down scripture in plain language

Feet – It might sound at first like people in the Bible had a real foot thing going on, but actually this was just a culturally acceptable way to talk about sex. Same goes when it mentions a woman "making herself known" to a man, or him "coming to know" a woman. Like anything else, of course, context matters. Sometimes feet are just feet!

Zarephath – An ancient Phoenician city between Tyre and Sidon that suffered from three years of drought. The drought was said to have been imposed on the city at Elijah's request to God, because of King Ahab's ungodly ways. It would have been in the farthest northern region of what the Israelites considered Cana, or part of the promised land.

Points to Ponder

First Thoughts

I would be curious to hear what proponents of the idea that the Bible exclusively advocates sex only after marriage would have to say about this Ruth text. Seems that it could be interpreted that Ruth sexually seduced Boaz before he married her, and at the behest of her mother-in-law, no less.

Oh and just in case you feel like men are sorely under-represented throughout the Bible, this week offers us a healthy dose of patriarchy, alright. Sons are a blessing to their fathers, but never mind about daughters or wives. At least things balance out a bit in Kings and Mark, given that the heroes of these stories are women. Unfortunately, though, they have to do more than simply be born to earn such recognition.

Digging Deeper
Mining for what really matters . . . and gold

Though I was being a little bit cheeky about the patriarchy all over the texts this week, women do have a significant role. In the case of Ruth, bringing her and Boaz together was masterminded by Naomi. And though ultimately Boaz decided to marry Ruth, it was Ruth who initiated, arguably even seduced, Boaz.

In the Kings text, we could easily focus on Elijah as God's prophet. However, the story goes nowhere without the widow. She is, in many ways, the very embodiment of what Naomi is trying to protect Ruth from becoming. And yet despite being on the brink of starvation, she offers the gesture of faithful generosity that is the catalyst for the miracle. It's not dissimilar to the story of the feeding of the multitudes in the Gospels in which (in some ways, erroneously perhaps) we talk about Jesus being the one who feeds the crowd. In fact, the food comes from a little boy, and the miracle comes only after the offering is made.

Finally, in Mark we see Jesus offering a condemnation of those in power who take advantage of the vulnerable who, in this case, he describes as widows. Then just after this (at least for the sake of the story), it is another widow who offers up all she has, just like in Kings. In this gesture, Jesus sees the miracle already. While people tend to look toward him as the source of such things, he keeps trying to redirect their attention back to these small, unremarkable moments.

We have this tendency to get fixated on the result, while missing what's really at the source. And in each case here, it is the most vulnerable who are the miracle workers. Also important to note is that the drought, which is believed to be brought upon the community because of some godless happenings in Ahab's court, affects the poor, the widows, and children the most. And if we understand a bit more about Ahab, we see yet another feminine connection, albeit a less miraculous one this time.

Ahab is married to a Phoenician woman named Jezebel. She is a bit of a religious fanatic, but not for the God of Israel. Rather, she hangs so passionately onto her cultural deities (Baal and Asherah) that she persuades Ahab to accept her gods as the focus of their territorial religion. So in her position of power, Jezebel is the one who triggers this regional calamity, while the most profoundly affected among them is the spark of hope that will, ultimately, change the course they're on toward destruction.

The darkness of a vast space may feel oppressive, overwhelming, and impossible to overcome. And yet one solitary candle can bring light to so much.

Heads Up

Connecting the text to our world

Rosa Louise McCauley was born into adversity in more ways than most of us will ever experience. Born on her family's farm, she moved with her mom to live with her grandparents, both former slaves, when her mom left her dad. She walked to her one-room school when she could, which was so destitute that they often lacked desks or books, unlike her white counterparts in town.

McCauley remembers one day when her grandfather stood on the porch of their home with a shotgun while Ku Klux Klan members marched down the middle of their street. She attended all-black grade schools, followed by the Alabama State Teachers College for Negroes until leaving to return home to care for her sick grandmother. Rather than ever going back to school, she went to work at a local shirt factory.

At age nineteen, McCauley married Raymond Parks, an activist in the local NAACP, which was watched closely by local government and Klan leaders. Despite the dangers—or perhaps in some ways because of them—Rosa Parks became active in the movement for justice and equality for her black brothers and sisters.

We know the rest of the story, which unfolded when Parks took the city bus home after a day as a seamstress at a local Montgomery Ward on the afternoon of December 1, 1955, in Montgomery. What fewer may know is that her decision to sit in front of the line separating the black-and-white seating sections in the bus was part of a coordinated effort by many in the black activist community there. They had decided that it was time to challenge the oppressive laws surrounding segregation and subsequent disparities in treatment and services.

But even though many worked behind the scenes to help use this moment as a spark for a civil rights movement, it was because of Rosa Parks's brave act of nonviolent resistance that made the whole sequence of later events possible. For this reason, she will forever be remembered as one of the central faces of the ongoing racial equality movement in America.

All this, from one woman choosing to confound a broken system and choose for herself on behalf of others.

Prayer for the Week

God, help me shape the priorities in my life so that if I'm asked "What have you done for the 'least of these'?," I have something to say.

Popping Off

Art/music/video and other cool stuff that relate to the text

"The Rosa Parks Papers" (video, 2012) http://www.pbs .org/black-culture/explore/rosa-parks/#.WMr VvxjMzBI

"How Rachel Held Evans Became the Most Polarizing Woman in Evangelicalism," from the *Washington Post* (article, April 16, 2015) https://www.washington post.com/news/acts-of-faith/wp/2015/04/16/how -rachel-held-evans-became-the-most-polarizing -woman-in-evangelicalism/?utm_term=.7da72 c34288e

Destruction . . .
in a Good Way

Lectionary Texts For
*November 18, 2018 (Proper 28 (33) Twenty-sixth Sunday
after Pentecost)*

Texts in Brief
My dog ate my Bible!

First Reading
1 Samuel 1:4–20
A man named Elkanah has two wives, but has a special place in his heart for Hannah, who can't have children. Because of this, Peninnah, the other wife, taunts
her and she agonizes over it. She prays so fervently to
God at the temple that the priest Eli thinks she's drunk.
She explains her grief and Eli says God will help her.
She and Elkanah then bear a son together, whom they
name Samuel.

and

1 Samuel 2:1–10

Hannah offers a prayer of thanks for her gift of child-birth, containing elements of the "great reversals" we see so much in Luke. The poor and those without are raised up while those who are proud of their accomplishments will grieve. She speaks of a God of knowledge, power, and justice, and warns of the danger of pride or opposition to God.

and

Daniel 12:1–3

Daniel offers a fantastical picture of the world, which is undergoing hardship from all sides. The dead will be raised, the just and unjust separated, and those who are wise and lead others to justice will be held in high regard.

PSALM

Psalm 16

David seeks protection from God from earthly threats, natural disaster, and from death beyond life. In wisdom, life is found, while those who follow another God will find only suffering.

SECOND READING

Hebrews 10:11–14 (15–18), 19–25

The author talks of the futility of the offerings made by priests, which do not make up for human sin. Meanwhile, through Jesus's own sacrificial path, all sin is forgotten by God, once and forever. It is through such selfless sacrifice that we find ourselves fit to enter into the presence of God, which was made possible by Jesus, the one who showed the way. We're implored to cling to this hope, and to share it with others so they may join us in holding fast to it.

GOSPEL
Mark 13:1–8
Jesus's disciples are in awe of the human-built temple, but Jesus reminds them that it is all temporary, and that there will come a time when all that they see will return to dust. He warns them of buying into the deception of false prophets, or of succumbing to despair when present circumstances are hard. These upheavals and conflicts are indicators not of the end of all creation, but rather of something new being born from the rubble of the old.

Bible, Decoded
Breaking down scripture in plain language
Hannah – A descendant of Jacob from a tribe called the Kohathites, considered a revered priestly bloodline. Because so much of a woman's value at the time was tied up in her ability to bear sons, Hannah felt useless or even cursed by God. She is portrayed as deeply faithful to God and her husband, and as the picture of ideal motherhood.

Eli – A high priest among the Israelites, and the next to last in the line of religious judges or leaders of his people (the previous one was Samuel) before kings began to lead. Eli's two sons do not follow in his steps of faithfulness to God, and although God was said to have kept a promise that Eli's bloodline would continue forever, the males in his family tree would suffer. Both of his sons were said to be destined to die before they got old, and on the same day.

Daniel – Scripture portrays Daniel as a Jewish man of noble birth who is captured by the Babylonians, and ends up serving King Nebuchadnezzar and the kings that succeed him. Many scholars, however, agree that Daniel was not a historical figure, and that the book of Daniel may actually have been about the Greek king Antiochus IV in the second century BCE.

Points to Ponder

First Thoughts

While we tend to get hung up on the idea that apocalyptic literature, which many of these are this week, is about horrible things to come, it's actually a glimpse beyond tragedy and upheaval to the hope on the other side of it. There's a curious tendency in human nature to focus on the negative, sometimes to a degree that we miss the bigger point.

There is another theme in some apocalyptic literature that, I think, may say more about humanity's need for vindication and our own sense of justice to be carried out rather than God's notion of reconciliation and wholeness. After all, if the high are made low and are crushed while the meek and oppressed are raised up, we still have the same issue of disparity and suffering. And if you believe in God's vision being one in which all suffering will cease and we will become one in the spirit of unconditional love, I'm not sure this can be reconciled with our need for the unrighteous to get what we think they deserve.

Digging Deeper

Mining for what really matters . . . and gold

At the risk of your eyes glazing over, I want to pull out two big fifty-cent words used in theology nerd circles. It has to do with whether we think these texts are *eschatological* or *apocalyptic*. It's easy to get one confused with the other, but they're definitely, and importantly, different. And depending on which theology nerds you ask, there would probably be a lot of different understanding of the terms and how they relate.

In *Preaching Through the Apocalypse*, Cornish Rogers and Joseph Jeter recognize that, sometimes, the terms are used interchangeably. Apocalyptic, though, contains what they call a "creative negativity." Something today has to die or succumb to destruction in order to make way for something new. It's a joyous, hopeful sort of revolution.

Eschatology, on the other hand, looks at the present and anticipates the effect it will have on the future. What we do now will help determine what comes later. The present and future are linear and directly related. Apocalyptic is more dualist in its outlook. With this in mind, we can see Daniel as eschatological since it sees what's going on now as directly related to events to come.

But then we have Jesus's description of the destruction of the temple not as something to be feared, but as something necessary to clear a path for something far more remarkable.

One way I like to think of the difference is that eschatology looks toward the future in order to change something about the present. Thinking like this, the way Al Gore portrayed the future of our climate based on present behavior—as well as how we can change that outcome—would be more eschatological. Someone seeing the ruin and decay in inner urban Detroit and imagining what could emerge from the bleakness would be more apocalyptic.

Jesus was an apocalyptic preacher, but in a good way. We think of that word as terrifying, but for him, apocalypse was about that creative negativity Rogers and Jeter describe. The only way that should seem scary, then, is if we lack the vision or faith to release the present to make way for the promise of a radically different future.

Twenty-first-century Christian religious institutions need to think more apocalyptically. I don't mean we need to talk more about the terrible imagery of the end of the world that the bullhorn-wielding sidewalk preachers are notorious for. I mean we need to look past the decline and seismic upheaval taking place within our religious systems and see new possibility with hope. But sometimes that beautiful apocalypse can only be realized if we stop thinking so eschatologically about our role in *making* that future happen.

Heads Up
Connecting the text to our world

One of my favorite animated movies (and the list is growing with so many good ones continuing to come out every year) is *Wall-E*. It's a sweet story about a robot who is one of many left behind on earth to clean up the mountains of waste and refuse after humans have consumed it to the point of inhabitability, after which they escape to space until the robots make it livable again.

As he digs through the layers and layers of garbage like a junkyard archaeologist, he collects things. His array of findings are his only company for part of the movie, but his favorite of all is a small plant sprout. What happens with the sprout is critical to the plot, so I won't ruin it for the three people in the universe who haven't seen it yet, but for *Wall-E*, it's sacred, holy, a relic of what once was and, at the same time, what could be.

While all of humanity looked around the decimated planet and saw nothing but death for themselves, it took a bloodless worker droid to find the promise of life in the middle of it all. From their outer-space perspective, they see a world drained of all hope because of their collective choices. But Wall-E, who endured the consequences of their sins, saw something worth saving that they all missed.

It's not that the cute, primitive robot is the perfect Christ figure, but he is an apocalyptic visionary. He sees potential where the rest find nothing but rubble. For humanity, the whole exercise of cleaning up one mountain of crap after another might have proven overwhelming. After all, to what end? Clear one mound away, only to find another. Best to hole up in their makeshift resort in the sky that kept them pleasantly distracted from reality miles below them.

They may have been alive, but they weren't actually living. One the other hand, Wall-E witnessed the smallest miracle, easily snuffed out by carelessness or neglect. And with that tiny thing, he had enough to become a savior.

Prayer for the Week

God, help me imagine with divine inspiration, so that I might find hope greater than the fear that keeps me from being able to let go of the present and any illusion that I have ultimate control.

Popping Off

Art/music/video and other cool stuff that relate to the text

"The End," by Jim Morrison/The Doors (song, 1967)

Wall-E (movie, 2008)

An Inconvenient Truth (movie, 2006)

Preaching Through the Apocalypse: Sermons from Revelation, Cornish Rogers and Joseph Jeter, editors (book, 1992)

Wrong Kind of King

Lectionary Texts For

*November 25, 2018 (Reign of Christ, Proper 29 (34)
Twenty-seventh Sunday after Pentecost)*

Texts in Brief

My dog ate my Bible!

FIRST READING

2 Samuel 23:1–7

Samuel recounts King David's final words about how rulers who are just will be honored by God, as will those whom they lead. Leaders who rule without God's wisdom and blessing, however, will fail and ultimately perish, mired in conflict.

and

Daniel 7:9–10, 13–14

Daniel offers a fantastical vision of the Messiah—one who will come in human form—whom all will serve, as he will be directly appointed to lead all of humanity.

PSALM

Psalm 132:1–12 (13–18)

A prayer on behalf of David to God, but also a poem of remembrance for all who read it about his deeds and God's promise to him and his people. David is celebrated for returning the Ark of the Covenant to Jerusalem, and the psalm suggests David's kingship is a fulfillment of prophecy. Any who oppose him, God will foil, and David's kingdom will long endure. The poor will be fed and all will find salvation from God.

and

Psalm 93

God is touted as king and lord over all the world. God's house is sacred and God's commands for humanity are enduring, as is the earth, God's own handiwork.

SECOND READING

Revelation 1:4b–8

John, believed to be author of Revelation, speaks of Jesus as the fulfillment of prophecies by the likes of Daniel. He is the king over all earthly kings; he speaks of Jesus's resurrection ("firstborn of the dead") and his role in realizing salvation for the world. The text concludes with a vision of Jesus's return after death to establish God's kingdom in the world for all time.

GOSPEL
John 18:33–37

Pilate, the provincial leader assigned to the region where Jerusalem is, questions Jesus about being called King of the Jews by his followers. Jesus responds that his kingship is not a physical earthly one, but rather his reign is something beyond that of a tribal leader. Pilate presses him, and Jesus responds that he has, and is, living out his intended purpose.

Bible, Decoded
Breaking down scripture in plain language

Ephrathah – The ancient name for Bethlehem. It is cited in the Gospels as the birthplace of Jesus, and was believed to be one of the sites where the Ark of the Covenant was kept.

Jaar – This is the only place in the Bible when a town is referred to by this name, but it is believed to be a place known elsewhere in scripture as *Kiriath Jearim*. Located about ten miles outside of Jerusalem, it would have been a border town of the kingdom of Israel. It was also believed to be one of the other places where the Ark of the Covenant was housed for a period of time.

Pontius Pilate – The governor of the territory of Judea where Jesus was arrested, which he oversaw. Assigned by the Roman Empire as their regional leader, he was in charge of Jesus's arrest and imprisonment. Later, he infamously washes his hands (figuratively and literally) of any culpability in ordering Jesus's crucifixion, having found no crime committed, yet allowing a crowd assembled at his palace to determine which man—Jesus or Barabbas—would die.

Points to Ponder

First Thoughts

It's worth noting that this text in 2 Samuel is actually one of just under a dozen places in the Hebrew Bible that claim to contain the last words of David.

Having these texts together in one week makes it clear how desperately many of the people of Israel wanted an earthly king to help establish the permanence, sovereignty, and prosperity of their people. It's understandable, given their long, troubled history of displacement, enslavement, struggle, and occupation. It's also understandable how deeply disillusioned people were when they thought this was what Jesus would end up being for them, and then he refused. Centuries, even millennia, of waiting led them to this Messiah who didn't end up being what they expected.

John is thought to have written Revelation from a prison on the Island of Patmos. There are several theories about the vibrant, surreal imagery employed throughout the text. Some have suggested he was suffering from a mental breakdown, or that he had to encrypt his writing in a way that would not be deciphered and destroyed by his captors. But given how similar it is in tone to the Daniel excerpt, it seems he's pulling a bit from the *midrashic* tradition of imitating the style and imagery used by former prophets. This might have been to assert that this was divinely inspired, as was believed of previous prophetic texts.

Digging Deeper
Mining for what really matters . . . and gold

We've spent enough time with the telling of David's reign, as well as his own words, to recognize that this testimonial looking back on his time as king is rather inflated. Beyond just pumping up the good bits about him and ignoring the notable negatives, he's actually elevated to a point that one might mistake him as the messiah prophesied elsewhere in the Hebrew texts. If we consider the accounts of David chronologically, it's pretty obvious that his mythology only grows over time. This is not uncommon today as well, as approval ratings for former American presidents tend to improve the longer they're out of office: even more so after they die.

But in this case particularly, the veneration of this all-too-human king may tell us more about us than it does about him. We like our authority figures and celebrities to be bigger than life. We have this insatiable need, over and again, to add on to the stories of their greatness the longer we have sat with their story. While, on the one hand, we crave real, human connection with those we look to for guidance, wisdom, or protection, we also want them to be as near to gods as we can muster.

Here's where Jesus ran up against so much resistance within his own community. Granted, many of them came to welcome the idea of him as an other-worldly anointed king. They recognized in his teaching, his life, and his acts of healing and provision the touch of God among them. But that was not enough. They wanted their messiah to act as a physical, earthly ruler in the tradition of David, Solomon, and others, reestablishing the nation of Israel as independent and finally free of the perennial yoke of oppression and exploitation. It helps us understand how profoundly disappointed they must have been when he did not fight back, allowing the "powers that be" to treat him like a criminal, a peasant, another throwaway Jew, trampled under the boot-heel of tyranny.

It seems to beg the question if John isn't revisiting this human longing for an earthly king yet again with the book that concludes the Christian biblical texts. Taken at its word, Revelation portrays a sort of kick-ass-and-take-names Jesus who will ride in on bolts of lightning with teams of horses and fire-breathing dragons, causing the heavens to shake. Maybe so, but if we're talking human mythology, this sounds more like a Marvel comic film or an episode of *Game of Thrones*.

We can see how hard it must have been to try and continue down this path of Christ if, after expecting this earth-shattering return, we got more calls to peace, more commands to serve, work with our own hands on reconciliation, and no ending in which the bad guys get what we think they deserve.

It would be incredibly hard to follow or, despite the disillusionment, to be able to see the good news, even in this unexpected turn. We might even endeavor to kill him, all over again.

Heads Up

Connecting the text to our world

This wouldn't be a real pop culture resource if I didn't make at least one allusion to *Star Wars*, and since this is the last study in the church year, I can't resist. There are loads of classic mythology and biblical allusions throughout the *Star Wars* saga. Many people have suggested that the force the jedis can channel after the proper training is much like the pantheist philosophies in many ancient and contemporary world religions. Particular to Christianity, we have the rebel alliance fighting mightily against the oppressive empire, a dynamic that pervades entire decades, a long series.

But if ever there was a Christ figure in popular culture that stood above the rest to me, it's Ben Kenobi, aka Obiwan. Of course he was the sage who guided Luke Skywalker through his own jedi training, helping him tap into the force and teaching him how to use his instincts to perfect his light saber skills. But the moment when he truly embodied the essence of what it meant to be a jedi was at the moment of his death.

During a fierce battle with Darth Vader, lord of the empire, he lowered his weapon and surrendered to death. It wasn't that he didn't think he could beat Vader. He wasn't tired or giving up all hope. This was the most radical act of subversion in the entire series so far. He stood at total peace as his enemy struck him down, ending his life.

And yet his spirit lingers. He waits patiently as his metaphysical self, guiding those who listen toward the light. Granted, there are moments when this notion of the way of the Jedi being nonviolent engagement could be challenged, like when Kenobi's spirit helps

Skywalker as he launches the final torpedo to blow up the Death Star. But even then, he doesn't implore Luke Skywalker to fire at will. Rather, his words to Luke before the rebels complete their mission are "let go."

Of what exactly, he doesn't say. So we're left to wonder, much like when Pilate asks Jesus if he is king of the Jews. The closest he comes is by saying to Pilate "You've said I am." In doing so, he's letting go. He's releasing any sense of control over his future (in the physical sense) to his enemy, which is about as welcome to his fellow Jews as Kenobi's death is to Skywalker. Luke expects him to fight back, to kill Vader and help finally overthrow the empire.

But he doesn't. Luke may complete the work, helping to destroy the empire's grip on the rebels once and for all. He could help establish a new galactic order, in which the good guys rule and the villains get a taste of their own medicine. Maybe Kenobi will return, setting justice right after all.

Or maybe it will end up with something none of us can imagine.

Prayer for the Week

God, help me see and understand the radical power of release, surrender, and nonviolent engagement. Help me set aside expectations and focus on what I'm called to do, here and now.

Popping Off

Art/music/video and other cool stuff that relate to the text

Star Wars Episode IV: A New Hope (movie, 1977)

Invictus (movie, 2009)